George Wa

George Washington Parke Custis

A Rarefied Life in America's First Family

CHARLES S. CLARK

Afterword by Matthew Penrod

McFarland & Company, Inc., Publishers

Jefferson, North Carolina

LIBRARY OF CONGRESS CATALOGUING-IN-PUBLICATION DATA

Names: Clark, Charles S., 1953– author.
Title: George Washington Parke Custis : a rarefied life in America's first family / Charles S. Clark.
Description: Jefferson, North Carolina : McFarland & Company, Inc., Publishers, 2021 | Includes bibliographical references and index.
Identifiers: LCCN 2021033676 | ISBN 9781476686622 (paperback : acid free paper) ∞ ISBN 9781476644110 (ebook)
Subjects: LCSH: Custis, George Washington Parke, 1781–1857. | Custis family. | Washington family. | Slaveholders—Virginia—Biography. | Arlington House, the Robert E. Lee Memorial (Va.)—History. | Alexandria County (Va.)—Social life and customs—19th century. | Alexandria County (Va.—History—19th century. | Plantation owners—Virginia—Biography. | BISAC: HISTORY / United States / Revolutionary Period (1775–1800) | HISTORY / United States / 19th Century
Classification: LCC E312.19.C87 C53 2021 | DDC 973.4/1092 [B]—dc23
LC record available at https://lccn.loc.gov/2021033676

BRITISH LIBRARY CATALOGUING DATA ARE AVAILABLE

ISBN (print) 978-1-4766-8662-2
ISBN (ebook) 978-1-4766-4411-0

Front cover image: George Washington Parke Custis, between 1844 and 1849 (Library of Congress)

Printed in the United States of America

McFarland & Company, Inc., Publishers
Box 611, Jefferson, North Carolina 28640
www.mcfarlandpub.com

For Ellen,
Washington scholar and wife

Table of Contents

Custis Family Sites

Audley
Annefield
Arlington
Chatham
Fredericksburg Cedar Grove
Popes Creek
Romancock
RICHMOND White House
Williamsburg

WASHINGTON D.C. AREA

POTOMAC RIVER

MARYLAND

Arlington House
D.C.
Tudor Place
Ravensworth Abingdon Mount Airy
Hope Park Mount Vernon
City of Alexandria Woodlawn

VIRGINIA

Acknowledgments

This work was conceived in 2018 during the author's reporting and tourist visits to Arlington House. That led to stimulating lunches with Park Ranger Matt Penrod, who consulted and wrote the afterword. In 2019, I retired from my Washington journalism career and travelled to do research in archives in Washington, D.C., Virginia sites at Mount Vernon, Alexandria (where I lived for 15 years), Richmond, Williamsburg, Charlottesville, and Lexington, as well as Durham, North Carolina. The real writing started in January 2020. The pandemic hit weeks later, the forced lockdown prompting a focus on polishing and fact-checking by email. I'm forever grateful to the highly professional archivists who adapted their own situations and continued to help remotely.

The work was financed in part by a Washington Library research grant from the Mount Vernon Ladies' Association, for which I'm indebted to Stephen McLeod, director of library programs, and Kevin Butterfield, executive director, of the Fred W. Smith National Library for the Study of George Washington.

Drafts of the book were read by Arlington attorney-historian George Dodge and by Arlington history activist Bernie Berne. Some chapters were reviewed by Mary Thompson, Mount Vernon's research historian and able expert on the enslaved men and women who worked there. Their suggestions were invaluable. I'm also grateful for publishing advice from Hope LeGro, assistant director of Georgetown University Press, and Nadine Zimmerli, editor for history and social sciences at University of Virginia Press. Equally valuable guidance came from fellow Custis specialist Cassandra Good, assistant professor of history at Marymount University in Arlington, and Seth Bruggeman, associate professor of history at Temple University.

Progress was eased greatly by the dedicated National Park Service staff at Arlington House, who provided access to their unique archives. They include Curator Kimberly Robinson and rangers Mark Maloy and Dean DeRosa, as well as press spokesman Aaron LaRocca. I also spoke with retired ranger Ed Bearss, whose late daughter Sara wrote some of the best work on Custis. (Ed died in 2020.)

Thanks to Mount Vernon library Special Collections Librarian Katherine Hoarn and Reference Librarian Samantha Snyder as well as Manager of Visual Resources Dawn Bonner. I must equally thank Virginia Historical Society Director of Library and Research John McClure, Reference Coordinator Matthew Guillen and Collections Management Assistant Andrew Foster; Tudor Place Archivist Wendy Kail and Collections Manager Bryn Cooley; Alexandria Library's Pam Walker and colleagues; Library of Congress Manuscript Reference Librarian Edith Sandler; City of Alexandria Research Historian Daniel Lee; City of Alexandria Gadsby's Tavern Museum & Stabler-Leadbeater Apothecary Museum Curator Callie Stapp; Library of Virginia Library Specialist Lisa Wehrmann; Maryland Historical Society Special Collections Archivist Sandra Glascock; Historical Society of Washington Research Services Librarian Jessica Smith; New-York Historical Society Reference Librarian Mariam Touba; Museum of the American Revolution (Philadelphia) Associate Curator Matthew Skic; New York Public Library (Brooke Russell Astor Reading Room for Rare Books and Manuscripts) Librarian Meredith Mann; Historical Society of Pennsylvania archivists Lee Arnold, Jon-Chris Hatalski and Andrew Williams; Washington and Lee University Special Collections and Archives Senior Assistant Lisa S. McCown; the reference team at the Albert & Shirley Small Special Collections Library, University of Virginia; College of William & Mary Swem Library Special Collections Research Center Assistant Carolyn Wilson; Duke University Libraries Research Services Librarian Elizabeth Dunn; Syracuse University Libraries Learning Commons Librarian Tarida Anantachai; Catie White, Research Center Assistant at the Connecticut Historical Society; and Stratford Hall Director of Research and Library Collections Judy Hynson.

Thanks for special consultations from manuscript dealer Gary Eyler of the Old Colony Shop in Alexandria, Virginia; Steve Hammond, the Black Heritage Museum of Arlington and the Syphax family; Don Strehle and Daniel Froggett of Alexandria Masonic Lodge; the design team at Mariner Media; my brother-in-law Grant Franks of St. John's College for help with Latin; Ann Rauscher for fine indexing; and my boyhood friend Steve Williamson of Richmond for scouting the Custis sites on the Pamunkey River.

Thanks for years of generous support and stimulating talk from fellow Arlington Historical Society members Mark Benbow, Tom Dickinson, Cathy Bonneville Hix, Gerry LaPorte, Karl VanNewkirk, Eleanor Pourron, John Richardson and Johnathan Thomas.

Last but hardly least, I'm indebted for life to Ellen McCallister Clark, the Washington scholar and library director at the Society of the Cincinnati. She married me in 1982 after I showed up at Mount Vernon on the pretext of a "research project," now in your hands.

Introduction

To be well-born back when the United States was young would have cut two ways. For an aristocratic Virginian named George Washington Parke Custis (1781–1857), it meant flung-open doors and a lifetime of answering to a world-famous name. But those impossible expectations! Custis could have used his special privileges to scale new heights of accomplishment, in the manner of, say, John Quincy Adams, a president who "descended from glory" from another president, John Adams. Or Custis could have squandered his life in the manner of, say, John Payne Todd, the adopted son of President James and Dolley Madison who pained his family with dissipated years of drinking and gambling.

Remarkably, Custis traveled a third path. He traded on his step-grandfather's name and devoted his adult life to preserving George Washington's unique historical stature. But on gaining adulthood at the dawn of the nineteenth century, this first presidential "son" broadened himself into architecture, farming, political oration, and even the fine arts. He commissioned a temple-like building for the nation's capital skyline called Arlington House. He spent decades there blowing trumpets for the Father of the Country. None of it was either predicted or required of him—especially after he broke Washington family hearts by under-performing at three of the young country's prestigious colleges.

Adopted and raised at Mount Vernon, Custis grew up on conversational terms with early America's luminaries, from Lafayette to "Light-Horse Harry" Lee. There were high hopes for him. In Edward Savage's famous painting of the nation's first presidential family, the long-haired boy aged eight is portrayed standing next to a seated George Washington—the child's hand on a globe. Custis's elders might have wondered, would that gesture foretell far-reaching vision?

He was not a great man. Though he tried (once), he never held elective office, and garnered only a few minor appointments: a cornet in the Army (briefly), chair of the Alexandria committee on retrocession, and justice of the peace. But the coincidence of George Washington Parke Custis's birth just as the Revolutionary War was concluding would mold his emblematic life. His father, John Parke Custis, died just six months after the boy arrived, a few weeks after the British surrender at Yorktown. And George Washington, after resigning as commander-in-chief of the Continental forces, raised the boy as "American royalty" in a country that had just fought a war to sever ties to monarchal rule. Young "Wash," as he was called, both resented and relished what such privileged circumstances had thrust upon him—a contradiction that shaped his personality and actions. He came of age with the new American republic. Only eighteen when George Washington died in 1799, he then reached his majority, age twenty-one, just when his grandmother died in 1802, leaving him one of the young nation's most prominent inheritances. (The Custis name, for much of the eighteenth century, carried greater status in Virginia than Washington's.)

That life bridged America as it evolved between the Revolution and the Civil War. That allowed Custis to weigh in as an essayist and orator on the top-tier issues: domestic economic independence, farming innovation, collapse of his beloved Federalist Party, the advent of the steamship and the railroad, protection of the rights of Irish Catholic immigrants, and the first federal benefits for war veterans. He greeted, advised and entertained uncounted influential guests. And his intimate descriptions of life under George Washington's roof delighted listeners and readers for decades.

But Custis the philosopher was a practitioner of slavery. Do we need another book on a white male American enslaver? He had inherited one of the nation's largest enslaved workforces, and Custis's handling of the peculiar institution is central to America's tale. In modern times, his former home—in 1972 officially renamed by Congress as "Arlington House—The Robert E. Lee Memorial"—closed in 2017 for renovations so the National Park Service could bolster its presentation of slavery. Its archive is rich in source material. Scholarship in recent years has achieved consensus: truth to the nineteenth-century rumors that Custis fathered at least one child with an enslaved woman, likely more. Those secret events as collected here form a sort of climax to this biography. The enslaved persons in his possession can now come across as individuals.

Much of Custis's historical impact was the product of chance. When his daughter married the young Robert E. Lee, Custis could never have known that within years of his death, the long-threatened secession of the southern states would unfold, and violently. Or that his son-in-law would lead the main Confederate army. Or that his cherished Arlington House would no longer merit top billing on land now the site of the world-famous Arlington National Cemetery. "Surrounded by all that was best in the way of colonial refinement and culture, Custis stamped the impress of his own character on the home he established," said one late-nineteenth-century

Washington guidebook. "The location and architecture of the house indicate culture and refined comfort, while the immensity of the estate, the beauty of the lawns, the broad and well-kept drives, and the ample provisions everywhere for the comfort of both man and beast show the indelible traces of the genial and hospitable gentleman."

This volume constitutes the first detailed biography of Custis, capturing all phases of his eventful life. Until now he has been sketched as a bit of a cardboard figure, making cameo appearances in dozens of treatments of George Washington and Robert E. Lee. And the overexamined Lee, who lived full-time at Arlington House for only a fraction of the years that Custis held court there, is today being subjected to a twenty-first-century demotion.

Custis conveyed little of the manly strength of the emmarbled Lee or Washington. But he did put across a gentle, approachable and contagious patriotism. Where his two more famous relatives were handsome, soft-spoken and duty-driven, Custis was short, beak-nosed, verbose, paunchy and playful. In other words, approachable. "In stature," wrote his daughter in introducing his recollections, "Mr. Custis was of medium. height, and well-formed; his complexion fair and somewhat florid; his eyes light and expressive of great kindliness of nature; his voice full, rich, and melodious; his deportment graceful and winning; his courtesy to strangers extremely cordial; and his affection for his friends, warm and abiding." There's no doubt that Custis possessed a mellifluous voice that, in an age before microphones, could enthrall hundreds in a room or public square. In modern parlance, he was a *must-invitee* who knew the first fifteen U.S. presidents. (Now *that* is networking.)

Yes, Custis had detractors. Jeffersonians mocked him as a George Washington pretender, "the inevitable" after-dinner speaker stuck in the past. He was one of the last in the nineteenth century to appear in knee breeches and ruffled shirts, and he sang Revolutionary War–era songs well into the 1850s. His life was a strange amalgamation of mediocrity and national greatness. But "he read much, his memory was quick and retentive, and his knowledge of history and the public affairs of the world was remarkably full and accurate," recalled his colleague on the ill-fated freed-slave-deportation project championed by the American Colonization Society.

This author's approach to portraying Custis's actions (and the reactions) is to allow, whenever possible, the denizens of the eighteenth and nineteenth centuries to do the speaking. The book is intended as a vivid account, warts and all, of the highly American experiences of Custis and his intimates. There is a more local motive: If there is a single individual founder of my hometown of Arlington, Virginia, Custis is he.

CHAPTER 1

A Fruitful Reunion

Hosting the touring hero Lafayette in the "fairy-like" ambience of Arlington House; debating slavery; drawing inspiration for a unique American memoir.

At the invitation of President James Monroe, the celebrated French military officer Lafayette in 1824–25 journeyed to the United States four decades after his heroics in the American Revolution. He visited all twenty-four young states to bask in cheers from thousands of Americans.

Among the many old comrades and notables sharing the hosting during his souvenir-commemorated trip was George Washington Parke Custis. Known variously at the "First Son," a "child of Mount Vernon" and, later, "Old Man Eloquent," Custis (1781–1857) was himself a household name. Average Americans would have noted his appearance since the 1790s as a child member of the nation's first family in widely circulated engravings of the famous group portrait by Edward Savage. Adopted and raised on George Washington's estate as the founding father's step-grandson (and only male heir), Custis first met the Marquis de Lafayette (1757–1834) at Mount Vernon at the age of three. Custis was forty-three when Lafayette returned in 1824 to dine at his spectacular home at Arlington House. The marquis confided to him a memory of his first sighting of the boy on the Mount Vernon portico in 1784: "a very little gentleman, with a feather in his hat, holding fast to one finger of the general's remarkable hand, which (so large that hand!) was all, my dear sir, you could do well at the time!"[1]

It was natural that Lafayette's packed itinerary would include hours traveling with Custis to Revolutionary War sites as well as intimate conversation at Arlington, the interior of which exhibited a unique collection of relics—portraits of the Washington and Custis families, Martha Washington's china, and the bed on which George Washington died. In the account of the Frenchman's trip written by his private secretary, the mansion, with its lush woods and elaborate flower and kitchen gardens, is recalled as "built on scaled plans of the Temple of Theseus, standing on one of the most beautiful situations that one could imagine. From the portico, the eye can embrace, at the same time, the majestic course of the Potomac, the commercial activity of Georgetown, the rising City of Washington, and, in the distance, the vast horizon below which are the fertile fields of Maryland."[2]

Their first supper, on October 15, 1824, was delayed until evening by the marquis's visit to the Washington Navy Yard with Federal City dignitaries and dinner with President Monroe. The Frenchman was accompanied across the Long Bridge in a carriage by his son George Washington Lafayette (whom Custis had befriended when both were teenagers) and four other carriages ferrying U.S. military officers. Lafayette "set out at dusk, crossed the Potomac Bridge and ascended the heights of Arlington by the devious road and through the park," wrote one witness. They approached in time to enable the family to "illuminate the mansion." The torchlight effect "was at-once beautiful and grand," the unnamed participant wrote, with each window of the home bright, and the torches throwing their "lustre over all the surrounding objects." The relations that host Custis assembled in the dining room included his wife Molly and daughter Mary; several of his half-siblings from the Stuart family of Hope Park in Fairfax, Virginia; brother-in-law Thomas Peter of nearby Tudor Place in Georgetown; and his wife's brother William Fitzhugh and his wife Anna Maria Sarah Goldsborough of the Ravensworth mansion, also in Fairfax. "The general, with his usual politeness, saluted the ladies," the witness recalled. Mrs. Custis presented the general with a "fresh bloom rose from Mount Vernon, plucked that morning." Lafayette took notice of Custis's daughter, sixteen-year-old Mary, and kissed her hand. The guests enjoyed the repast prepared and served by the enslaved persons of Arlington House.[3] At 10:00 p.m., when the Frenchman's party departed by the awaiting carriage, the ladies stood under the lighted portico and waved handkerchiefs. Custis had arranged for his enslaved servants to walk alongside Lafayette's carriage with torches to assure a safe exit along the winding road. In the "'fairy like' scene," the romantic writer said, "the slumbering sheep, whose heads had been pillowed on the verdant turf, now began to open their eyes and raise themselves to behold what had interrupted their tranquility."

The witness regretted that Lafayette's visit did not afford a daylight view of Arlington's "spreading oaks and elms" along with the "fleecy flocks, and ornamental … trees here and there left in clumps to afford shade for the flocks and herds which graze on the open lawn," the fields of corn and extensive forest all set against a stirring view of the federal towers downtown and the steeples of Alexandria City.

During this encounter (or perhaps a later one), Lafayette expressed to Custis's wife his admiration for their riverfront plantation, urging her to "cherish these forest trees around your mansion. Recollect, my dear, how much easier it is to cut a tree down than to make one grow."[4] Among the extended conversations with Custis, the marquis made no bones about his philosophical opposition to American slavery. "If Mr. Custis employed only a dozen well-paid free workers," the visitor mused, as expressed in his secretary's memoir, that "instead of a large number of indolent slaves who ate up his produce and left his roads in bad repair, I am sure that he would not have been long in tripling his revenues and in having one of the most charming properties, not only in the District of Columbia, but also in all of Virginia."[5]

Lafayette's grand tour—conducted by barge, steamer ship, horseback and stagecoach—also afforded him visits with Custis's three sisters, whose acquaintance he had also made at Mount Vernon at the end of the Revolution. Eliza Parke Custis Law remained especially close to the French family, receiving a thank-you note from Lafayette's son declaring, "Your carriage was of great assistance to him, we had indeed to repair it from time to time. I know that your tender affection for my father has made you think of him every day since we are traveling, that you followed him step by step."[6]

What Lafayette shared with Custis and his own son was experience in viewing the adulated George Washington as a personal father figure. Lafayette had been but nineteen when he arrived in the America in 1777 to join the Continental Army, and his Washington namesake son resided at Mount Vernon in the late 1790s to shield him from French Revolutionaries who had imprisoned his aristocrat father.

Planners of the 1824–25 trip would unite the three at numerous symbolic sites. The week before the Arlington House dinner, Custis met with the French party at Fort McHenry near Baltimore, where the battlefield tents used by George Washington in the Revolution (owned and lent regularly by Custis) were pitched.

The sentimental journey continued on October 17, in an emotional ceremony at Mount Vernon. Their party on the steamboat *Petersburg,* which included Secretary of War John C. Calhoun, was greeted by Washington relatives Lawrence Lewis and John Augustine Washington II. Lafayette's son reminisced about playing as a boy on the lawn. Then Custis, the only male child of Mount Vernon, led Lafayette's party to the tomb of George Washington, where he called the sixty-seven-year-old Lafayette the "last of the generals of the Army of Independence." He then presented Lafayette with Washington's Masonic sash and an engraved gold ring containing a strand of the hair of George and Martha Washington (a joint gift from Custis and his sisters Nelly, Martha and Eliza).[7] "Will you never tire in the cause of freedom and human happiness?" Custis asked rhetorically. "Is it not time that you should rest from your generous labors, and repose

Harper's Magazine, Benson Lossing engraving of Arlington House, 1853 (courtesy George Washington Memorial Parkway).

on the bosom of a country which delights to love and honor you, and will teach her children's children to bless your name and memory?"[8]

Lafayette responded: "The feelings, which at this awful moment oppress my heart, do not leave me the power of utterance. I can only thank you, my dear Custis, for your precious gift and pay a silent homage to the tomb of the greatest and best of men, my paternal friend."[9]

Soberly, the entourage walked from the tomb before Custis stopped and handed the ribbon of the Society of the Cincinnati—the elite group of Revolutionary War officers once headed by George Washington—to the major who'd provided the military escort, telling him to divide among the young men on the boat. The sailors fought for scraps as souvenirs. The boat was pushed off for the trip to the battlefield at Yorktown—scene of Lafayette's heroics before the British surrender. Custis in 1824 made sure the battlefield tents were erected there in their exact location from 1781.

The peripatetic Lafayette was pulled by multiple invitations. In December, his son notified Custis that they must postpone a visit to Woodlawn, the stately home near Mount Vernon built for Custis's sister Nelly and husband Lawrence Lewis; the marquis was being honored by a resolution in the U.S. House and Senate.[10] (The Woodlawn visit took place later in December, during which Nelly Custis asked Lafayette for a lock of his own hair as a keepsake for herself and her brother.) In early January, Lafayette's son wrote Custis affectionately, saying, "My father being able to dispose of himself on Wednesday, will do himself the pleasure of dining at Arlington. It's so long since I wished for that satisfaction myself, and I most sincerely rejoice at the anticipation of it. You know, my friend, how happy I was when we met at Baltimore. Since that day, I felt every day more and more, how much our two hearts were calculated to understand each other."[11]

At that next dinner in January, Custis presented Lafayette with a treasured umbrella and a cup and saucer of the "states" china belonging to the Washington family.[12] Just before Lafayette sailed back to France in September 1825, the Frenchman met President John Quincy Adams and an envoy from Colombia at the White House. There, Custis and Lafayette cooperated in arranging the gift of a portrait miniature of George Washington and a gold medal given to Martha Washington by the town of Williamsburg to be forwarded to Simon Bolivar, the popular liberator of oppressed South American nations.[13]

For Custis, one benefit stood out from Lafayette's "guest of the nation" tour. The two enjoyed enough private dialog to inspire Custis to write a series of essays he would call "Conversations of Lafayette." Eventually reaching sixteen installments, they showcased Custis's natural journalistic talents—he took no notes at ceremonies and meals with the Frenchman, but assembled the vivid details later in private. That feat was all the more remarkable given Custis's record as a poor college student back when his education was being paid for by a frustrated parental figure, George Washington.

Published first in early 1825 in *Alexandria Gazette* and a Baltimore paper, the series was then picked up by the District of Columbia–based *National Intelligencer*. Many of the reports concerned the Frenchman's early life and the mixed reception he received when he returned from the newly independent United States to a France and Europe in political turmoil. "The

French journalists have accused me, without cause, of my forgetting that I am a Frenchman—of treating the memory of Louis the 16th with disrespect etc.," Lafayette told Custis.[14] "As to the first charge, I plead not guilty. I have never forgot, for a moment, my allegiance, love and duty, to my native country."

The *Gazette's* introduction to one essay lent a political tinge to Custis's writings, touted as addressing a "matter of deep and feeling interest to the South, and evinces the paternal and benevolent solicitude of the General Lafayette for all which relates to the welfare and happiness of our country, and his ancient desire for the better condition of a very large class of human beings. On the other hand, the gentleman with whom these conversations have been held is himself a southerner and a large slave proprietor." The editors cited the Latin poem, "*Quaeque ipse miserrima vidi; et quorum pars magna fui,*" which translates as "and those terrible things I saw, and in which I played a great part."[15]

Thus began a rich discourse between the two men on the toxic topic of slavery. "I have been so long the friend of emancipation," Lafayette told Custis in installment 16 on "Slavery and Colonization," particularly "as regards these otherwise most happy states that I behold with sincerest pleasure the commencement of an institution, whose progress and termination will, I trust, be attended by the most successful and beneficial results." With candor, the Frenchman admitted that he would "probably not live to witness the vast changes in the condition of man, which are about to take place in the world; but the era is already commenced, its progress is apparent, its end is certain—France will, ere long, give freedom to her few colonies. In England, the Parliament leaders urged by the people, will urge the government to some acts preparatory to the emancipation of her slave-holding colonies." He went on to ask, "Where then, my dear sir, will be the last foothold of slavery, in the world? Is it destined to be the opprobrium of this fine country?"

Lafayette expressed openness to Custis's current work with the American Colonization Society, the near-decade-old group organized under such personages as James Monroe, Thomas Jefferson, James Madison, Henry Clay and Washington nephew Bushrod Washington. Its agenda was not outright abolition but an organized campaign to free American slaves by sending volunteers among them to Africa to a planned economic community in what became Liberia. Custis used this sixteenth "conversation" with Lafayette to explain the logical complications. "The idea is that the master should give one day in the week to the slave, as a day of grace," Custis wrote, "in which the slave may earn something toward his liberation. At the usual rates of hire, it would require sixteen years for a valuable slave to earn his price. The great difficulty will always be the increase, since if

Marquis de Lafayette by Dutch-French artist Ary Scheffer in 1824 (Office of Art and Archives, U.S. House of Representatives).

they were to serve only sixteen years, the system would be without end: the children, and children's children, would rise up in regular succession, and we shall have only 'scotched the snake, not killed it,' and slavery would be interminable."

With two million enslaved persons in the country, U.S. shipping would never have the capacity to take even a small portion to Africa. So Custis toyed with "humble" adjustments to the policy while imploring the owner to "bargain with himself" to not continue to enslave the next generation. Lafayette in their talks suggested giving owners an additional two years of a slave's service. Custis pressed for persuading "proprietors" of enslaved Blacks to implement the society's relocation agenda, promising, "A change like this, my dear general, would form the millennium of the South."

The impact of Custis's popular conversations was not success for the American Colonization Society. But publication of his words lit a spark in his imagination and sent his life in new directions. With encouragement from a Philadelphia and New York–based historian named John Watson, Custis hit on the notion that the American public would take interest in his own recollections of the private life of Founding Father George Washington.[16] Thus began his own series of "Recollections" published in several newspapers, notably the *National Intelligencer*. The eventual work included anecdotes of the Frenchman's heroics on the American battlefield and the memoirist's own sentimental attachment.

Custis's friends on the *Intelligencer* by 1828 felt a need to explain their handling of Custis's unfolding first-hand portrayal of Washington. "We understand that the publication of Recollections and Private Memoirs of the Life and Character of the Pater Patriae, which has been for some time expected by the American public, is delayed from the author not being as yet enabled to avail himself of the kind and paternal invitation of General Lafayette, to visit La Grange, where the valuable memoranda, to be obtained from the lips and papers of the general, have long since been tendered to the author's acceptance."[17]

Sadly, Custis's long-nourished dream of sailing to France to gain exclusive access to Lafayette's papers (which he considered endangered) was foiled by shaky finances and a denied request for a loan of $12,000. In a letter, Custis implored a District of Columbia officer of the Bank of the United States to grasp that he was working on a project "of no little interest to the American people, in particular, 'The Private Memoirs of the Life and Character of Washington.'"[18]

Lafayette, writing from La Grange in Paris in August 1828, looked back fondly on his Custis ties, saying in letter to Eliza Parke Custis, "Your brother has promised to come over, but I see nothing from him. I had lately a much welcome letter from Nelly.... Remember me more affectionately to the Woodlawn, Arlington, Georgetown branches wherever they and their offspring may be situated."[19]

Financial frustrations would haunt the land-rich, cash-poor Custis for much of his adult life. But the bond he cemented with the great French figure on that visit was a turning point in his multi-pronged contribution to the American story.

CHAPTER 2

A Youth in High Places

The Virginia orphan is taken in by the Father of the Country, breaks bread with society's elite, is presented at Washington's inauguration as "first son" but flunks out of two top American colleges.

The triple-branded name of George Washington Parke Custis was from his birth a gleaming calling card—even by standards of eighteenth-century Virginia gentry. It flavored a rarefied upbringing and head start in life that, while marred by missteps, rooted Custis's adult life deeply in George Washington's values of patriotism, military glory, Federalism, the dignity of farming, and a moral ambivalence toward slavery.

The descendant of three heralded Virginia families was born, April 30, 1781, in *Maryland*. Mount Airy in Prince George's County was the family estate of his mother, Eleanor Calvert, a granddaughter of the sixth Lord Baltimore. She had married Custis's Virginian father, John "Jacky" Parke Custis, when he was nineteen and she only sixteen. It was a courtship that Jacky's stepfather, George Washington, sought to discourage until the boy finished his studies (a drama repeated a quarter-century later when G.W.P. Custis was at college).

The father knew the infant for only six months before Jacky's death in November 1781 from "camp fever" caught weeks earlier during the Siege of Yorktown. Both of them, however, in different decades would bear the distinction of being raised at Mount Vernon by the Father of the Country. As an infant born as the nation was being transformed to an infant republic, Custis received a special welcome as his family's first male heir. His sisters were Elizabeth "Eliza" Parke Custis (born 1776, also at Mount Airy); Martha Parke Custis (born 1777 at Mount Vernon); and Eleanor "Nelly" Parke Custis (born 1779 most likely at Abingdon Plantation, then in Fairfax, Virginia).

Custis's lineage remained conspicuous throughout his adult life. His family's roots in European royalty, in England, Belgium and the Netherlands, were documented in books published during his lifetime.[1] He would keep letters and display portraits of those ancestors—Virginia planter-settlers and soldiers of fortune such as colonial governor's counselor John Custis IV and tobacco planter Daniel Parke Custis—and regale visitors with tales of their exploits.[2] When traveling to New Kent and King William counties north of Williamsburg, George Washington Parke Custis would emulate multiple generations of the Custis, Parke and Washington families in attending St. Peter's Episcopal Church in New Kent.

Noteworthy forebears included Colonel Daniel Parke, Jr. (1664–1710), a nonconformist favorite of English Queen Anne who held offices in England, the Virginia colony and the Leeward Islands in the Caribbean.[3] A pivotal family event set in motion by him was a stipulation in his will that "inheritances were to be confined to the persons either already bearing the name of Parke or adopting it." Enforcement spawned protracted lawsuits to assure that heirs who "use my Coat of Armes" honored the wish. (A suit by another with the name of Parke demanding payment of past debts haunted George Washington for decades after he took on administration of his wife's inheritance in 1759.[4]) Both the names Parke and Custis persisted in the high-status names of Custis's grandfather, father, three sisters and himself.[5]

The wealthy Parke married his daughter Frances to John Custis IV (1678–1749), who would build the importantly named Arlington Plantation on Virginia's Eastern Shore. A marriage held together less by love than land and inheritance, it generated gossip that came down through the centuries: the couple spoke only indirectly, through their enslaved servants. Once John Custis IV invited Frances on a carriage ride. "Where are you going, Mr. Custis?" she asked, observing that her husband had driven the horses into the Chesapeake Bay. "To hell, Madam," he replied. "Drive on," she said. "Any place is better than Arlington."[6] A century later, John Custis's prickly personality and frigid marriage were recounted in the memoirs of George Washington Parke Custis, notably his verbatim quotation of his ancestor's self-inscribed tombstone (still viewable on the Eastern Shore site). The mid-nineteenth-century Custis said the mid-eighteenth-century inscription was designed to "perpetuate his infelicity" following a marriage in which "the connubial bliss was short":

> Under this marble tomb lies the body of the Hon. John Custis, Esq., of the city of Williamsburg, and the Parish of Bruton, formerly of Hungar's Parish on the Eastern Shore of Virginia, and the County of Northampton, aged 71 years, and yet lived but seven years, which was the space of time he kept a bachelor's home in Arlington, on the Eastern Shore of Virginia.[7]

The sole offspring of the doomed Eastern Shore marriage arrived as Daniel Parke Custis (1711–57). He would grow up to be a politician and wealthy planter with properties along the Pamunkey River east of Richmond. Of most significance for G.W.P. Custis's future was Daniel's courtship and marriage in 1750 (at St. Peter's Church) to Martha Dandridge (born 1731). She had grown up more modestly nearby at Chestnut Grove in New Kent County. "She was the most attractive belle at the court of Williamsburg," Custis would later write of his grandmother.[8] The groom's father, John Custis, nearly rejected her as "much inferior" on fortune.[9] But the marriage proceeded and provided Martha with fine clothes, luxury wines, and enslaved property. The couple had four children, though only Martha Parke and John Parke ("Jacky") survived early childhood. George Washington Parke Custis later wrote that it was his grandfather's broken heart over the loss of two children that hastened Daniel Parke Custis's death at forty-five, probably of a heart attack.[10]

It took only a year for an ambitious young surveyor and soldier from Westmoreland County named George Washington to learn of the marital eligibility of the widow Custis. They would meet and marry, he age twenty-six, she twenty-seven, on January 6, 1759, at the Custis family property known as White House. Washington had recently made his reputation in the French and Indian War. He moved his new family to his inherited home at Mount Vernon along the Potomac River. There he would assume duties as stepfather to Jacky and Martha (called "Patsy"), striving—as his military obligations wound down—to coach them in proper education and marrying well. The two fatherless Custis children would keep a family name that, at the time, carried greater prestige than Washington's.

Young Jacky Custis grew accustomed to creature comforts supplied by enslaved persons at the Mount Vernon household and farms. His schooling struggles caused anguish in George and Martha Washington. Despite a prestigious and skeptical tutor in the Rev. Jonathan Boucher in Annapolis, Maryland, young Jacky had trouble focusing on his studies. Blame the local attractions. When he was sixteen, Jacky's mind seemed focused on "dogs, horses and guns," as well as "dress and equipage," Washington complained.[11]

Noting that Jacky had been introduced to both Greek and Latin, Washington hopefully described his stepson as "a boy of good genius, about 14 years of age, untainted in his morals, and of innocent manners." Early on, he considered Jacky "a promising boy" and expressed anxiety that as "the last of his family," who would be coming into "a very large fortune," he wanted to see him made "fit for more useful purpose than a horse racer."[12]

Jacky didn't help himself when he displayed insensitivity during a return visit to Mount Vernon in 1773, as the family was confronting the death by epilepsy of his sister Patsy. In a rudely delayed condolence letter

Massachusetts portraitist Edward Savage took seven years to complete this image the Washington family posed for New York City in 1789. It was exhibited in 1796 and circulated to the public as ink and watercolor on paper engravings starting in 1798. The original is today in the National Gallery of Art (courtesy Mount Vernon Ladies' Association).

to his mother, Jacky dwelled on his own troubles at college. His stepfather's plan that he postpone marriage to complete his studies at King's College in New York City proved unenforceable. Jacky's campus work product comprised uncompleted assignments, unpaid bills and an elitist attitude common to the period's young men secure in a pending inheritance.[13]

George Washington was appalled when his stepson in 1772 announced that he had met, during social hours in Annapolis, Maryland, heiress Eleanor "Nelly" Calvert. The student planned to marry her. When Washington complained about the distraction to the tutor, Boucher pushed back:

> Miss Nelly Calvert has merit enough to fix him as any woman can.... She is the most amiable young woman I have almost ever known.... She is all that the fondest parent can wish for a darling child; warmed with the Ideas of her merit, I can almost persuade myself to believe. That the advantages which may be derived to his morals from this engagement, rash as it has been, are enough to compensate for the ill influence it may be supposed to have on his intellectual pursuits. There is a Generosity, a Fortitude, a Manliness & Elevation of Mind which such Gallantry inspires, that is not so easily otherwise taught....

Upon the whole it appears to me, considering his temper and situation, that his friends have rather reason to rejoice than be uneasy at this engagement.[14]

After Eleanor's father met with the Washingtons, the engagement was approved. Jacky and Eleanor wed on February 3, 1774, in the great hall at Mount Airy.[15] Jacky was later described by his daughter Eliza as a "most enraptured lover" on that wedding day. "I have been told," she wrote in 1808, "that when arrayed in white, which was the fashion of that day, and standing in the midst of their numerous connections to receive the Nuptial Benediction, they looked as if some inhabitants of celestial regions had descended to gladden the children of Earth."[16]

The young couple were ensconced both at Mount Vernon and in New Kent County, where Jacky tended to his Pamunkey plantations. After the first shots of the Revolutionary War, he followed the action largely from home, though he received letters directly from his stepfather, commander-in-chief of the American forces. The young man avoided service, the exception being a brief role reportedly as a battlefield messenger in Cambridge, Massachusetts, in 1776.[17]

Two years later, Jacky Custis alienated his warrior stepfather by running successfully for the Virginia House of Delegates. "I do not suppose that so young a senator as you are, so little versed in political disquisition, can yet have much influence in a populous assembly, composed of gentlemen of various talents and different views,"

Left: John Parke "Jacky" Custis (father of G.W.P.C.), watercolor on ivory by Charles Willson Peale, 1774. *Right:* Eleanor Calvert Custis Stuart (mother of G.W.P.C.), unknown artist, watercolor on ivory done in 1782 (both courtesy Mount Vernon Ladies' Association).

Washington counseled him. "But it is in your power to be punctual in attendance."[18]

Jacky also entered into a risky real estate venture that would affect the fortunes of his entire clan. In 1777, he agreed with fox-hunting friend Robert Alexander (of the founding family of Alexandria) to buy Abingdon Plantation along the Potomac. "Nothing could have induced me to give such terms but the unconquerable desire to live in the neighborhood of Mt. Vernon," Jacky wrote to Washington, having been encouraged by his stepfather to invest in land.[19] (Washington in 1774 had himself purchased timber-producing land along Four Mile Run in Alexandria County—which would one day devolve to his step-grandson.[20])

But the battlefield general was appalled at the terms, not only of the Abingdon proposal, but of Jacky's handling of other properties east of Richmond. "I am afraid Jack Custis in spite of all the admonition and advice I gave him against selling faster than he thought, is making a ruinous hand of his estate," he worried.[21] Jacky was undeterred, and the young investor agreed to pay twelve pounds per acre over twenty-four years. "I can only say that the price you have offered [for Abingdon] is a very great one," Washington wrote from the Valley Forge winter encampment. "But as you want it to live at [it]; as it answers yours and Nelly's views; and is a pleasant seat and capable of improvement, I do not think the price ought to be a capital object with you, but I am pretty sure that you and Alexander will never agree … for he is so much afraid of cheating himself."[22]

Jacky Custis's purchase and survey of a forested Potomac-side property would present a model for his son's later creation of his own riverside estate.[23] (A legal fight over ownership of Abingdon unfolded between Alexander and David Stuart, the physician, planter and later stepfather of George Washington Parke Custis, who sought to protect his stepson's future inheritance. It was resolved by arbitration in 1792.[24])

Jacky and Eleanor settled in at Abingdon, though dividing their time across the Potomac at Mount Airy. She gave birth in rapid succession to seven children with Jacky, though only four would survive. In one letter composed weeks after the boy-heir's birth in April 1781, Jacky wrote to Washington, "I am very sorry to inform you that a very painful complaint (a kind of bloody flux) has for some time past prevailed in my family. I did not apprehend that it was dangerous or epidemic until I brought Nelly and her little boy home, they were both soon seized of it. Nelly has recovered, but I fear my little son will not, he is now in a dangerous situation."[25] The infant Custis survived; his father would not.

It was weeks later that major events unfolded that would bring the end of the Revolutionary War. Beginning in June 1781, the Continental Army linked up with troops led by French General Jean-Baptiste Donatien de

Vimeur, comte de Rochambeau, who had sailed to Newport, Rhode Island, a year earlier. The allied forces then executed their famous march to York-town, Virginia, to entrap the British enemy.

For Washington personally, that meant an opportunity for a long-wished-for visit to Mount Vernon. He arrived in September, and 26-year-old Jacky and wife Eleanor rode out to Mount Vernon in a char-iot to greet him. Jacky was inspired to volunteer as an aide-de-camp.[26] So the unseasoned soldier rode with the armies to Williamsburg and York-town wearing a green ribbon identifying him as one of the military fam-ily. Just before the surrender by Lord Cornwallis, Jacky Custis caught a cold and "camp fever" (possibly typhus). Confined to bed in mid–October, he never recovered. He was transported to Eltham, in New Kent County, home to Martha Washington's sister. Washington himself was summoned from his Williamsburg headquarters but arrived just in time for Jacky's death on November 5.[27]

Hence six-month-old George Washington Parke Custis, along with his three older sisters, became fatherless. The older daughters, Eliza (now five) and Martha (now four), would remain with mother Eleanor at Abing-don. The younger two, Nelly (now two) and baby George Washington Parke Custis still nursing, were moved to Mount Vernon. The two were under the direct care of and Englishwoman named Anderson, and Elizabeth Foote Washington, wife of the farm's manager Lund Washington. After inquiring among relatives as to who should best take the young children in, Washing-ton finally resolved, "From this moment on, I adopt the two youngest chil-dren as my own."[28]

A Mount Vernon Boyhood

Nicknames, in a family packed with sound-alike relatives, were inevi-table for George Washington Parke Custis. The boy was known variously to intimates as "Washy," "Tub," and, as he matured, "Wash" or "Washington." None other than the Marquis de Lafayette wrote to George Washington in 1786 promising children's books, saying, "I beg leave to send under separate cover to you a few titles to be presented to Tub and his sisters."[29]

Remembered for his fair hair and blue eyes, the chubby boy was favored by Martha Washington, while the general, relatives said, was par-tial to his sister Nelly. "Grandmamma always spoiled Washington," Nelly recalled. He was the "pride of her heart."[30] His grandmother offered smoth-ering thoughts in letters to her intimates, updating them on her invest-ments in his diet and health: "My pretty little Dear Boy complains of a pain in his stomach.... I cannot say it but it makes me miserable if he ever complains, let the cause be ever so trifling."[31] In 1784, Martha would boast to her niece, "My little Nelly is getting well, and Tub is the same clever boy you left him—he sometimes says why don't you send for cousin—you know, he never makes himself unhappy about absent friends."[32]

Young Washy received gifts from the steady stream of high-powered visitors to George Washington's home. In the summer of 1784, a visiting French dentist named Jean-Pierre Le Mayeur brought the three year old a toy wooden horse.[33] The Mount Vernon account books kept by secretary Tobias Lear recorded the purchase of a ball and marbles.[34] And the boy would have been among guests when Washington, in 1787, paid eighteen shillings for the unusual treat of bringing a live camel to a party.

The young Custis's early education was supervised by a succession of private tutors, who also established social relationships. In May 1785, pioneer lexicographer Noah Webster offered to tutor Nelly and Washy in exchange for access to the general's papers. Washington declined, favoring instead his personal secretary Lear, who worked with the boy in Mount Vernon's North Garden House.[35] A Virginian named William Shaw, brought in to tutor and organize Washington's papers, left after thirteen months after the general faulted him for a lax work ethic.[36] Washington then engaged Gideon Snow of Boston, with whom the adult Custis would correspond, sharing memories that the boy in July 1787 wrote to send his love, but faulting Snow for skipping a Sunday visit. The boy implored Snow in a dictated letter, "When will you send my waggon to me? For my old one is almost worn out, and I shall have none to get in my harvest with."[37] (More than sixty years later, Snow would recall planning Custis's instruction in Latin and the purchase of "handsome soft black cloth" for his coat and overalls.[38])

Washy's teachers inculcated social finesse. "I wish it was in my power to make you some return for so valuable a present," the polite six year old wrote on January 17, 1788. It was a letter to Martha Washington's friend Elizabeth Willing Powel, wife of the mayor of Philadelphia, thanking her for a book called *Children's Friends*. Powel had written to Washy's grandmother of her plan for the gift the previous November. "I have sent our little favorite Master Custis the work I promised him.... I shall distrust my skill if he is not a child of penetration and genius. He has sweet conciliating manners like your charming little Eleanor." Martha replied on January 18: "My pretty boy is so pleased with the book you sent him that he read it over and over and over and says he will write to Mrs. Powel and thank her himself, for her kind remembrance of him."

Washy assured the Philadelphia matron, "I have nothing worth your acceptance but my best thanks and assurances that I will endeavor to imitate the good characters which I find described in the book."[39] That same matron also presented Washy with a camera obscura.

General Washington, his adoptees would recall of their Mount Vernon upbringing, was never to be disturbed when working at his desk after the afternoon meal. But the great man did not ignore Washy, and mentioned him in his postwar and presidential-era correspondence. "Your young friend is in high health, and as full of spirits as an egg is of meat," he wrote to New England clergyman-historian William Gordon on March 8, 1785. In November that year he described the four year old as "a remarkable fine one and my intention is to give him a liberal education; the rudiments

Custis at age four by Robert Edge Pine (courtesy Washington and Lee University, Lexington, Virginia).

of which, shall, if I live, be in my own family."[40] Wash and Nelly attended Sunday services at Christ Church in Alexandria and at Pohick in Fairfax County. Their comings and goings for dining and clothes shopping were recorded in Washington's diaries.

They were exposed early to prominent portrait painters. Well-connected British artist Robert Edge Pine arrived on April 28, 1785, to paint Washington and Martha Washington's four Custis grandchildren, rendering Washy as a four-year-old Greek god.[41] Massachusetts portraitist Edward Savage captured the family in what, after Washington became president, became a nationally distributed portrait of the first family.[42]

English painter James Sharples portrayed Wash at age fifteen, adding to the boyhood influences on Custis when he took up painting as an adult.

As they came of age, Wash and Nelly led luxurious lives on the Mount Vernon estate that meant service from enslaved persons who served sumptuous home-grown meals. "Bad bread was entirely unknown at Mount Vernon; that too was mixed every night under the watchful eye of the mistress," Custis recalled of his grandmother's discipline. The chef Hercules Posey "was something of a tyrant, as well as a capital cook."[43] Wash also knew "old

Billy" Lee, the body servant who had served Washington during the Revolution (and whose nephew Philip would later be Wash's valet).

The general instructed Wash that "system in all things should be aimed at, for in execution it renders everything more easy." The boy could take a gun out before breakfast, but must be back for the meal. An hour before dinner, "confine yourself to diligent study," Washington instructed. The boy could amuse himself in the afternoon before tea, and then study until bedtime. On Saturdays, Wash could go riding or hunting. But he had to be on time for meals. "It is not only disagreeable but it is also very inconvenient for servants to be running here and there and they know not where, to summon you."[44] The siblings became close, with Nelly confining to a friend her confidence that Washy would take good care of her dog Frisk.[45]

The future plantation owner would absorb George Washington's interest in experimental farming and some of his military-style management, if not his study habits. After Washington became president in 1789, with Washy age eight and his sister ten, the children were now prepared for presentation to the public as the nation's original First Family. They relocated, first to New York City, then to Philadelphia, the capital from 1791 to 1800.

The chief executive's packed schedule often shorted family togetherness, and Martha Washington took on the parenting. After she declined to accompany Washington to the historic Constitutional Convention in Philadelphia in May 1787, the general wrote to delegate Robert Morris of Pennsylvania, "Mrs. Washington is become too domestic, and too attentive to two little grandchildren to leave home."[46] She and the children had also missed the April 30 Inauguration.

But on May 16, 1789, Martha and the children set out for New York after an emotional send-off attended by the extended family. Escorted to the gate by Washington's nephew Robert Lewis and an entourage of enslaved servants, they made the two-week journey in a London-built coach that had been given to Martha Washington by the state of Pennsylvania. The stone-colored vehicle was bedecked with scenes of seasons, green superfine cloth and silk. The "wretches," as Lewis called the Mount Vernon enslaved in a diary, were "much affected," and Wash and Nelly were bawling at the prospect of leaving. Wash's older sister Eliza Parke Custis later described it, "I remember well what I felt when the Negroes came to take leave of their mistress, to bid her farewell, and bless her for all her goodness to them—I see them now, bent down with years, and infirmatives, their heads silver'd by time uncover'd as they bow'd, and their voices resound in my ears. 'God bless you all' as the carriage drove off."[47]

The party arrived in Manhattan two weeks later to a temporary house on Cherry Street near Franklin Square. Martha wrote to a friend: "The children were very well and cheerful all the way.... Dear Little Washington [Custis] seemed to be lost in a mass at the great parade that was made for us all the way we come."[48]

The initial quarters Congress rented from Postmaster Samuel Osgood was "a mansion of very moderate extent," as Custis later described it.[49] They provided cramped space for himself, Nelly, the president and Mrs. Washington, Lear "as principal secretary, Col. [David] Humphreys, Lewis and [Thomas] Nelson as secretaries, and Maj. William Jackson as aide-de-camp." Soon the first family moved to a more spacious home at 39 Broadway, built for Scottish merchant Alexander Macomb.[50]

In the city both children were exposed to the arts. Nelly was given harpsichord lessons, and Washy taken to the theater, where he enjoyed plays on his grandfather's lap.[51] Washington took the boy to performances by the "Old American Company," at which they were often greeted with cheers.[52] The two pre-teens played with the children of other government officials and enjoyed an attic full of toys, among them watercolor paints, skates, drums and a small cannon. They performed plays for the amused president at home. The family attended St. Paul's Chapel and Trinity Church, and the children were driven around Manhattan and out to the country in carriages when Washington wanted to "exercise." They enjoyed Pintard's museum and a waxworks featuring a likeness of George Washington.[53] Young Washy, a future poet, was exposed to verse recitals by Washington aide (and future ambassador) Humphreys, one of Yale College's famous "Connecticut Wits."

Nelly attended a New York boarding school as a day student and studied painting with William Dunlap.[54] Washy was outfitted with a private tutor, George Wright, a graduate of Trinity College, Dublin, though eventually the boy was sent to a Greenwich Village school with seven other boys taught by Patrick Murdock. His playmates included William Duer, a son of the treasurer of the Continental Congress, and Walter Buchanan, a godson of the president.[55]

In 1791, after Congress moved the capital and the First Family to Philadelphia, Washy and Nelly settled into the President's House at Market and 6th streets, a stone's throw from Independence Hall. In that small household filled with books, newspapers and magazines, they witnessed the drama of Mrs. Washington's lady maid, Oney Judge, escaping in the Quaker State, prompting Washington and his wife to castigate her for "ingratitude." Washy inhabited a bedroom shareable with Martha Washington's nephew Bat Dandridge and even his tutor, Washington's private secretary Tobias Lear. The tutor and bookkeeper recorded that Washy contracted measles and was treated by the prominent Dr. Adam Kuhn.[56]

In the new capital, twelve-year-old Nelly and ten-year-old Wash took dancing lessons from James Robardet. They attended Christ Church and St. Peter's at Third and Pine.[57] The "best" people came to Wash's birthday party, Martha noted, where they enjoyed ice cream molds. They watched July 4 fireworks atop the presidential mansion. The family visited the museum of natural history assembled by painter Charles Willson Peale. Occasionally, they travelled back to the fledgling Federal City and Mount Vernon—Wash at age twelve witnessed the laying of the cornerstone of the Capitol on September 18, 1793.[58] And he would later recall witnessing at age ten, in the president's house in Philadelphia in early 1792, Washington's tense interview with the

George Washington Parke Custis and sister Eleanor "Nelly" Parke Custis, circa 1789, by unknown artist (courtesy Mount Vernon Ladies' Association).

disgraced General Arthur St. Clair.[59] (One of Washington's favorites during the Revolution, St. Clair in November 1791 had ignored the chief's warnings about Indian threats in western Ohio. The officer left his camp unprotected, which allowed an attack that cost him 900 killed or wounded—as well as Washington's good graces.[60])

Martha Washington, by August 24, 1794, was able to write, "My grandchildren are every much grown. Nelly is a woman in size—and Washington [Custis] begins to be a sturdy boy."[61]

In 1795, Wash accompanied the president to a Philadelphia naval shipyard, later recalling visiting "the *United States* Frigate at Southwark, when her Keel was laid, & stem & sternpost only up. The Chief expressed his admiration at the great size of the Vessel that was to be."[62]

Wash's mother, meanwhile, having married physician-politician David Stuart (after consulting George Washington) and living at Hope Park in Fairfax, followed the glory via letters from Lear. She thanked her son's tutor for his educational efforts, but delivered gentle skepticism about Martha Washington. "Had I known you had ever given up your authority over Wash, I would have been miserable about him," Eleanor wrote. "For although his good grandmama will, I am sure, do all she can, yet her excessive affection will blind her at times to the failings that may require immediate checks."[63] Boasting that her children raised elsewhere continued to obey her, she wrote Lear in Philadelphia expressing wishes that the same advantages had been afforded to her two older children, Martha and Eliza, asking him to "shake hands with My Dear Boy … don't let him forget he has a mother."[64]

Education Anguish at Princeton

"You are now extending into that stage of life when good or bad habits are formed," President Washington wrote Wash on November 28, 1796, on the eve of the youth's first journey to a distant college, "when the mind will be turned to things useful and praiseworthy, or to dissipation and vice."[65] The teenager's schooling thus far in Philadelphia—Lear had arranged for him to commute to the College, Academy and Charitable School, the preparatory school that would later feed into the University of Pennsylvania— had produced mixed results. "I clearly see that [Wash] is on the high road to ruin," warned Lear as early as 1791, citing the boy's having been "born to such noble properties … and the servile respect the servants are obliged to pay him." But what to do? "The president sees it with pain, but, as he considers Mrs. W's happiness bound up in the boy, he is unwilling to take such measures as might reclaim him, knowing that any rigidity towards him would perhaps be productive of serious effects on her."[66]

Wash's grandmamma Martha wrote to her niece Fanny Bassett Washington of her worries on September 29, 1794: "As constant as the day comes, but he does not learn as he might if the master took proper care to make the children attentive to their books."[67] She also blamed the problem on Wash having so many friends in a metropolis teeming with distractions. "In this city, everyone complains of the difficulty to get their children educated," she wrote. "My dear little Washington [Custis] is not doing half as well as I could wish … and we are mortified that we can't do better for him."[68]

There followed a three-year struggle that unfolded on two other campuses—a generation-gap drama that Custis and his own daughter in later life would lay open in their jointly written memoir.

George Washington had spent years assembling an extensive library at Mount Vernon in hopes, first, of giving his stepson Jacky, and later, his step-grandson Wash, the classical education he himself lacked. (Of special importance, Washington stressed, was Latin.)[69] In a repeat of the pattern with Jacky, Washington wrote in frustration to the unformed student who had wandering eyes. Though Wash responded with fawning replies filled with over-promising rhetoric, the president of the United States complained separately to relatives and the college presidents who had welcomed their prestigious charge. At different times, Washington would consider sending his only male heir to Yale College, or the Alexandria Academy he had helped found. After his presidential travails, while at home at Mount Vernon, Washington was still planning: "The more I think of his entering William and Mary, unless he could be placed in the bishop's family, the more I am convinced of its inutility on many accounts, which had better be the subject of oral communication than by letter," the retired president wrote to Wash's nominal stepfather David Stuart, in 1799. The president and Mrs. Washington both rejected the idea of sending Wash to Harvard, he added, "the most eligible seminary to have sent him to; first because it is on a larger scale than any other; and secondly, because I believe that the habits of youth there, whether from the discipline of the school, or the greater attention of the people generally to morals, and a more regular course of life, are less prone to dissipation and excess than they are at colleges south of it." Toward the end of his life, the retired president summarized: "I believe Washington [Custis] means well, but has not resolution to act well."[70]

On November 8, 1796, a fifteen-year-old Custis enrolled as a member of the sophomore class at the College of New Jersey (later called Princeton). There in Nassau Hall he joined eighty-seven students, paying eight pounds per year for tuition and rent, payable at two dollars a week.[71] He enjoyed being roommates with Cassius Lee, son of Richard Henry Lee, and joined the Whig Society. In the spring of 1797, Custis received ceremonial pistols and a sword from the first president of the United States, who had a direct relationship with Princeton's president, the Rev. Samuel Stanhope Smith. That clergyman would give Custis personal attention and a classical curriculum.

Custis began his tenure high-mindedly, writing to his benefactor on March 25, 1797:

> The Roman History I have finished, reviewed, and am perfect, translating French has become pretty familiar, and the great deal of writing attending which has probably improved my hand. I have read a great many good authors this winter and have paid particular attention to Hume, have obtained a tolerable idea of geography, and sir, in justice to myself and my own endeavors, I think I have spent my time in nowise to be complained. Arithmetic, I must confess, I have not made as much progress as could be expected, owing to a variety of circumstances, and the superficial manner in which I first imbibed the principles, but the ensuing summer shall make up the deficiency.[72]

But Princeton instructors reacted less favorably. On May 24, 1797, Washington wrote to the Reverend Smith saying his latest report from campus "filled my mind (as you naturally supposed it would) with extreme disquietude" concerning Custis's study habits. "From his infancy, I have discovered an almost unconquerable disposition to indolence in everything that did not tend to his amusements."[73]

Custis assured his benefactor that he was studying Joseph Priestley's lectures on history and English history by David Hume and Tobias Smollett. He expressed alarm that he hadn't heard directly from Washington, but the threatening letter that finally came in May (the text is lost to history) appeared to prick the student's guilty conscience. From Nassau Hall on May 29, 1797, a chastened Custis replied:

Dearest Sir

Words cannot express my present sensations, a heart overflowing with joy at the success of conscience over disposition is all I have to give—Dearest Sir did you but know the effect your letter has produced it would give you as consummate pleasure, as my former one did pain—My very soul tortured with the sting of conscience at length called reason to its aid and happy for me triumphed, the conflict was long doubtfull till at length I obtained the victory over myself and now return like the prodigal son a sincere penitent. That I shall ever recompence you for the trouble I have occasioned is beyond my hope, however I will now make the grand exertion I will now shew all is not lost and that your Grandson shall once more deserve your favour....[74]

Custis took a break from classes, and weeks later acknowledged to Washington his lack of discipline. "While I look up to that Providence which has preserved me in the late contest with my passions, and which has enabled me to do that which will redound to my honour, permit me to make this humble confession ... that if in any way or by any means I depart from your direction or guardianship, let me suffer as I and such an imprudent act deserve," he wrote to the retired president now home at Mount Vernon on June 8, 1797: "During my recess from college I was by no means idle, having with Dr. Smith complete studied the use of the globes.... The course he means to produce this summer privately I do know except Priestley's elements of natural history, which I shall begin immediately with Smith's Constitutions." He added that he would "take particular care in eating fruit and drinking water, as I have seen so many fatal instances of intemperance in both."[75]

To an errant Custis the adoptive father gave some ground, writing on June 4 that "it is not my wish that, having gone through the essential, you should be deprived of any rational amusement *afterward;* or, lastly, from dissipation in such company as you would likely meet under such circumstances, who, but too often, mistake ribaldry for wit and rioting, swearing, intoxication, and gambling, for manliness."[76]

Even so, his step-grandson's contrite missive, Washington replied, "eased my mind of many unpleasant sensations and reflections on your account ... and if your sorrow and repentance for the disquietude occasioned by the preceding letter, your resolution to abandon the ideas which were therein expressed, are sincere, I shall not only heartily forgive, but will forget also, and bury in oblivion all that has passed." Washington grew mildly concerned with young Custis's ambitious practice of writing independently to his stepfather Stuart, his former tutors Lear and Zechariah Lewis, and his brother-in-law, the Georgetown land speculator Thomas Law.[77] The cocky fifteen year old wrote to Law in 1796, on the eve of the man's engagement. "I very much wish to see the happiness of my sister with the man she loves," he said, adding lofty thoughts about the new Federal City being the "pride of future ages."[78]

Custis at age fifteen, pastel done in 1796 by James Sharples (courtesy Washington and Lee University, Lexington, Virginia).

Initially, Washington assured the young student: "Far be it from me to discourage your correspondence with Doctor Stuart, Mr. Law, Mr. Lear or Mr. Lewis." But Washington later wrote Lewis himself urging the tutor to "impress upon [Wash's] mind" the importance of study. He described his ward as distracted by "an indolent temper, amusements, at present innocent but unprofitable."[79]

In July 1797 the youth ambiguously described to his step-grandfather his leisurely doings at Princeton:

> The fourth July was celebrated with all possible magnificence. We fire three times 16 rounds from a six-pounder and had public exhibitions of speaking.... At night the whole college was beautifully illuminated. My ideas of impropriety proceeded from a distaste of such things during a recess from them, as I was confident all relish for study would be lost, after such enjoyment, for there is a difference in the minds being entirely taken off an object, to which it can return with increased vigour and a momentary relapse without anything more than whetting the appetite when it cannot be satiated.[80]

Classes resumed, and Custis on July 30 assured Washington that he was "now engaged in geography and English grammar.... The senior class will leave college in about a fortnight, and we shall become junior or second class, not in studies, as we do not commence mathematics til next session. The time appears to glide away imperceptibly."[81] By then, it may have been too late for the would-be scholar. On September 7, 1797, George Washington Parke Custis was suspended by the Princeton faculty. Decades later, his daughter wrote in their memoir that "we know not why Mr. Custis was removed from Princeton."[82]

It wasn't until the twentieth century that the mysterious reasons were revealed by a scholar reading the minutes of the college faculty. They read: "Mr. George W. Custis having been guilty of various acts of mean[n]ess & irregularity, & having endeavored in various ways to lessen the authority & influence of the faculty and was suspended and ordered to leave the college."[83] Washington had no choice but to settle unpaid tuition (delivered by Lafayette's son). On October 7, 1797, he sent the college president a note saying Custis "will have himself only to upbraid for any consequences which will follow."[84]

Distractions in Annapolis

Back at Mount Vernon, the wayward Custis resumed his leisured life, enjoying hunting and visits to the race track. Washington had long envisioned the boy as a horseman, having thanked the dentist le Mayeur for his gift of a toy horse by writing, "He finds beauty in every part, and tho' shy at first, he begins now to ride with a degree of boldness which will soon do honor to his horsemanship."[85] Custis's love of horseback adventures was also suggested in a letter from his sister Nelly to a friend around this time:

> I had business a fortnight ago in Alexandria, and for a frolic went up one morning with my brother on horseback. My beast is a pretty iron grey, 4 years old, 15 hands high, gentle, goes well except starting—called Sir Edward Pellew. The morning was fair and very damp, before we got far from home, it began to rain, however, as I never like to give up any undertaking after once engaging in it, & wished also to accustom myself to riding in all weathers, I kept on, two mile[s] from Alexandria the rain poured violently, my brother and self rode to town full gallop, and got our faces very nicely washed before we could get to a place of shelter.[86]

(Custis also rode with Washington himself. In his memoir, he recalled witnessing the rare event of the *Pater Patriae* falling from his horse, during a leisure-time ride home from Alexandria with a neighbor named Peake and son-in-law Lawrence Lewis, in November 1799. Washington assured his companions that "it was owing to a cause that no horseman would well avoid or control."[87])

But George Washington hadn't given up on Custis's schooling. In

Annapolis, Maryland, where he had famously turned in his military commission in 1783, lay the campus of St. John's College, where the Washington family had sent other members.[88] Its "able" preceptor John McDowell, an attorney and classical scholar, could offer special attention, and the town—where Wash's father Jacky had been distracted—was well policed. "There is less of that class of people which are baneful to youth in that city, than in any other," the ex-president wrote to David Stuart.[89]

Neither of the men performing the role of parent was confident in the seventeen-year-old's maturity. "His habits and inclinations are so averse to all labour and patient investigation," Stuart wrote, expressing an "opinion that not much can be expected from any plan."[90]

In January 1798, Stuart accompanied Wash on the trip to Maryland's Chesapeake Bay, and the parenting by letter began anew. "I was so fortunate to get in with a Mrs. Brice, a remarkable clever woman, with whom I live and am well contented," the student wrote Washington in March, referring to landlady Juliana Jennings Brice. Wash said he was "pursuing the study of Natural Philosophy, and hope to distinguish myself in that branch as well as others. Arithmetic I have reviewed, and shall commence French immediately with the professor here."[91]

Again writing discreetly, Washington warned school head McDowell that "Mr. Custis possesses competent talents to fit him for any studies, but they are counteracted by an indolence of mind which renders it difficult to draw them into action."[92]

The St. John's preceptor replied on March 8: "His proficiency in literature does not indeed appear to be adequate to the opportunities, which he has enjoyed and the time that he has spent at school. But with diligence and application, he may yet acquire a good stock of valuable and ornamental knowledge."[93]

To Custis, the step-grandfather was more tactful. "The wise man you know, has told us (and a more useful lesson never was taught) that there is a *time* for all *things*; and now is the time for you to lay in such a stock of erudition as will effect the purposes I have mentioned," he wrote on March 19, 1798. "Let these continue to be your *primary* objects and pursuits; all other matters, at your time of life, are of secondary consideration ... for it is on a well-grounded knowledge of these your respectability in mature age; your usefulness to your country; and indeed your own private gratifications, when you come seriously to reflect upon the importance of them, will depend."[94]

Custis was expected every fortnight to write a letter home detailing his academic progress. The youth responded cheerfully on April 2: "I am very happily situated, perhaps better than many." Addressing the "'principles' Washington recommended," he wrote, "It is them that elevate the soul and prompt us to good works, I conceive that misfortunes are intended as awful example for us to profit by and are proportionate to the degree of prevalence which the passions have over us. What, then, could have been a greater misfortune to me than your displeasure? What a greater happiness than your confidence?"[95]

Custis was rising to make 6:00 a.m. classes, promising Washington, "I attend college regularly, and am determined that nothing shall alienate my attention."

An early request for money rubbed Washington wrong. On May 10, the general reminded him that Stuart had brought with him a trunk and a "quarter's board paid in advance, except for your washing, and books when necessary, I am at a loss to discover what has given rise to so early a question." Custis backtracked in a May 26 response: "I did not mean to insinuate that I was actually in want, but supposed you had placed money in the hands of someone to whom I might apply."[96]

The youth added that he had "opened accounts with a shoemaker, tailor.... I took a couple of pieces of [nankeen] for summer breeches and a gingham coat," he wrote. "My hat might have last much longer had it not been a most worthless one and broke, tho not from ill usage. I have been very careful of my clothes and frequently revise them myself.... Far from being addicted to frequent taverns I am not fond of such sociability and assure you that I have not spent a farthing in that way. Tis true that I am fond, when among friends at my own time, to enter into a little superfluities, such as toddy, etc. but farther I sacredly deny any dissipation." The student did allow that, like his father, he loved the local families. "I am charmed with Annapolis and also its inhabitants and have received every attention from them," he wrote in May to his future brother-in-law Lawrence Lewis.[97]

Custis also caused a stir in his new situation by presuming to offer advice on the marriage prospects of his sister Nelly. Back in the rising Federal City, Nelly was being pursued by the eligible bachelor Charles Carroll, Jr., the son of a signer of the Declaration of Independence. After dancing with him at a tavern in Georgetown, however, Nelly was put off: he "too often told of his merit and accomplishments," she complained.[98] But talk has spread among the young people. In an April letter to Washington from his campus, Custis thought it appropriate to express his approval of Carroll as a suitor, calling him "a young man of the strictest probity and morals." Washington scolded Custis with the comment, "If his object was such as you say has been reported, it was not declared here; and therefore the less said on this subject, particularly by your sister's friends, the more prudent it will be until the subject develops itself more."[99]

More threatening to his step-grandfather's support were the rumors that Custis, like his own father, had become serious with a local woman.[100] Having not heard from Custis in weeks (their letters crossed in the mail), Washington on June 13 admonished, "We have with much surprise, been informed of your devoting much time to paying particular attention to a certain young lady of that place!" After a world-weary warning against pre-occupation with the "gratification of passions," the Father of the Country wrote: "I am sure it is not a time for you to think of forming a serious attachment of this kind … might … involve a [consequence] of which you are not aware." In a passage later printed in Custis's memoirs, Washington added, "This is not a time for a *boy of your age* to enter into engagement which might end in sorrow and repentance."[101]

Custis wrote back on June 17 to defend himself. He had disclosed to his mother earlier that he had "solicited her affection, and hoped, with the approbation of my family, to bring about a union at some future day." But now he told Washington that "the report, my mamma tells me, of my being engaged to the young lady in question, is strictly erroneous. That I gave her reason to believe in my attachment to her, I candidly allow, but that I would enter into engagements inconsistent with my duty or situation, I hope your good opinion of me will make you disbelieve." To bolster his case, Custis added, "However rash and imprudent I may be, I have always remembered my duty and obligation to you."[102]

By mid-summer, Custis could write that he had nearly finished reading six books of Euclidian math, and was anticipating the adjournment of the college in late July. He would flatter his benefactor with a letter on July 12 congratulating Washington on his newly revived status as commander in chief in a possible war with France: "Let an admiring world again behold a Cincinnatus springing up from rural retirement to the conquest of nations and the future historian in erasing so great a name insert that of the *Father of His Country*."[103]

Custis's final days at St. John's, before he took a stagecoach home, were marked by a small budgetary confession he sent to Washington on July 23: "The only object I apologize for is an umbrella, which I was unavoidably obliged to procure, as I lost one belonging to a gentleman."[104] Behind the youth's back, Washington was preparing for the worst, complaining to Custis's stepfather and mother. "If you or Mrs. Stuart could by indirect means, discover the state of Washington Custis's mind, it would be to be wished," he wrote on August 13, 1798. "He appears to me to be moped & stupid, says nothing—and is always in some hole or corner excluded from company."[105]

McDowell tried to be encouraging on the fate of his well-connected pupil. On the same August day Washington wrote him, the educator wrote to Washington that Custis "has of late been much more attentive to business; and has applied himself to the study of Euclid with such advantage, that he is now pretty well acquainted with as much of the elements, as is usually read in our schools."[106] In early September, as the academic year was starting, Washington wrote McDowell asking him to "admonish him seriously of his omissions and defects." He asked to be informed "if you should perceive any appearance of his attaching himself, by visits or otherwise, to any young lady of that place, that you would admonish him." The retired president was merciless. "There seems to be in this youth an unconquerable indolence of temper, and a dereliction, in fact, to all study, it must rest with you to *lead* him in the best manner, and by the easiest modes you can devise, to the study of such useful acquirements as may be serviceable to himself, and eventually beneficial to his country." Washington confessed to being "at a loss to point out any precise course of action of study for Mr. Custis."[107]

Wash would never return to campus. The reaction among the family was mixed. Sister Nelly appeared unsuspecting of the drama. In July she reported to a friend, "My brother will come home in August to pass his vacation. He is much pleased with Annapolis, & studies very well."[108] Grandmother Martha Washington sounded when she wrote to her one-time romantic rival Sally Fairfax, back in England, in 1798: "The youngest daughter, Eleanor is yet single and lives with me, having done so from an infant, as has my grandson, George Washington—now turned seventeen—except when at college, to three of which he has been, viz. Philadelphia, New Jersey and Annapolis."[109]

To end the ordeal, George Washington wrote to Martha's brother Bartholomew Dandridge on January 25, 1799, to say he found it "impracticable to keep him longer at college with any prospect of advantages; so great was his aversion to study; though addicted to no extravagant or vicious habits, but from mere indolence & a dereliction to exercise the powers of the mind."[110]

The episode trailed Custis for life. Even his daughter Mary, in their late-life memoir published after her father's death in 1857, diagnosed Custis's upbringing under Washington as limited: "The public duties of the veteran prevented the exercise of his influence in forming the character of the boy, too softly nurtured under his roof, and gifted with talents, which, under a sterner discipline, might have been made more available for his own and the country's good."[111]

The Call of Home

During his struggles on campus, Custis continued to participate in family events at Mount Vernon and surroundings. When he returned for visits, the teenage Custis bonded for life with the son of the Marquis de Lafayette, George Washington Lafayette. The younger Frenchman, who had been given safe harbor from French Revolutionary fervor in the United States, was permitted to live at Mount Vernon now that Washington was a private citizen.

Also during Custis's teen years, there were family weddings. His sister Martha, the second oldest, was first of the four to marry. On January 6, 1795 (George and Martha Washington's anniversary), she wed prominent Washington, D.C., (Georgetown) businessman and landowner Thomas Peter. The celebration was held twenty miles out in Fairfax County at the Hope Park plantation of David Stuart and Custis's mother Eleanor. (She by this time had given birth to twelve children with her second husband.)[112]

The Peters' marriage was followed on March 20, 1796, at the same site by the wedding of Eliza Parke Custis to Thomas Law. Seventeen years older than Eliza, he was a speculator and developer of the Federal City with children from another relationship in British India. (It was a match that prompted gossip—President John Adams wrote to his wife Abigail that Eliza had married an "English East India Nabob" twice her age.)[113] The new couple would settle in a handsome home in Southwest Washington.

Perhaps most meaningful to Custis was the marriage of his sister Nelly to Washington's nephew Lawrence Lewis. "An event occurred on the twenty-second of February 1799 [what would be Washington's final birthday]," he recalled in his memoir, "that while it created unusual bustle in the ancient halls, shed a bright gleam of sunshine on the last days at Mount Vernon."[114] The candlelight ceremony was performed by the Rev. Thomas Davis of Alexandria. General Washington, having raised Nelly as his own, bequeathed

Nelly Custis, oil on canvas done in 1804 by Gilbert Stuart (National Gallery of Art, Gift of H. H. Walker Lewis in memory of his parents, Mr. and Mrs. Edwin A.S. Lewis, Accession Number, 1974.108.1).

the couple a distillery and farmland for the building of Woodlawn plantation—within sight of Mount Vernon.

One mysterious event marred Custis's homecoming. Though details are scarce, legal records in the nearby town of Alexandria showed a brush with the law. Little noticed (until a city historian found it in the 1980s), the notice from the Court of Oyer and Terminer read:

> At an Examining Court appointed & held for the Town of Alexandria 25 June 1798 for the Examination of Geo. W. Custis. Present—John Dundas, William Harper, Johan Thompson, Philip Marsteller, and Dennis Ramsay. George W. Custis, who was recognized to appear before the Court this day to answer a suspicion of Felony in entering the house of John Gadsby, an innkeeper and feloniously Stealing & Carrying away two Silver Spoons of the value of Four Dollars being this day solemnly called and failing to appear it is ordered that his recognizance be prosecuted.—John Dundas.[115]

The absence of a follow-up suggests the case was settled out of court, a mystery remaining as to why the wealthy youth would pilfer silver from a prominent city establishment.

Better news lay ahead. As perhaps has a consolation prize for his failure to graduate, George Washington Parke Custis in 1799 received a military rank. The context was the recruitment of qualified officers and formation of the "New Army," envisioned by Alexander Hamilton as a contingency for countering the expected threat from the French Army now controlled by Napoleon.[116] In preparation, Washington, as the reappointed commander, wrote to David Stuart on December 30, 1798, saying he felt "a thorough conviction that it was a vain attempt to keep Washington Custis to any literary pursuits, either in a public seminary or at home under the direction of any one." Hence, the general said, he had the idea of "bringing him forward as a Cornet of Horse … without encountering the dangers of war." The Troop of Light Dragoons was a cavalry used chiefly for reconnaissance. An added benefit, Washington wrote, was that the title "might divert his attention from a matrimonial pursuit (for a while at least) to which his constitution seems to be too prone."[117]

Actually, Washington already made the move two weeks earlier, proposing the appointment to Adams Administration Secretary of War James McHenry on December 14, 1798. The commander in chief expressed worry about Custis being his "only son indeed, the only male of his family." Washington said he would "further pray that no mention of his name be made until the result is known." He had not yet cleared the plan with Martha Washington or Custis's stepfather Stuart. Tobias Lear, however, jumped the gun. He informed the seventeen-year-old Custis, who was thrilled. On January 10, 1799, Custis received a letter from McHenry: "I have the honor to inform you that the President, by and with the advice and consent of the

Senate has appointed you a Cornet in the Army of the United States. You are requested to inform me, as soon as convenient, whether you accept or not the appointment, that I may notify the same to the president."[118]

The youth's precise rank was left unspecified, to "obviate misconception" because "a want of materials" meant the number of officers needed was not yet clear.[119] He was assigned to Charles Cotesworth Pinckney of South Carolina as an aide de camp. But just two months later, Washington again importuned on Custis' behalf. "May I ask if there would be any impropriety in letting Mr. Custis step from a Cornecy, into the Rank of Lieutenant?" he wrote McHenry. "But it is not my desire to ask this as a favor. I never have, nor never will, solicit any thing for myself, or connections."[120]

Washington's involvement didn't end there. On June 7, 1799, he wrote to longtime factor Clement Biddle, in Philadelphia: "Sir, my Ward, Mr. Custis, having entered into the Service of his Country as a [subaltern] Officer of the Dragoons, I wish to equip him with every thing suitable thereto; in a handsome, but not an expensive style."[121] Though the letter was likely not delivered, its itemized requests to be delivered on the "one of the first packets bound to Alexandria" included a pair of pistols and horseman's sword, a saddle and proper halter, a "proper horseman's cap." The closest thing to action the young Custis would see was some drilling at Harper's Ferry, Virginia, after which he was discharged with the brevet major rank. The youth would fire more bullets as a hunter in the Mount Vernon deer park than as a soldier. Washington counseled him there too, advising, "Fire with ball, use no hounds, and on no account kill any but an old buck!"[122]

CHAPTER 3

Building a Future Legacy

Custis uses an ample inheritance as a Washington reli-
quary, marries Virginia gentry and creates a monument on
the Federal City skyline.

Still under the age of majority with his formal education stalled, George Washington Parke Custis was living the high life at Mount Vernon in 1799 when he experienced his life's most momentous event.

To set the stage: His sister Nelly, living at Mount Vernon following her marriage to Lawrence Lewis, had been given 2,000 acres of nearby land by George Washington, on which they would build a handsome mansion known as Woodlawn. In late November she gave birth to her first child (Frances Parke Lewis) on whom Washington doted. Soon after, Custis, at eighteen and the future male heir, traveled southward with brother-in-law Lewis to inspect the Washington and Custis properties in New Kent County, Virginia.

On December 14, America's first president died in his bed at Mount Vernon, victim of a throat infection that came on after a horseback ride in wet weather. Attended by his wife Martha, friend and physician Dr. James Craik, two other physicians and secretary Lear, Washington is said to have asked for the young Custis.[1] (Craik had the unlikely distinction of having been present at the deaths of both Custis's father Jacky in 1781 and George Washington's eighteen years later.)

The heirs who were traveling were notified by a messenger bearing a letter from Lear. "It is with extreme pain that I have to communicate to you a melancholy event," Lear wrote to Custis on December 15. "Our beloved friend, General Washington, is no more!" The secretary described Washington's initial dismissal of his illness as "trifling" and the arrival of three physicians, saying the general "suffered extremely." Lear added that "Mrs. Washington and Mrs. Lewis bear the afflicting loss with as much virtuous fortitude as could be expected." He asked Custis and Lewis to "return to us speedily."[2]

On arriving at Mount Vernon (he missed the funeral), the step-grandson would learn his future as spelled out in Washington's will. "Whereas," read one clause, "it has always been my intention, since my expectation of having issue has ceased, to consider the grandchildren of my wife in the same light as I do my own relations, and to act a friendly part by them; more especially by the two whom we have reared from their earliest infancy—namely—Eleanor Parke Custis & George Washington Parke Custis." The deceased's two wards received far more than their siblings Martha and Eliza. "Actuated by the principal already mentioned, I give and bequeath to George Washington Parke Custis, the grandson of my wife, and my ward, and to his heirs, the tract I hold on Four Mile Run in the vicinity of Alexandria, containing one thousand-two hundred acres, more or less—& my entire Square, Number 21, in the City of Washington."[3] As executors, the general named his wife, George Washington Parke Custis (when he came of age), and five nephews: William Augustine Washington, Bushrod Washington, George Steptoe Washington, Samuel Washington, and Lawrence Lewis.[4]

Nothing—including Washington's unusual emancipation of some 123 slaves held in his name—would take effect until the death of Martha Washington. She would live on to 1802. A portion of the Founding Father's enslaved help would be freed in January 1801, under a deed of manumission she signed the previous month. Washington's will, filed in Fairfax Courthouse, directed that the mansion and surrounding land of Mount Vernon (along with the general's papers and library) would go to nephew Bushrod Washington. But as a Custis, the teenager once known as Washy could look forward to an immense estate through his natural paternal line: Jacky Custis, though he died without a will, left the family some 18,000 eastern Virginia acres, more than 200 enslaved persons and 30,000 English pounds.[5]

Following the sudden blow (Washington was sixty-seven and only two-and-a-half years out of the presidency), Martha Washington, her mansion creped in mourning, closed the master bedroom and took to a room on the third floor. She took comfort from having her grandson across the hall. "Washington Custis, in whom she seems quite wrapt up, was indisposed, and she seemed very anxious on his account," recalled Anna, the wife of William Thornton, the man Washington had picked to design the U.S. Capitol (where the first president's body was originally slated to be interred).[6] More than a year after the president's death, widow Martha mentioned her grandchildren in a letter to her niece Martha Dandridge: "I have been and am at this time very much indisposed. Nelly has been very unwell and Washington ill, thank God he is getting better."[7]

Soon after his guardian's death, an ambitious nineteen-year-old Custis wrote and circulated a letter praising the youth of America, drawing accolades from Revolutionary War General Henry "Light-Horse Harry" Lee. (He was the statesman who had delivered a famous eulogy to Washington before Congress: "First in war, first in peace, first in the hearts of his countrymen.") Of this early example of Custis's rhetoric, Lee wrote him in February 1800, "The sentiments which it breathes do honor to your heart; and I ardently pray as similar spirit may pervade the rising generation throughout these states."[8]

In October 1801, during the Jefferson administration, Custis helped host a visit from a future president—another "first son" named John Quincy Adams. In an October 28 diary entry, the thirty-two-year-old Adams described a family trip to Mount Vernon from Georgetown, via ferry through Alexandria, to dine and stay overnight. (The New Englander called Custis's sister Nelly "a very pleasing and beautiful woman."[9])

Martha Washington, back in September of 1800, had drafted her own will in the handwriting of her granddaughter Nelly. She died on May 22, 1802, and her testament was probated that June. It dealt mostly with Mount Vernon's furnishings, specifying that a public auction be held to sell household items not listed in the will. Bequeathed to the now-twenty-one-year-old Custis were "all the silver plate of every kind of which I shall die possessed. Together with the two large-plated coolers, with the bottle castors, and a pipe of wine if there be one in the house at the time of my death...." More substantively, Custis inherited the unique family paintings, a set of tea china, mattress bolsters, beds, Martha Washington's ancestral books (Bushrod inherited Washington's library), and a desk that had belonged to his grandfather Daniel Parke Custis.[10]

Martha's will also required that a large share of the goods be sold to retire debts. At the advertised auction held on July 20, 1802, Custis used his privileged access to buy (with borrowed funds, competing against other Washington and Custis relatives) many more of the first family relics. He and his three sisters purchased as many as 200 items.[11] By spending $4,500 (about $100,000 today) at auctions for both George and Martha's belongings, he acquired other paintings, Washington's battlefield tents and farm implements and livestock. Custis's offer to buy Mount Vernon itself was rejected by Bushrod Washington.

The value of the household goods was petty compared with the worth of his father's plantations on the Pamunkey River, and, off of Virginia's Eastern Shore, Smith's Island, smaller properties in central Virginia and Washington's Northern Virginia land along Four Mile Run. With the accompanying 200 enslaved Black men, women and children, young adult Custis found himself among the top one percent of slave owners in his state.[12] Included in that morally burdensome count were G.W.P. Custis's share (with his sisters) of the 153 "dower slaves" (89 adults and 64 children)—those from the Custis side of Martha Washington's family, who, pointedly, were not included in the group Washington slated for emancipation.[13] Several of those were among the Mount Vernon house servants with whom Custis had grown up.

In a buy-out agreement (with an annual payment) reached with his mother and her second husband, David Stuart, Custis inherited ownership of fifty-seven Blacks who would now involuntarily serve him, after he built his own estate on the Potomac.[14] The names of four dozen of those enslaved survive in an Alexandria deed book: Doll, Phill, Nat, Zachariah, Judah, Ibby, Winney, Will, Doll, Morris, Southy, Joseph, Edmonds, Agga, Moll, Peg, Bett, Jim, David, Mingoe, Con, Ned, Paul Jancy, Fanney Janey, Austin, Dina, Larry, Alley, Coelia, Mason, Amma, Paul, Peter, Joe, Molly and her child, Rachel, Joe, George, Harry, Harry, Amy, Caesar, Randolph, Beck, Julius Beck, Daniel and Issac.[15] In addition, a March 4, 1802, codicil to Martha Washington's will specified that she gave Custis "my mulato man Elish—that I bought of Mr. Butler Washington to him and his heir for ever."

In mourning the loss of the only father he knew, Custis was now eager both to honor the nation's *pater patriae* and to imitate Washington's feat of helping design a prestigious colonnaded home. His oldest sister Eliza, married to Thomas Law, had honeymooned at their elegant townhouse on the southwest corner of the Washington City.[16] Custis's sister Nelly and husband Lawrence Lewis were at work on their mansion called Woodlawn (built from 1800 to 1805). And his sister Martha and her husband Thomas Peter were soon to construct the handsome Tudor Place on a hill in Georgetown (built 1805–1816). Custis conceived of a residence that would double as a memorial. He called it Mount Washington.

His chosen riverside location, on a commanding 200-foot bluff with a view of the emerging capital city, was the most promising portion of the 2,300 acres he inherited from Jacky Custis (the bluff) and Washington (the forest two miles away along Four Mile Run). Congress, under an 1801 act passed a decade after the Maryland side of the Potomac site had been selected for the Federal City, formalized the Virginia side as Alexandria County. (The Maryland land was given the now-obsolete name of Washington County.) Hence Custis, born in Maryland and raised in Virginia, became a new District of Columbian.

The designated land for his project of a lifetime traced back to a 1669 grant by Sir William Berkeley, governor of Virginia, to Robert Howsing, a Welsh tobacco merchant,[17] and later to Gerard Alexander. Acreage nearby had been purchased by a young George Washington in 1774 from James and George Mercer, the site just five miles down the Potomac from the Abingdon plantation built by the Alexander family (for whom Alexandria City is named). Abingdon—where Custis lived as an infant and later visited regularly—was previously owned by his father Jacky (and occupied by his mother Eleanor and her new family before they settled 20 miles out in a Fairfax manor called Hope Park).[18]

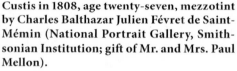

With promising black soil and abundant forests of oak, chestnut and hickory trees, the elevated site was near two convenient ferries (one owned by neighbor John Mason and another named for an earlier neighbor named Captain Henry Awbrey). The Alexandria Turnpike taking shape nearby would be suitable for future transport of supplies and crops—an advantage Custis learned from Washington himself.[19]

Custis in 1808, age twenty-seven, mezzotint by Charles Balthazar Julien Févret de Saint-Mémin (National Portrait Gallery, Smithsonian Institution; gift of Mr. and Mrs. Paul Mellon).

Who should design Custis's memorial home? As befitted their wealth and social status, the Custis sisters' homes at Woodlawn and Tudor Place were the creations of Capitol architect William Thornton. For reasons not documented, Custis in 1802 instead engaged one of Thornton's competitors.

Award-winning English architect George Hadfield (1763–1826), an immigrant graduate of the Royal Academy in London, had made an unsuccessful bid to revise the design of the U.S. Capitol, on which he had worked supervising construction. He did make his mark on some of the earliest buildings for U.S. Cabinet departments and Washington's City Hall. But he fell into disfavor with federal building commissioners.[20] Like many contemporaries in the young United States, Hadfield was inspired by Roman and Greek classical architecture. The preference for columns and peaked roofs had already been modeled by Thomas Jefferson and James Madison, who expressed through their grand homes an admiration for ancient Republics associated with the birth of democracy. The style known as the Greek Revival also showed up in the Capitol and the Executive Mansion, built around the time Hadfield and Custis drew up their plans. (Those documents vanished from the historical record.)

In summer 1802, Custis, after a brief stay in the City of Alexandria with his friend Washington Craik, set up shop in a four-room brick cottage on the Potomac's muddy flats once owned by the Alexander family. There were outbuildings from previous tenant farmers.[21] The home was damp and rat-infested, jeopardizing the priceless Washington heirlooms stored there in this era before curatorial sciences.[22] The enslaved workers set to work constructing wood cabins for their own homes. Custis also hired Scottish and Irish-born laborers. After a false start with a man named John Wither, he engaged war veteran John Ball as manager. Ball, whose family would be central to the future Arlington County, placed an advertisement in the *Alexandria Gazette* in November 1803 for a manager of a planned market garden.[23] For the formal gardens, Custis enlisted William Spence, the gardener at Mount Vernon. "Custis has finished a wing of his building," remarked Custis's aunt Rosalie (Stier) Calvert, writing from her Maryland plantation called Riversdale, to her mother in December 1803.[24] It "will be very handsome and will be seen from all points in Washington."

Custis never expected his Potomac-side project to be a primary profit center, counting on his two large plantations on the Pamunkey to finance Mount Washington. He could never have predicted that the agonizingly slow progress—due to economic vicissitudes and the War of 1812—would stretch out construction for 16 years.

Portrait of Mrs. George Washington Parke Custis, 1807–8, by Cephas Thompson. Oil on canvas, 27¼" H × 22⅜" W (Virginia Museum of Fine Arts, Richmond, gift of Mrs. A. Smith Bowman).

He did know that his dreams required one more essential ingredient: The love of his life. Like his hero George Washington, Custis planned to marry well. Through long-standing elite family connections, he became acquainted with sixteen-year-old Mary Lee Fitzhugh, then residing seven miles down the Potomac at her parents' Alexandria town home on Oronoco Street. Her father William Fitzhugh, a wealthy slave owner, had built the Georgian-style Chatham Manor across the river from the heart of Fredericksburg, Virginia, where Mary was born in 1788. Her mother was the former Anne Bolling Randolph, from another branch of Virginia gentry. By the late 1790s, the Fitzhughs were spending more time near the new Federal City in Alexandria, having put Chatham up for sale. A slave revolt in Fredericksburg in 1805 cemented Fitzhugh's decision to relocate, and where he had already built a mansion in Fairfax County called Ravensworth.

Daughter Mary, a devout Christian known to family as "Molly," became engaged to Custis early in 1804. "Custis is going to marry Chatham Fitzhugh's youngest daughter," reported Custis's aunt Rosalie. "It is a good choice which all the family is happy about."[25] The aunt described his intended as "a very pleasant woman and quite well-bred, despite the fact, as you noted, that her mother was a woman without education and her sister a fool."[26] (Rosalie's husband George attended the wedding, but she stayed home due to impassable roads.) Custis himself confided to his Pamunkey plantation overseer about his choice, "Accidents happen—in the best of families."[27]

The couple was married that July 7 in the Fitzhughs' Oronoco Street home. The service was performed by a Washington family intimate, the Rev. Thomas Davis, rector of Alexandria's Christ Church.[28]

The new husband did not make an impression as a romantic honeymooner. "Washington Custis spends most of his time at home," wrote Molly's friend Cornelia Lee in a letter dated August 24, 1804.[29] By October the new husband was off to inspect his southern properties at New Kent and King William counties.[30]

In the ensuing four years, the couple conceived four children, including a son they named Edward Hill Carter Custis, a daughter Martha Elizabeth Ann Custis, and an unnamed daughter. Those three died in infancy (Edward lived 14 months). Only their daughter Mary Anna Randolph Custis, born October 1, 1808, at the Annefield plantation in Clarke County, Virginia, would reach adulthood. "Custis's young wife is a very amiable person, but the poor girl lost her first two babies—the first lived only a few moments and the second, a delightful little girl, just died recently," Rosalie Calvert reported to her sister.[31]

Molly Custis became her husband's partner in the grand project that would become their home on the Washington horizon. One decision made early in their marriage, as evidenced in correspondence beginning in 1804, was the abandonment of the name "Mount Washington." Homes and jurisdictions invoking the *pater patriae* were becoming common (even Custis's sister Eliza, newly separated from Thomas Law, named her new home in Alexandria "Mount Washington"). So George Washington Parke Custis changed course. His choice of the name Arlington House was a tribute to his ancestor John Custis IV's plantation on Virginia's Eastern Shore.

KNOW all men by thefe Prefents,

That we *George Washington Parke Custis and William Fitzhugh*

are held and firmly bound, unto the United States of America, in the full and juft fum of one hundred and fifty dollars, to the payment whereof, well and truly to be made, we bind ourfelves, our heirs, executors and adminiftrators, jointly and feverally, firmly by thefe prefents: Sealed with our feals and dated this *the 6th* day of *July* — 1804

THE CONDITION of the above obligation is fuch, that whereas, there has this day iffued a Licenfe from the Clerks office of the Circuit Court of the Diftrict of Columbia for the County of Alexandria, for a Marriage intended between *George Wm. P. Custis and Mary La. Fitzhugh*

Now, if there is no lawful caufe to obftruct the faid Marriage, then the above obligation to be void, or elfe to remain in full force and virtue.

Sealed and delivered
in prefence of

Marriage deed for Custis and Molly Fitzhugh, July 6, 1804 (Library of Virginia and Arlington County Clerk).

That property he inherited (which by his lifetime was in disrepair) had, in turn, been named, most likely, for the ancestral village of Arlington in the British hill country of Gloucestershire. (That supposition would later be debated, prompted by an assertion published by Custis intimate William Meade, later Bishop of Virginia, that John Custis IV named his Northampton, Virginia, plantation to honor Henry Bennet, a seventeenth-century Earl of Arlington.[32])

As construction on Arlington House proceeded, financial constraints forced the Custises to concentrate first on the two wings (believed to have been completed by 1804). That architectural work-in-progress was where the family accustomed to elegance lived until the signature center block with its porticos became habitable, around 1818. One clue to Custis's tight budget was that no stone would be used in the construction. The house was made of red bricks covered with stucco and painted to resemble sandstone. The waterproof stucco plaster that would cover the columns was invented by a relative, David Meade Randolph.[33] The exterior wings of Arlington House were built at 40 feet long, 25 feet wide and its center 60 feet wide and

40 feet deep, with the eight Doric columns placed 25 feet out. In a painstaking process that required waiting months for materials to settle, the entablature above the columns and roof structure was built of wood and painted to resemble marble (true marble being beyond Custis's means).

Custis brought brick molds from Mount Vernon.[34] Invoices survive showing he ordered supplies from local merchants: Rye, straw, and corn shucks from a Joseph Birch; nails and a padlock from John Maffit; wheelbarrows and stacking from a John Murdock; nutmeg, cloves, allspice, salt, ginger and indigo from a George Gordon.[35] Both he and wife, invoices show, patronized the Stabler-Leadbeater Apothecary in Alexandria, which sold medicine, soap, perfume, combs and brushes, window glass, paint and varnish and artists' supplies.[36] Custis showed signs of being a stern taskmaster. A worker named William doing the flooring was "a first-rate laborer and fellow of good taste," Custis wrote Molly in 1810 while she was away, "but a worthless vagabond otherwise."[37]

The fully executed Arlington House, completed in 1818, was finalized by contractor Cornelius McLean, who billed Custis for $1,550.[38] The completed interior included a center hall, a first-floor family parlor with archways, a morning room (where Custis executed his paintings), a second parlor, a dining room, a conservatory, an office-studio, a "hunting hall," a guest chamber, a pantry and a school and sewing room. The upstairs accommodated the family bed chambers and dressing rooms. A basement housed a wine cellar (some bottles inherited from Mount Vernon) and a winter kitchen. The enslaved persons who provided the indoor service occupied quarters to the rear of the main house, also done in stucco, near the stables. The exception was the cook's quarters, which became part of the summer kitchen when weather was too hot for cooking in the main house. A drywell outside allowed storage of milk and eggs.[39]

Because not all his riverside land was arable, Custis embraced the English technique of creating a park between his house and the turnpike. But the farmland was active. Produce from the market and kitchen gardens (some of which the enslaved were permitted to keep) included peas, beans, potatoes, corn, asparagus, strawberries, cherries and pears, some used to produce brandy. Marketing the foodstuffs as well as timber from nearby Washington Forest, though seldom profitable, was made easier once the Long Bridge crossed the Potomac in 1809.[40]

Bread for the Arlington House community, as of 1807, came from a primitive mill (replaced in the 1830s by Custis's more elaborate grist mill, a four-floor stone structure) built about four miles away on Four Mile Run stream near a turnpike. A sawmill was erected alongside. Neither would be profitable; at one point early on Custis tried to sell them. "The corn-meal business has been found to answer remarkably well at these mills," read his advertisement in the *Federal Republican* for September 8, 1813, seeking either to dispose of them or attract a partner.

Custis's vision of a Washington memorial was grand. His fortune was replenished in 1809, when Molly's father William died, bequeathing her 800 acres near Ravensworth.[41] But even though Custis was raised in eighteenth-century Virginia affluence, his finances as an adult forced restraint. "I would tell you my countrymen, to beware of luxury," he said in 1811 at one of his many sheep-shearing parties held on the property. "It has been the bane of Republican governments. It sapped the foundation of the splendid systems of Rome and Athens."[42] By 1817, Custis was again strapped for cash and scrambling to sell land. He is recorded in a letter to an attorney challenging a revenue office threat to confiscate some of his property for back taxes. Seeking "a course of common justice," Custis instructed the counsel to threaten an "appeal to the Congress of the United States to whom, as last resource I shall be obliged to report. I hope, however, that this unpleasant business may be settled without such reference, which would make more noise that such a sum is worth."[43]

Custis wrote to Molly of his hopes that "our castle" would soon be finished as they made plans for new clothing. By the time the basics of Arlington House were complete in 1818 (improvements would continue for decades), Custis enjoyed a growing reputation as a political orator. With Arlington House he had a landmark in the capital city visible from all sides except from the west. It was the nation's first temple-like mansion, and the first fully completed monument to the glories of George Washington.

Not everyone who beheld it approved. In March of 1818, a writer described as a "new England gentleman" took a swipe at the architecture in a newspaper critique of President James Monroe. He referred to the "ruins of the Capitol, where from my chamber I have a view of the majestic Potomac, the plain on which Washington is to be built, the president's home, Commodore Porter's chateau, and Custis' Folly."[44]

But Arlington House—whose stout columns would one day become the symbol of a county called Arlington—won early plaudits long before it was praised by architectural historians. A traveler identified only as "a stranger" in May 1811 published a letter to the editor of the *National Intelligencer* praising its "picturesque views" across the Potomac: "His seat is on a superb mount, and his buildings are begun in a superior stile of taste in elegance."[45]

Decades later, Custis's daughter, in introducing her father's memoirs published in 1860, wrote fondly of the honeysuckle and laurel-bedecked enclave where she grew up: "It is a most lovely spot, overlooking the Potomac; and from the noble portico, that adorns its front, so conspicuous from every point of the federal city and its vicinity, he saw that city grow into its present grand proportions, from a humble and uninteresting village."[46]

CHAPTER 4

A New Gentleman Farmer

An agricultural reformer boosts domestic manufacturing, manages three slavery-dependent plantations and ventures into the sheep industry.

Among the published works owned by President Thomas Jefferson (whose collection would form the core of the Library of Congress) was an 1808 pamphlet honoring agricultural societies. "Bread for the poor; industry for the people—and independence to the nation," read the editor's preface printed in Alexandria, Virginia.[1]

The author was George Washington Parke Custis. Only six years after embarking on his career as a gentleman farmer, the twenty-seven-year-old heir joined the many Americans concerned about an overreliance on goods imported from England. Agriculture is the "great basis of all national prosperity, the key stone that centers the arch of government, and the great impetus that moves the machine of national wealth and individual industry," he wrote. In explaining why he has been "a labourer in its cause," the well-born Custis acknowledged that he has "endeavored to take an active part as my situation and means of knowledge would admit." He trumpeted American's "vast maritime coast, and rivers visiting the internal parts of every state, [shows] its disposition by Providence, for a great agricultural, manufacturing and commercial commonwealth." The young nation should aim for a global presence in the farming trade, he offered. He complained of a status quo in which "even the *flag of our country* is made of foreign manufacture, and our legislators and patriots, while delivering the most dignified and national sentiments are clothed in the produce of a foreign land."

Custis's pamphlet was a prospectus inviting investors to take out subscriptions for his experimental breed of sheep—"The Arlington Improved—originally delivered from the best improvements at Mount Vernon—or the American long-wooled sheep," as he labeled it. Some farming opportunities to create the best wool for clothing was now coming

48

from Custis's inherited Smith's Island, the isolated site off Virginia's Eastern Shore named for English explorer Captain John Smith. A young Custis had visited there in 1800. "The Smith's Island wool is, without question, one of the finest in the world, and has excited the promise and astonishment of all who have seen it," he said in his pitch designed to discredit the popular Spanish-born breed of Merino sheep. "The only question is the texture. If the Merino is finer in grain, the Smith's Island is so fine as to answer to which the other can be appropriated."

Sheep raised at his Arlington House or on Smith's Island, Custis forecast, would do particularly well in the U.S. southern states, where farm management is "deplorable," he jabbed, and would help them "emerge from their native lassitude, and apathy, and become aroused to a due sense of their political situation."

What qualified Custis, pampered as a youth and un-studious in college, to become a leader in American agriculture? His eventual role as an innovator, policy advocate and technician who suffered with other farmers through market downturns, marked an astonishing maturation.

The farmer newly installed at Arlington House could draw from a rich heritage. His great-grandfather John Custis IV became known in the Williamsburg, Virginia, region for innovative tobacco planting and lush garden design. But even more important, the nineteenth-century Custis descendant had the advantage of having been raised at Mount Vernon under the direction of a part-time gentleman farmer named George Washington. (In Custis's posthumous recollections, his daughter published a long-treasured text of "Agriculture Directions" from Washington written to his nephew George A. Washington in 1789. That text was more technical than inspirational: "The profit of every farm is greater or less, in proportion to the quantity of manure which is made thereon, or can be obtained by keeping the fields in good condition," the elder Washington wrote. The first president had also practiced crop rotation and experimented with sheep breeding.)[2]

Custis inherited, with Martha Washington's name inscribed, a timely instructional book published in Glasgow, Scotland, in 1798, by John Naismith. It examined farm innovations in tenant rights, land ownership and debt in the County of Clydesdale.[3] From his father and great-grandfathers, Custis also inherited other British classics such as *Salmon's History of Plants* (1710); *A Dictionary of Animal Husbandry, Gardening Etc.* (1717); and *The Compleat Housewife* (1734).[4] And he was familiar with the famed statistical compilations of Scotsman John Sinclair (1754–1835), a reformer who created the British Agriculture Board.

More tangibly, Custis inherited or purchased farm implements and livestock from Mount Vernon, including, the inventory shows, a corn drill, a flax break, a potato tool, six harrows, a boat and blacksmith tolls.[5] His animals included mules, a ram, five cows, one foal and a horse, with the proprietor eying stud fees as source of income.[6] He also purchased prized Mount Vernon ewes and Persian rams.

Custis may not have expected the Potomac-side Arlington to be a commercial-scale money-maker. Tobacco being in disfavor in Northern Virginia as damaging to soil, he planted primarily corn and wheat. He also cultivated fisheries for shad and herring on the residential property he envisioned chiefly as repository of George Washington's relics. For steadier profits, Custis counted on his plantations east of Richmond. Romancock (an Indian name for circling of water) was near West Point in King William County. It comprised 4,656 acres including 1,200 acres of marsh, and boasted a grist mill. Ten miles northwest, across the Pamunkey River in New Kent County, was the larger plantation of more than 5,000 acres called White House (where George and Martha Washington were married). There Custis built a distillery for delicacies such as apple brandy and port wine.

For decades to come, Custis from his Arlington home would hire and depend on distant overseers to keep his southern plantations operational. He confided to them in letters about family events and financial troubles. Travel—first by horse and schooner and later by steamer—was by necessity infrequent. In 1804, Custis hired James Anderson, a well-regarded Mount Vernon manager, to run the Pamunkey River plantations. He had served George Washington effectively, running his distillery, but annoyed his patron by resigning early.[7] Anderson and Custis immediately visited Smith's Island for sheep-grazing possibilities, salt mining and the possibility of building a school.

On November 28, 1804, Custis wrote to Anderson that he had procured a Captain Wallis, for $100, "to sail tomorrow," and the distillery will receive a stock from a $750 received. "Your salary will be drawn from that first payment," which Custis enclosed. "I beg you to prepare his cargo: wool, cotton, beef salted. I am quite out," the frugal farmer said. "The price is too high to be purchased here." Wallis would also transport to Arlington a load of flour.[8]

Custis demonstrated sophistication in planning. "I approve of the sale of any mare or colt and would wish you to deliver under the name of Arlington," he wrote Anderson in an exchange on housekeeping in early February 1806. "I truly hope you will be able to do something handsome in the fishery this year which will pay off many little matters. In regard to the salt works, the probability of war and taking our vessels will greatly enhance the value of salt."[9] He promised to ship Anderson a boar pig from Arlington. On February 27, Custis followed up with advice on ways to keep rats from raiding supplies of oil used as a preservative. He also reported on shipping, that "Captain Milestone arrived safe here on 21st and delivered his bill of lading in good order a few turkeys." Custis confessed his financial constraints: "If prices are not much altered for the better at Norfolk, you can load this man for Alexandria again as soon as possible," he instructed. "If you have received the money for the mare, please remit, as I am poor as charity."[10]

Anderson replied that "the distillery house is nearly finished." He supplied an inventory of pork produced, along with a list of the two plantations' live colts, cattle, sheep and lambs. His ledger broke down 143 enslaved Blacks into categories of tradesmen, field men, women, boys, women, girls, house slaves, invalids, sick, and children.[11] The team at White House had also begun selling clay to builders in Richmond.[12]

Custis sought to impress Anderson with the potential for Smith's Island sheep. "I thought you would not like the legs of my fine sheep," he wrote his Scottish caretaker in June 1810. "But as I knew the pastures in your country were very large and the grass not very fine, I thought I would send you a fellow well qualified with legs to scramble over them. His wool is immense—14 inches measured at the shew—the young lamb you will like the better as he grows more."[13]

Meanwhile, Custis's plan for a school for poor children on Smith's Island, to be financed through sales of sheep and cattle, hit resistance. A correspondent wrote him on October 2, 1807, to say they might find 20–25 "scholars" in the neighborhood of the selected facility. "Your school will be very thin."[14]

At his still-primitive home on the Potomac, Custis was embarking on his major effort at agricultural innovation. Ambassador David Humphreys, a Washington intimate Custis knew as a boy, returned from Spain with a flock of 100 special sheep known as Merinos.[15] His delivery to mills in Connecticut would spark high-impact competition across the young United States. In response, Custis on March 8, 1803, took out an unusual ad in the *Alexandria Gazette*, promoting "An American Breed of Sheep." He promised a premium of $40 for any farmer who could deliver, within two years, a "finest ram lam." The strategy lay in fattening the animal with nourishment that produces the most high-quality fleeces and consumable mutton. He began offering sheep stud services and sending wool specimens to agricultural authorities in Philadelphia, New Jersey, upstate New York and even to England. (John Sinclair himself took notice.)

Custis also tapped Alexandria County Revolutionary War veteran John Ball, another alumnus of Mount Vernon, to manage the Arlington House plantation.[16] But what Custis called the Arlington Institution for the Promotion of Agriculture and Domestic Manufactures "is solely the work of one individual, having neither association nor support from any other person," he declared.[17] Custis was credited with holding the first American agriculture fair, launching a tradition in multiple jurisdictions at which he would appear regularly for the rest of his life.[18]

Breeding Sheep to Change a Nation

To overcome skepticism, Custis used his connections. In 1805 he followed through on his advertisement by holding the first of what would become a famous series of competitive "sheep shearings." The annual events were held on his birthday, April 30 (also the anniversary of Washington's first inauguration)—at his own expense. The public exhibitions of wool clipping drew as many as 300 guests. Architect William Thornton, after attending, recalled the beauty of Washington's battlefield tents on display, decorated with laurel and honeysuckle.[19] Prizes for the most promising sheep included engraved silver cups, cash, and, later, waivers from the tolls at the Custis flour and meal mills on Four Mile Run.

In the well-publicized shearing in April 1808, Custis's brother-in-law Lawrence Lewis exhibited a large, long-wooled lamb called Dishley. He competed against entries from Custis's other brother-in-law Thomas Peter and neighbors John Mason of Analostan Island, across the Potomac, and William Lee of Burgundy Farm, near Mount Vernon. The winner for woven fabric was Miss Peggy Fields of Fairfax, whose work was described as "white, exceeding fine thread, pattern Marseilles, of small figure very soft, even and extremely beautiful, 7–8 yards wide."[20] Mason made a motion to the crowd that at the next sheep shearing, "visitors should appear clad in American manufacture."

The experimental shearings drew praise from Revolutionary War hero Charles Cotesworth Pinckney, who had known Custis as a teenager. "I sincerely congratulate you on the successful progress you have made in improving the valuable article of manufacture and on the discovery of the Smith's Island breed of sheep," he wrote from Charleston, South Carolina, on September 17, 1807, inviting Custis to be a member of his state's Agricultural Society. "The most beautiful wool I ever beheld."[21]

Custis presented Jefferson with a waistcoat made from homespun "Arlington cloth."[22] "I took that pattern to Mr. Jefferson, then the third President of the United States, and requested him to have it made up and wear it on the evening Nation's Jubilee," Custis recalled decades later. "Accordingly, at his levee [reception] on the succeeding 4th of July, Jefferson wore the first vest made out of domestic cloth ever worn in this country."[23]

The Arlington entrepreneur also publicized plans to provide homespun for the American military. In 1808, he gave Dolley Madison the year's best cotton cloth. But husband James Madison, who was inaugurated in

1809 in garb made from Merino sheep, was only mildly interested. Having put off Custis before, he replied saying only that "in the economy of our rural establishments, we ought, by reducing the number of black cattle ... [create] additional value lately given to wool."[24]

Custis's ambitions also rose to investing in a clothing factory on the Potomac shores. His advertisement recorded in the Raleigh, North Carolina, *Star*, read:

> George Washington Parke Custis, the Farmer of Arlington, and proprietor of Smith's Island near the capes of Virginia, so famous for its sheep—proposes the establishment of a woolen manufactury by a company, between Mount Vernon and the Federal City; to be managed by the commissioners of the Arlington Institution. The stock to be invested in 150 shares of 20 pounds each. The site of the factory, stone, timber, etc. to be gratuitously given by Mr. Custis. Subscriptions are open at Alexandria, Arlington, and other places.[25]

Custis's coarser cross-breeds required him to keep up with the purer and softer merinos. He approached local landowners like James Hooe, of Alexandria and Franconia in Fairfax County, writing in 1810, "I perceive by the *Gazette* that you have a few Merinos for sale—that may be the price & terms of payment.... I would be glad to purchase a few more, but of the last sales were so far beyond my means to prevent my offering a single bid."[26] Customers near Custis's New Kent County property bought in, having read the news coverage. "I concluded from the quantity of wool that your sheep must be an excellent breed," wrote neighbor Nathaniel Atkinson. "State in a line to me the general properties of this breed of sheep, say, the average quantity that the ewes and wether will yield."[27]

As storm clouds gathered for war with England, Custis continued to arrange shipments of Smith's Island fine wool to the old country. On February 17, 1810, the child of Mount Vernon received confirmation of plans and encouragement from a George Logan of New York City: "At this momentous crisis," the merchant wrote, "it becomes the duty of every good citizen to smother the spirit of party and all unite as Americans with the feelings of Washington."[28] Similarly, a Federal City recipient of Custis's specimens the next year sent word that he would present them to the Davis Society for the Promotion of the Arts and Manufactures, "The example you have exhibited is rare, and requires [more] than ordinary patriotism," he wrote Custis. "I am [inclined] to believe that Americans feel ingratitude with regard to Washington."[29]

Not everyone warmed. "Merino rams are becoming more fashionable with you than English horses," chided competing New York planter Robert Livingston, with whom Custis traded technical advice.[30] Others questioned the feasibility of shipping sheep from isolated Smith's Island, reporting that ewes and rams fought when caged for transport. But Custis continued to compete against pure imported merinos. "It has always been my labour to impress upon my countrymen the propriety of cherishing their native flocks," he wrote. Imported expensive merinos have left "the humble produce of our own clime … forgotten or despised." He added a protectionist argument: "The great farmer may be able to take care of himself. But the little farmer deserves every care from his country."[31]

Such allusions to political discourse were not lost on pro–Jeffersonian critics of Custis's Federalist leanings. In July 1810, a sneering letter signed by an anonymous "Cornplanter" appeared in the Republican-leaning Richmond, Virginia, paper called the *Spirit of Seventy-Six*. "Here is the little ram again," the critic wrote of recent coverage of the orator, whom he accused of elitism, drunkenness and plagiarism. "His own sheep are not more distinguished from those of his neighbors…. Custis talks of 'keeping his sheep not for show' but 'to prepare them for sharing the slender hospitalities of his poor neighbors' farms," Cornplanter jabbed. "You contemplate him between the handles of a plough, 'without gloves or umbrella' setting good examples to the effeminate sons of luxury and sloth or cultivating the fine arts in the character of painter or poet; or giving the public a schedule of his Smith's Island, and other property; or telling the world how much richer he might be if he chose it."[32] Cornplanter questioned President Madison's decision to appoint Custis a justice of the peace in Alexandria County. And in a political swipe, he admonished, "Let him relinquish or the present, or at least pursue with less precipitate and overweaning zeal, the small, but delicate project of 'renationizing' the whole people of the United States."

Custis replied in print, questioning why he should be blamed for his bid "to seek in our domestic institutions, that industry and prosperity we so admire in others…. If these are crimes, I glory in my sin," he said in a gambit to rise above party. "I would not change, to be sovereign of the popular sentiment. No, sir, my politicks are Mount Vernon…. In those principles have I lived & labored."[33] Not humbly, Custis declared that his destiny is "so interwoven with the glorious destiny of the nation that whatever our domestic interests are hailed as the guardian genius of our clime, my humble service will not be forgotten."[34]

By the time the shearings ended in 1811, Custis had failed to situate Arlington Improved or Smith's Island breeds as fixtures in the American markets. But the exhibitions helped Custis influence local farm groups such as the competing Columbia Agricultural Society in Georgetown, and they helped spawn agricultural fairs throughout the mid–Atlantic region. The events also established him as a host with regional fame. A visitor in May 1809 wrote, "We are all united in our admiration of the amicable and yet truly dignified deportment of Mr. Custis, which I never saw excelled on any similar occasion."[35] The *Boston Patriot* newspaper ranked Custis, along with

Humphreys, Robert Livingston and George Washington himself, as among "the nation's most distinguished farmers."[36]

And the shearings would enhance the resources and visibility of the Arlington plantation. His domestic fishing operations had been expanded to exploit the Potomac's stocks of sturgeon, shad and herring. He was harvesting timber and quarrying stone from his Four Mile Run property and had put his sawmill and stone grist mill in operation by 1808.[37] A ferry operation helped link him to the new Federal City and the ports in Georgetown and Alexandria. In 1816, local newspapers reported, as many as 1,500 beef cattle were fattened in Arlington for the District of Columbia butchers.[38] Dry goods made from Smith's Island herds were by then valued at $80,000.[39]

Custis wrote joyfully to his wife Molly, sharing private thoughts as she was resting in Milford, Virginia, that their messenger "arrived today & delivered the intelligence that you look full and as … sweet as when you were married…. Believe me this good news has improved my health & Spirts." He informed his wife that he had moved earth in their Potomac-side estate, creating new kitchen gardens by employing ten horses and adding floor partitions to their home.[40]

Trouble Down South

Their joy wouldn't last. "This is to inform you," came the letter from Custis friend Will Costin in Northampton County, April 9, 1814, "that the British landed on Smith's Island and took from thence about 60 head of sheep and cows."[41]

The War of 1812's trade embargoes, and the nation's later economic downturns in 1819 and 1837, would combine over the decades to destabilize Custis's farming enterprise. From his office in Arlington House, he was forced to make changes, to sell excess property, alter personnel and adopt new transportation technology.

"The distressed and confused situation of the business," his White House caretaker wrote to him in November 1814, "has been such that I have not been about to write satisfactorily and postponed it from time to time hoping every day to have it in my power to inform you of the quantity of corn delivered and the proceeds—you no doubt, sir, have been astonished at my not writing."[42]

From Arlington House, Custis had already begun selling Washington family lands in western Virginia. Even the Four Mile Run property was considered for the auction block, with Custis marketing it as filled with first-rate timber. However, "it is very certain that the character of the lands belonging to the heirs of George Washington has been grossly misrepresented," wrote one unimpressed correspondent.[43] In July 1813, Custis had the Washington Forest tract of 123 acres surveyed by a team of John Gilpian and Thomas Trammell for a Mr. Sommers. Custis told helpful landowner Hooe that he was "anxious to avoid [the] inconvenience of a public sale of my land." A few months later, he added that the Washington Forest tract was "tampered with by certain persons and … defeated by the operations of the war."[44]

Custis and wife Molly had earlier sold smaller tracts near the Eastern shore, but had trouble unloading the 500-acre ancestral Arlington plantation.[45] (A survey there in 1820 found only a chimney remaining.[46]) The surveys were not always definitive. A surveyor named Christopher Johnson wrote Custis on July 1, 1818, to defend his measure of Romancock. Custis had wanted the work redone before purchasers came to make offers. "I can assure you that I have used every exertion and extension of boundary to give you a true and accurate quantity of land," Johnson wrote, asking Custis to travel down before requiring a second effort.[47]

As his operations expanded, Custis hired crews for the schooners *Lady of the Lake* and *American Eagle*, which moved produce from Georgetown and Alexandria to and from the Pamunkey. Beginning in 1820, he sought to trim expenses by outfitting his paid laborers and enslaved workers with self-designed wooden-soled shoes. "They have done most famously of all the modern economics; they are the *chef d'oeuvre*," he boasted in a farm journal, citing his leather dealer's assertion that using wood reinforced by iron nails has reduced Custis's costs by 75 percent.[48] "My people at first apprehended broken shins, broken necks, and all the ills which flesh is heir to—but now declare nothing would induce them to return to leather bottoms," he wrote in 1825. "The rogues now admit that their feet are always warm."

Custis's technical knowledge deepened. He compared timber by price versus quality and extolled the benefits of fertilizers such as marl (lime-rich mud), oyster shells and Peruvian guano. He described landscaping and construction of water-tight enclosures for reclaiming marshland. "I attacked an ash pocosin [a wetland] with Irishmen, some four years ago," he wrote to *American Farmer*, "ditched it with a dyke of 1–2 feet base, and 3 feet high, and ditch of 8 feet in width, which kept out the tide, and drained the surface sufficiently for cultivation."[49]

"The corn crop was very good," as was cotton, and trees will produce a barrel of brandy, Custis was informed by new Pamunkey overseer William Bromley in 1824. "Tobacco is not good," Bromley added, describing efforts to treat illnesses among the enslaved. "The woman Betsey's girl Judy is dead."[50] Bromley had been recruited by a short-term caretaker after, J.B.

A caretaker's inventory from Custis' plantations on the Pamunkey River, combining enslaved persons with livestock (Virginia Museum of History & Culture).

Walden, who had arrived the previous year, had prompted reports that he may been have been mistreating the enslaved.[51]

By 1832, Bromley's accounts showed that White House plantation was functioning with 97 "Negroes," 16 horses and mules, 2 colts, 47 cattle, 6 calves, 149 sheep, 94 hogs and 60 pigs. Nearby Romancock, he wrote to Custis, had 59 "Negroes," 9 horses and mules, 2 colts, 94 cattle, 11 calves, 145 sheep, 125 hogs and 50 pigs.[52]

In the ensuing decades, Custis would use agricultural fairs and historical societies to deliver some of his best oratory—interweaving farming topics with politics and patriotism. "Providence has given us a genial climate and a teeming soil, and we will and ought to be independent," he told the Fairfax Historical Society in 1850.[53] By age sixty-nine, he had not strayed from the rhetoric in the pamphlet he published at the age of twenty-seven. "Agriculture will give more benefit to the state and happiness to the individual than any other occupation in human affairs," he wrote in old age. "May be the heraldry of America became the plough and the loom."[54]

CHAPTER 5

The Federalist Orator

Regaling crowds with patriotic rhetoric, irking political critics, endorsing military heroes for president while supporting Irish immigrants and veterans.

Though blessed—one could say *burdened*—with a world-famous name, George Washington Parke Custis was never destined to be a political leader. At age twenty-one, he declared his candidacy to be a delegate to the Virginia General Assembly from Fairfax County, in 1802. Echoing the Federalist tendencies of his upbringing, he spurned personal campaigning and defended property qualifications for voter eligibility. To the Jeffersonians' desire to expand the rights of suffrage, Custis warned that Americans would soon learn "whether the powers of rhetoric ... would carry more conviction to the minds of the people than a proposition extracted, not from books, but from grain or fruit." He placed only third among four candidates for two seats.[1] But Custis vowed to press on, writing to the *Alexandria Gazette,* "The light of truth will yet flash on the mind hardened by prejudice."[2]

Instead, Custis would satisfy his goal of preserving his step-grandfather's legacy and remain active in various Washington societies, which, as political parties intensified their demands for loyalty, leaned Federalist.[3] His mark on politics would be made as an orator, in causes ranging from Federalism to Irish independence to national unity to dignity for military veterans. His was a career in public speaking that brought special invitations to historic ceremonies that would afford Custis unique status as probably the sole American who could say he personally knew the first fifteen presidents.[4]

In an age before electronic amplification, Custis had to rely on his own projection to capture the attention of rowdy crowds. "Scarcely of the middle stature, he is erect, with a full-made person, and a fine, intellectual face, a good head, very considerably bald, a few light flowing locks, a large Grecian nose, and two bright grey eyes," wrote a correspondent on hearing

59

the orator at a Bladensburg, Maryland, barbecue in 1848. "His voice is full-toned and rich."[5]

Custis was enamored of Revolutionary War officers, in particular, George Washington's military and political associates Alexander Hamilton and Henry "Light-Horse Harry" Lee (the father of Custis's future son-in-law, Robert E. Lee). He personally wrote profiles of the older men that were later included in his memoir. "In the illustrious Alexander Hamilton were united the patriot, the soldier, the statesman, the jurist, the orator, and philosopher, and he was great in them all," Custis wrote.[6] Henry Lee, who would spend his later years disgraced by debt, was a "highly gifted man," Custis testified. "With the advantages of a classical education, General Lee possessed taste, and distinguished powers of eloquence; and was selected, upon the demise of Washington, to deliver the oration in the funeral solemnities of the Pater Patriae."[7]

Deploying rhetoric flush with classical references, exclamatory patriotism and, yes, hyperbole, Custis embarked on a speaking career befitting a man who proclaimed that his destiny was "interwoven with the glorious destiny of the nation."[8] In one of his earliest speeches, he warned an Alexandria crowd at an 1804 July Fourth celebration against the rise of parties, countering criticisms of the late George Washington that grew louder during the Jefferson administration. "We have viewed the history of republicks, and observed the blessings that form of government affords," he said. "Would we close the tale without remarking the dark side it presents? Ingratitude has been a leading figure in the ancient system, and is not unknown in the present day.... May the rage of political intolerance cease to affect this favored clime. May the persecution of party life lose its force."[9]

Yet Custis backed patriotism over party enough to treat statesmen with the respect he was raised to display. In March 1809, on returning from the inauguration of James Madison, Custis and two Federalist friends spotted a lone horseman on Pennsylvania Avenue. He was none other than newly disempowered President Thomas Jefferson. "See gentlemen, how soon a great man becomes neglected and his services forgotten in America when he ceases to be the fountain of patronage and power!" Custis told his friends. "Whatever may be the revolutionary patriot and statesman's politics now, they were of the right sort in 1776, and led to the independence his country!" The three Federalists then escorted Jefferson down the avenue.[10]

Addressing farm-oriented crowds during sheep shearings, Custis spoke of Federalist politics and trade issues, enhancing his reputation. At an 1810 event at Arlington House, he broached foreign policy. "An enemy's anchor now clings to our soil," he said in praising the Spanish ambassador for his government's resistance to Napoleon. "May their glorious efforts be crowned with success.... May they grasp the temple of rational liberty, and crush with its ruins the oppressors of mankind!"[11]

His growing reputation set him up to deliver, in September 1812, his turning-point oration: His eulogy for the martyred Revolutionary War hero General James Lingan. It would endure through the ages as powerful defense of the father of the country as well as of freedom of the press.

Amidst a major split between America's political parties, Congress on June 19, 1812, declared war on the British, following years of trade embargoes and English ship crews' impressment of American sailors. Like many Federalists, Custis was critical of President Madison's interventionist policy, fearing, as did his compatriots in the Federal City area, economic damage to the ports of Georgetown, Baltimore and Alexandria.[12] In those troubled times, he was equally appalled by English "despotism" as by French Emperor Napoleon's European conquests.

That August, violence erupted between Federalists and Jeffersonian Republicans in Baltimore. A Federalist editor, Alexander Contee Hanson, back in June, had published criticisms of the Madison administration in the Baltimore *Federal Republican*, accusing the president of rushing to war. The Democratic press called for action. Within days, a mob with Republican sympathies numbering 400 laid siege to the newspaper office, prompting Hanson to escape to the safety of Georgetown. He continued publishing, returning to Baltimore on July 26 armed with muskets and escorted by eight sympathizers, including two war heroes. They were "Light-Horse Harry" Lee and James Lingan, who had made his name during the 1776 Battle of Long Island. (Lingan had later been captured by the British at Fort Washington and suffered in the notorious prison ship *Jersey.*)

Editor Hanson pressed on toward his publication's goal: "To participate in maintaining the rights of citizens and property, and defending the liberty of the press" against jingoists going to war.[13] He took possession of a house on Baltimore's South St. Charles Street and published another inflammatory edition. Democratic Party backers made several attempts to attack the house from nearby Fells Point. Lingan and comrades defended the newspaper office, and when authorities intervened, they agreed to go to the city jail for their own protection. On July 28, a mob met them there, shouting that Lingan was a "Tory Traitor." Hanson offered to give himself up, but the jailer declined to surrender the keys. The Federalist activists by now were mixed in with other prisoners. "Does this look as if I was a traitor?" Lingan is said to have demanded as he was clubbed, tearing open his shirt to expose the decades-old gash of Hessian bayonet. The mob tortured the old man, slicing flesh with pen knives and pouring hot candles in the eyes of the Federalists.[14] Lingan perished in the dank jail. Disputes persisted over the facts—did he plea for his life? Was his body really left exposed to the elements? A congressional investigation followed.

Custis was not the Federalists' first choice to deliver Lingan's eulogy. Originally, planners sought attorney Francis Scott Key—two years before he would write the "Star Spangled Banner"—but he declined for fear of new violence.[15]

On September 1, 1812, the crowd having grown too large to fit into St. John's Church in Georgetown, Custis addressed the mourners from a dais under George Washington's battlefield tent, erected nearby. The fact that Custis never met Lingan, the speaker said, assured that he himself spoke without political motives. (He was well acquainted, however, with Light-Horse Harry Lee.) "By what standard of patriotism shall we try your Lingan?" he thundered. Not by today's "mushrooms of yesterday," but by the "standard of 'Seventy-Six.'" Invoking classical Roman and Greek references, Custis described Lingan's heroics and shipboard imprisonment during the New York campaign. And, in a text that would be circulated as a pamphlet, he invoked George Washington. "Weep not my brethren, that our chief is gone. Dry up your tears; and thank the Author of divine mercies for having so long preserved our benefactor for our happiness." Custis was responding to "calumnies" he believed had come from Jeffersonians and Madisonians in the State Department. "I well remember the good old federal times, when the Father of his Country, blest with his virtues our rising empire," the orator said. "Then was the majesty of the laws supreme; then was the liberty of the press inviolate; and sure, if ever there was a time, when its licentiousness required a curb, it was, when its slanders were aided at the reputation of the first of men!"[16]

Those listening to the speech found it moving. "The profound silence of the audience, which, in number could not have fallen short of 1,800, was only interrupted by their sighs and tears," said a newspaper account. "To the eloquence of Mr. Custis, description wants power to do justice."[17]

But detractors inside the administration weighed in. The Federalists "could pick up nobody else to make use of but that ridiculous creature Custis, who is the standing laughing stock of the whole District of Columbia," said John Colvin, clerk to Secretary of State James Monroe.[18]

Even more snide was the commentary from "A.B." writing in the *American Watchman*. "This gentleman has been selected (for what reason God only knows) to deliver an oration at the funeral of Gen. Lingan," read the diatribe that mocked Custis's "Arlington sheepshearing park.... It is astonishing that the Federalists should not have had ... policy enough to have kept this absurd effusion from seeing the light and thereby prevented the author from being exposed to the contempt and ridicule of the discerning men even of their own party. Such a composition of inflated and pompous nonsense of affected pathos and ranting bombast has rarely been presented to the view of an enlightened public."[19]*

Yet the Arlington orator's reputation only grew. On June 5, 1813, Custis demonstrated a knowledge of foreign affairs in a speech he titled "A Celebration of Russian Victories" in turning back the marauding French Army of Napoleon in Eastern Europe.[20] Again, the Federalists put on an event to jab at Madisonians. Speaking at St. John's Church in Georgetown, Custis invoked inspirational events of conquest and resistance in Europe, returning, as usual to George Washington as a model. "When we fought for liberty, many were the foreign bosoms which beat in unison with our cause," he said. "Perhaps under the fur garment of the distant Russia, America and her efforts may have excited that cheering warmth which virtuous bosoms nourish." Napoleon's most recent march, he said, "is like the sirocco of the desert, spreading ruin and desolation around him—his course is known by the smoke of villages cooling in human blood." With the Russian ambassador in the audience, Custis implored, "Russia, go on! Thine own chains broken, break thou the chains of others." He then repeated a past prophecy for the fate of his own country, "that the heart which shall direct the energies of this great nation to the accomplishment of that high destiny the meritorious life of Washington founded, must feel the principles and be warned by the virtues of that immortal man."

The ongoing war with Britain continued to pit Federalists against the Madison administration. Custis feared that a British victory would dump cheap products in his country and hamper domestic manufacturing. But disapproval of the policy did not deter him from joining the military effort. Back in June 1810, the Virginia gentleman who had briefly been a cornet at age nineteen had been named captain of the Alexandria Light Dragoons (though he resigned a year later).[21]

When British troops first threatened Washington, D.C., in 1814, Custis volunteered. But he was rejected by the Madison administration due to rheumatism in his hands.[22] "Then I will go into the ranks," he told a reporter.[23] He would accept no pay. In the losing Battle of Bladensburg, Maryland, on August 24, Custis, as a thirty-three-year-old member of a battery led by Captain George Peter, fired the last shot from a field gun as the Americans retreated. Traveling back through the District, Custis stopped at the White House to verify that that the famous Gilbert Stuart portrait of Washington had been saved from British arsonists.[24] (Dolley Madison and two enslaved servants are credited with removing it.)[25] Custis continued to serve his

---

*In an historical sequel, Lingan's remains in 1908 were re-interred in Arlington National Cemetery, Custis's former property.

community by allowing families impoverished by the trade war to gather wintertime firewood at Arlington House.

Favored Politicians

Though as humiliated as any American by the British invasion of the capital, Custis took advantage of the situation to make a surprising new friend. In January 1815, Major General Andrew Jackson won a belated but inspiring victory in the Battle of New Orleans. The future president would be the first of several military heroes in whom Custis saw a worthy successor to George Washington. Custis won the privilege of escorting Jackson on a tour of Mount Vernon.[26]

They would meet again on the eve of Jackson's first run for president, New Year's Day 1824. Custis presented the general with the pocket telescope used in combat by Washington containing a Latin inscription affixed by Custis celebrating liberty. "Although it was in itself of but little value, there was attached to it recollections of the most interesting character. It had been raised to the eye of the departed chief in the most awful and momentous periods of our mighty conflict," he later recalled. "A memorial to the hero who triumphed to obtain liberty, it is now appropriately bestowed upon the hero who triumphed to preserve it." Noting that Jackson was childless, Custis asked that "at his decease," he leave the telescope, "as Alexander left his kingdom—'to the most worthy.'"[27]

After Jackson won the presidency in 1828, he and Custis would meet on numerous boat trips on the Potomac, and Custis's daughter hosted the president on a military posting after her marriage to Robert E. Lee. Custis's ambivalence about his partiality toward this exception to his Federalist leanings was evidenced in his defensive comment on Jackson's expansion of the spoils system of partisan appointments to government jobs. "When Jackson came in," he said, "this spoils carnival was simply the bursting of the gates from which Jefferson had drawn the bolts."[28]

Custis preferred to memorialize the wartime heroism of the Democratic Party's Jackson, publishing in 1829 in the Democratic-leaning *U.S. Telegraph* twelve stanzas of lyrics to a song that would eventually be performed at Washington's National Theater. Sample verse:

> Should a foe invade our land, Old Hick'ry with a Patriot band; Will hope once more to make a stand, And strike for Victory.[29]

Custis's belief that military heroism made presidential timber led him a decade later to enthusiastically back William Henry Harrison, the hero of the 1811 Battle of Tippecanoe. Harrison was nominated in 1840 by the

Federalists' successor party, the Whigs, founded in 1833 to oppose the Jacksonians. The "veteran Orator of Liberty ... who knows what General Harrison is, has consented to appear ... in favor of the Old Patriot and Soldier," read the newspaper announcement of a Custis appearance at a Whig barbecue at Pohick, in Fairfax, Virginia. "There will be something in listening to the adopted son of Washington speaking in the county in which the Father of his Country lived, and almost within sight of the spot where his ashes rest."[30] Custis spoke again to Alexandria Whigs at a streamer-decorated, illuminated parade the week after the election to celebrate the victory of Harrison and running mate John Tyler.[31] "Upon arriving in the public square, the procession filed in," wrote one reporter, "and Mr. G.W.P. Custis, the Orator of the Day, immediately took the stand and addressed the people in an eloquent, animated, and patriotic speech."[32]

The pattern repeated when Zachary Taylor, hero of the Mexican War, won the nomination in 1848. Custis announced his support at yet another autumn Whig barbecue in Alexandria, in which he hailed Taylor as in the same league as Washington and Jackson as a military man who can preserve the union. Taylor is "a man of wisdom and prudence, and a safe man, my fellow countrymen," Custis proclaimed. "Make him your president."[33]

At a speech in Washington that September, Custis delivered another stemwinder at a Whig meeting. "We are a nation of freemen, the proudest, the most prosperous and happy in the world," Custis said to uproarious applause. "My experience teaches me that there is nothing to fear from the just ambition of a military man at the head of the nation."[34] The *Alexandria Gazette* described that speech as "able and eloquent.... It called to minds the days of 1840. The Whig feeling is rising fast and high."[35]

Once in office, President Taylor hosted Custis for an evening dinner held in honor of Hungarian exiles fighting for liberty.[36] And Custis was invited to accompany the president and speak in Richmond in February 1850 at ceremonies surrounding the laying of the foundation for the Washington monument in Virginia's capital city.[37]

But Custis and Taylor would be tied together in history for a less auspicious reason. In the summer of 1850, Custis joined the president as a designated speaker at the July 4 celebration in the hot sun at the major Washington Monument under construction in the District of Columbia. Custis used the occasion to warn against planting seeds of secession. "While with joyous hearts we assemble to celebrate this anniversary, how comes, it my countrymen, that we hear the ill-omened sound of Disunion so rife in the land?" he said. "Of a truth, in my life's young day, it would have been a bold man who would have dared to utter the word."[38]

As recounted by Whig activist and newspaper editor Thurlow Weed, Taylor complained of a heart pain and giddiness. "The old hero sat in the sun at the Washington Monument during the long spreadeagle address by Senator [Henry Stuart] Foote [of Mississippi], with a tedious supplementary harangue by George Washington Parke Custis—exposed to the heat for nearly three hours. [The president] had drunk heavily of iced water and returned to the White House weary, fatigued and still complaining of headaches and dizziness." Taylor was reported to have then eaten cherries and milk to cool off. He died on July 9.[39]

A Guest for All Seasons

Over the decades, Custis would accept dozens of invitations to speak on subjects beyond George Washington and Federalism. "Old Man Eloquent," as the press dubbed him, addressed the economy, Irish Americans, European quests for liberty, the retrocession of Alexandria County from the District of Columbia and veterans benefits.

Perhaps his most formal address came early, delivered to Washington Society of Alexandria on February 22, 1820. "I am a volunteer on this occasion!" said the 38-year-old Custis in introducing a Washington's birthday fete. He filled his remarks with allusions to Greek and Roman military history as well as observations on the nation's economic troubles stemming from the downturn of 1819. "My address is not intended for graybeards only," he proclaimed. "I endeavor to portray the life and character of one who united so many of the rare and excellent qualities estimable in man." Custis reviewed Washington's "charmed life" going back to the French and Indian War and the lowest points of the Revolution: "It was at this gloomy and desponding period of our affairs that Washington formed that noble resolve, which, Americans, should be written in your books and treasured in your hearts—when asked if all is lost, he replied, 'Never, while we can defend the passes of the western mountains, and give liberty as an inheritance to our children.' Such, Virginia, was thy noble son."

Custis may have thought the Washington references would comfort those in poor financial straits. "The dilapidated state of our finances made it impossible to discharge and recompense the soldiery for their meritorious services and sufferings," he continued. "O Washington, unexampled man! May the remembrance of thy heroic life and actions inspire thy countrymen to preserve and perpetuate the last of the republics."[40]

Thinking globally, Custis was called upon in 1831 to raise money to support Polish freedom fighters battling the Russian Czar.[41] And during the 1848 uprisings that shook European capitals, he delivered a speech at Congress's behest in the District of Columbia praising "movements in Italy and prospects of Ireland joining in the benefits of the awaking of the people in Europe."[42] Again with members of Congress in attendance, Custis that April presided over a meeting of the Washington Repeal Confederation, whose purpose was to support freedom from monarchy and despotism in Europe.[43]

But no interest group attracted Custis's attention like the Irish-Americans. Their decades-long grievances against the domination of Ireland by the British won the heart of Custis, who, though raised as an Episcopalian, praised the Catholics' historic involvement in the Revolutionary army and enjoyed their annual St. Patrick's Day celebrations. The American Irish, many of whom occupied the lowest-status rungs among the white population, thrilled to the attentions of the well-born Custis. Their patron welcomed them to a land that recognized "no established church. Here every form of religion is tolerated and stand upon its own basis, and every religionist worships after the manner which the heart shall dictate," he said in one of many talks in the nation's capital. The Revolution brought "the rare spectacle of Protestant and Catholic, Jew and Gentile, fighting side by side for the power of self-government and the rights of mankind."[44]

On June 20, 1826, Custis's stature and enthusiasm were enough to give him an official role in the Irish cause, as chairman of the Friends of Civil and Religious Liberty in the District of Columbia. At their fourteen-member committee meeting at City Hall, Custis gaveled a vote on group's resolution "to express sympathy for the People of Ireland, and on an earnest desire and hope for a speedy amelioration in their condition."[45] The meeting's minutes, which would be published later in a British volume on liberty, included this toast from Custis: "May the Nations of the Old World, ere another half century shall elapse, be as independent and free, prosperous, contented, and happy as we."[46]

The British publishers included an account of Custis's speech weeks later at a July 4 event on the 50th anniversary of the signing of the Declaration of Independence. He invoked the name of Washington and the inscription his battlefield tent that read, "Honour and gratitude to Ireland, whose sons nobly contributed to the establishment of American independence." Custis pointed to a medallion and added a reference to Irish-born Revolutionary war hero Richard Montgomery, who was killed at the Battle of Quebec: "And thou, too, oh land of Montgomery, whose generous sons repaired to our friendless standard when first it was unfurled for resistance. Brave but unfortunate people! May the God of justice and mercy grant thee better destinies."

Custis also began private correspondence with Irish-American leaders far more blunt in their rhetoric. In March 1829, James Barry of the Hibernian Society in Alexandria wrote Custis thanking him for a recent oration he called "a happy combination of learned thoughts, appropriate liberal &

historic, and when the biggots of England will hear from the Catholic Association of Ireland that the adopted son of America's Washington is the willing friend, the eloquent orator, and mingling with the persecuted of their sister isle, what will be the confusion?"[47]

Custis was acknowledged no less effusively after he delivered, at an August 6, 1832, gathering of the Irish-Americans' National Volunteers, a petition on the birthday of Irish liberator Daniel O'Connell. It was signed by 24,000 and sent to St. Michael Parish in Dublin. Custis offered a "toast which will be remembered," a newspaperman wrote, "with the deepest gratitude by every honest Irishman, and re-echoed through the green hills and fertile valleys of old Erin."[48]

In talks at St. Patrick's Day gatherings, to Masons, to the Friends of Civil and Religious Liberty of the District, and the Washington City Benevolent Society, Custis continued to offer sympathy to a people who, as he put in in 1833, "deserve the support of the free all over the world in their coming struggle."[49] He was cheered by the Friends of the Irish Exiles. He risked British anger by backing a Catholic Emancipation and Reform bill pending in Parliament and proposing shipments of arms to rebels seeking Irish independence. "Ireland, like America, must endure her days of trial," he said at gathering during the Martin Van Buren administration. But, the "long agony over," Ireland "would finally take her rank among the nations," Custis said, expressing hope that his compatriots would plant a shamrock on his grave.[50]

Custis's wearing of the green also spurred detractors. His St. Patrick's Day speech given March 28, 1838, was dismissed as "twaddle" by a writer for the *Native American,* the organ of a nationalist group with an office in Washington. "This vast assemblage of three hundred and small odd sat down to feast their souls with the delicious rhapsody of the illustrious, hundred times illustrious George Washington Parke Custis, Esq., of Arlington House, on the opposite side of the Potomac River, and relation to _____, no, we will not mention *his* great name," the elliptical writer wrote. His screed mocked the gathering in a restaurant as a feast of the "thrice-told tale" with a "hiccoughed toast" to the "maudlin hypocrisy" of the Irish. After Custis, whose "appearance was that of an old man," bid the Irish to "light the fires of Erin's freedom by the flame of '76," the critic went on, "surely they must have winced under the terrible sarcasm. This half redeems the orator of Arlington."[51]

The orator was undeterred. On St. Patrick's Day on March 17 of the following year, Custis goaded the Irish exiles planning military action with doses of American patriotism and praise for the founding fathers. Of the prosperity of America over the past sixty years, he asked the cheering crowd, "Would such things have been under our old colonial system of vassalage and dependence on a mother country?" ("No, never!" came the response.) "The stranger when he visits our shores, exclaims, 'There's magic in these things.' … It is the magic of liberty," Custis said. "Courage, Ireland, and Ireland's friends. Better days are in store for you."[52]

The predicament of the Irish-Americans inspired a Custis poem, delivered to the Washington Benevolent Society in the District of Columbia on for St. Patrick's Day 1844. Its last stanza:

> From long Night of Darkness a Day-star now gleams;
> It heralds a bright rising Sun
> To cheer thee, Young Ireland, with Liberty's beams—
> Thy race of Misfortune is run.[53]

In September 1852, when Custis was seventy-one years old, the Irish Social and Benevolent Society of Baltimore at a special meeting unanimously elected him an "honorary member for life, with all the privileges of active membership without a contribution."[54]

Once Again a Virginian

The political issue on which Custis probably exerted the most influence was the decades-long question of Alexandria County's "retrocession" from the original District of Columbia. His role commenced in 1804, only three years after Congress enacted the law codifying the boundaries of the new federal capital that had been laid out in 1791. The surveyed ten-mile-sided square had roped in the northernmost Virginia side of the Potomac River.[55] That meant that Custis's residency at Arlington House, after he broke ground for it 1802, denied him, and other residents of Washington, D.C., the right to vote or seek office at the federal level.

Even so, Custis's Federalist beliefs in strong central government and his loyalty to southerner George Washington prompted him to defend the newly described capital even when critics began early to clamor that the Alexandria County land should revert to Virginia. In 1804, at age twenty-three, Custis chaired a group that drafted a petition to Congress to head off any such legislation. His letter, addressed to the Speaker of the House from Arlington House and dated December 11, was titled, "Enclosing Sundry Resolutions Agreed to by the Inhabitants of Alexandria County, relative to the recession of the Jurisdiction of that part of the Territory of Columbia, which was ceded to the United States by the State of Virginia." The text defended the existing District boundaries, reading,

> "Resolved, that the fundamental principles of all just governments, forbid that the citizens thereof should be ceded and transferred without their consent,

from one sovereignty to another, except in cases, where the national safety may absolutely demand it." Secondly, it resolved "that the cession of the people and territory of Alexandria County to the state of Virginia, or any other state, or sovereign power whatsoever, without such consent previously obtained, being not necessary for the national safety, will be subversive of our rights and injurious to our prosperity."[56]

But as his Virginia county ramped up economic development, Custis's views in the following decades would change. Through several administrations, the federal government failed to deliver expected placement of buildings, roads and military installations in Alexandria County. Congress also declined to fund the Potomac-side canal that was built in the late 1830s linking the Alexandria port to the Aqueduct Bridge into Georgetown. Such complaints appear in the debates over retrocession. The historical record is murky, however, on how the ever-salient issue of slavery may have also molded attitudes. Alexandria hosted a significant slave market in the 1820s through 1850s. As abolitionist sentiment expanded domestically and internationally, some Alexandrians likely feared that the slave trade would be abolished in the District (which would occur in 1850), perhaps influencing their views on retrocession. As petitions to the Alexandria City Council circulated in the 1820s and 1830s, the county itself appeared divided between the rural farm areas (that would later become Arlington County) and the residents in the city that hosted slave markets. In 1844, Congress rescinded an eight-year-old ban on petitions to Congress for ending slavery, a change that could have prodded pro-slavery interests to seek separation from a district that would also be more tolerant of abolitionism.[57] Some pro-slavery citizens feared that runaway slaves would find protection in rural Alexandria, and that tougher Virginia enforcement of the rights of slave owners would serve Alexandrians better.[58]

Custis was considered an informal leader on the question by the prominent families of rural Alexandria. He was chairman as they gathered on January 31, 1846, at Ball's Cross Roads tavern (today's Ballston section of Arlington). "High-handed and unauthorized measures" being pushed continually by Alexandria city leaders prompted Custis to complain that rural county residents were being treated "as so many swine in the market, without our knowledge, and most clearly against our express wishes."[59] Custis was also disappointed that Congress hadn't funded the Alexandria Canal built practically in his front yard.

But a subsequent resolution in support of retrocession by the Virginia General Assembly asked Congress to make it happen. A resulting "Act to Retrocede the County of Alexandria, in the District of Columbia, to the State of Virginia" passed the House by 96–65, and the Senate by 32–14, allowing President James Polk to sign it into law on July 10, 1846.[60]

The drama wasn't over. For Alexandria to rejoin Virginia, the law required a referendum of voting-age citizens of Alexandria (and, later, final approval from the Virginia General Assembly). Polk named Custis as chair of a five-member commission overseeing the vote, which took place in September 1846. Retrocession passed by 763–222. (Most in rural Alexandria opposed it, and Custis himself abstained.)[61]

Custis was appointed to travel to Richmond to lobby. Once approval came from the General Assembly, Alexandrians on March 20, 1847, celebrated with a parade, torches, flags and cannon. Custis was among the leaders who spoke in Market Square.[62]

He had made his peace with retrocession. In a letter to his caretaker on the Pamunkey that January, Custis wrote that he had intended to visit "the low country," but was too busy because "the citizens of this country (now a part of Virginia) did me the honor to elect me first" to one of their committees. Hence he declined, Custis told manager Francis Nelson, a proposal that he run for the Virginia House of Delegates.[63]

The issue was still on Custis's mind in that November on election eve, when he addressed a Whig barbecue in Bladensburg, Maryland. "Living, as I always have, within the limits of the District of Columbia, no vote was vouchsafed to me until the recent act of retrocession set that part of the of the District, where my residence is, to the State of Virginia. And I am about to give my maiden vote!" Custis told an enthusiastic crowd backing Zachary Taylor. "In doing it, I shall exercise a privilege enjoyed by no other voter in the nation—the privilege of casting the only vote that can be cast hailing from the sacred shades of Mount Vernon, and representing the family of the greatest and best of departed men, the Father of the Country!"[64]

Champion of Veterans

Throughout his public life, particularly as he grew old, Custis paid special attention to war veterans groups seeking public recognition and government pensions. He advocated universal training in anticipation of the next war, allowing active-duty Washington Guard troops in 1829 to drill at Arlington House, awarding a silver cup to the top marksman. Custis recommended "a wholesome and effective system, whereby the young men shall be embodied at convenient seasons and undergo a training and discipline which will fit them for camp and field: and after a limited tour of service in each year, for, say ten years, thereafter be exempt from all military duties, except … in case of invasion."[65]

And in one of his speeches to a banquet for Irish exiles, Custis honored the Revolutionary War heroics of Irishman Capt. John Fitzgerald of the 3rd Virginia Regiment under General Hugh Mercer. He also told a dramatic tale of imprisoned soldier John Byrne, calling him "a stout young Irish lad and weaver on the Mount Vernon estate when war broke out."[66]

On that formal Washington's Birthday, February 22, 1820, Custis spoke to celebrate an Alexandria-based militia called the Silver Grays. He made special mention of the role of banker William Herbert, a native of Ireland who was "ardently attached to the cause of American liberty" as a member during the war of Washington's Blue and Buff company: When "British vessels were in the Potomac and threatening the mansion of the General," Custis said, "Mr. Herbert repaired to Mount Vernon, and he was one of that familiar coterie who was always welcome as its guest at its great master's board."[67] In greeting the Mount Vernon Guards troop to his pavilion at Arlington in 1847, Custis gave a self-referential "hearty and right soldierly welcome of a veteran of Washington's last army and the days of 1799."[68]

In January 1855, an aging Custis spoke in the East Room of the White House to an audience that included President Franklin Pierce (himself a veteran of the Mexican War) and 1,000 members of the "old soldiers of 1812." Arriving from a meeting with American Indians at a nearby Presbyterian Church, these veterans wore cockades in their hats and marched to the White House to the strains of a Marine Band. Custis asked that Congress place these veterans, their widows and orphans—along with "our red brethren"—on the same footing as the veterans of the Revolution.[69] Custis made the same argument to the soldiers of 1812 the following January. The *Charleston Courier* reported that "the meeting passed resolutions declaring their conviction that our government was under the most solemn obligations to carry out the promises of the Continental Congress regarding provisions for the officers and soldiers of the Revolution, and petitioning Congress to supply the omissions of the former sessions for the care of soldiers and sailors of the war of 1812."[70]

In a more formal ceremony in December 1855, Custis came to Mount Vernon to greet travelers arriving by the steamer *George Washington*. The group, called the New England Veterans of the Stark, had worked for Manchester, New Hampshire's, Amoskeag Manufacturing Company making cloth bags vital for industry and the military. Many of them veterans of 1812, they came down the Potomac via Alexandria accompanied by a mounted guard and light infantry to a band playing "Yankee Doodle" and "Hail Columbia." On Mount Vernon's wharf, said an account in the *Baltimore Sun*, "the visitors and their associate were met and cordially welcomed by that venerable man, George Washington Parke Custis, extending both hands with a cordial welcome to the metropolis of our common country." At Washington's tomb, Custis invoked the Revolutionary War battles of

Lexington and Concord, saying, "No man would go from this place without being a better man, a soldier and patriot."[71]

Content with making his mark as a well-connected orator, Custis in later life would have one more brush with being a candidate for office. Having boosted Millard Fillmore as Taylor's vice president in 1848, Custis paid his respects to the nation's newly installed thirteenth chief executive at White House in August 1850. A reporter for the *North Carolinian* wrote that the visitor "had shaken hands with every man who had worn that honor. Perhaps there is no other man who can say the same? May he long live to see the succession of many others! From the health he now displays, we have no doubt he will be able to congratulate the next democratic president of the United States."[72]

Custis indeed would know Democratic victor Franklin Pierce. One of his several visits to Arlington House was preceded by anxious preparations, according to the diary kept by Custis's grand-niece Martha "Markie" Custis Williams. "All day, have Uncle [Custis] and I been sitting up. Uncle with his new brown vest on, [which] is the only change he ever makes for company and me with my black velvet spencer on the tip toe of expectation," she wrote in 1853, evincing exasperation at Pierce's poor etiquette in correspondence. "Uncle has been so preoccupied with his visit, anticipated, that he has not been enabled to settle himself to anything. The president has been canvassed and weighed and found *wanting*—at least in the manners which belong to his station."[73]

In 1856, months before the election that would bring Democrat James Buchanan to the White House, Custis's name was raised in a tongue-in-cheek proposal. As the anti-immigrant Know-Nothing Party gained prominence, some Whigs began pressuring former president Fillmore to accept the Know-Nothings' nomination.[74] (The secretive Know-Nothings took their name after new members were urged to reply to questions about their views with "I know nothing.") An essayist in the *Richmond Enquirer* wrote, "I beg that you will insert the following suggestion for the benefit of the Know Nothings, in the event of that deplorable contingency, namely, that if Mr. Fillmore should decline, George Washington Parke Custis shall be substituted in his stead."[75]

CHAPTER 6

Patriotic Curator

Custis pioneers historic preservation of Washington's legacy, lays groundwork for monuments, tours an underappreciated Bunker Hill.

Custis conceived of Arlington House as his public monument to the Father of the Country. But from the groundbreaking on, the uniquely positioned heir also established his private home as a reliquary.

The "Washington treasures," as he called them during an inventory by archivist-historian Benson Lossing, displayed in his front rooms included Mount Vernon furniture: The bed on which Washington died, a sideboard and tea table, special china emblazoned with the Society of the Cincinnati emblem, a punch bowl given to Washington by a French naval officer, a silver tea set, rich porcelain vases, mahogany chairs, the harpsichord that his sister Nelly famously was forced to play daily, notable letters to and from Custis ancestors and a large lantern that had illuminated the central hall of the mansion at Mount Vernon.[1]

The rare objects arrayed with scant security precautions included the model of the Bastille (carved from an actual stone from the prison) given to Washington by an English admirer.[2] The paintings that crowded the walls included the James Sharples childhood portraits of Wash and Nelly. "The wall of every room in the lower story, in addition to the hall, [is] covered with paintings and engravings," noted a group of Kentucky ladies who visited Custis in 1845. "Of the five original likenesses of Washington, by distinguished artists, that were taken of Washington, four of them are at Arlington House."[3] The dazzling display also included John Wollaston's portraits of Custis's grandparents, Martha and Daniel Parke Custis, and the older portraits of his ancestors Daniel Parke and John Custis IV. Visitors were also treated to works by Flemish masters, battle scenes, a portrait of Lafayette, an engraving of the Duke of Wellington and a full-length oil painting of Light-Horse Harry Lee.

"The dining room is adorned with, among other things, three deer heads, preserved from deer actually killed by George Washington," wrote a Civil War Union soldier who came through the abandoned mansion in 1861.[4] Custis actively promoted the popular circulation of George Washington images. In 1830 he commissioned the portrait artist Anson Dickinson to copy in miniature the full-length portrait of Colonel Washington in military garb done in 1772 by Charles Willson Peale. Custis had engravings made from Dickinson's portrait, which were sold for $1.

Outside on his property, Custis demonstrated reverence for his heritage by planting what would be called Pope's willow. As he wrote in the *Alexandria Gazette* in 1833, the tree was believed to be the source of all weeping willows across the United States. Custis's father, Jacky, he had been told, received, from a British officer at the 1776 siege of Boston, the slips from a tree in England overlooking the grave of early-eighteenth-century poet Alexander Pope.[5]

Custis's role as a preservationist also inspired him to advocate on the public stage, to weigh in on creation of the nation's earliest public monuments. His stream of published historical essays would tantalize American readers with eyewitness impressions and previously private Washington lore. And Custis would make his mark in a role resembling a curator and consultant, aiding historians, painters and even common-man autograph collectors. The American Antiquarian Society, formed in 1812 in Worcester, Massachusetts, to advance knowledge and assemble writings in the young nation's arts and sciences, quickly welcomed Custis as an officer. That placed his name alongside those of John Adams, Thomas Jefferson, John Quincy Adams, Noah Webster, Tobias Lear and David Humphreys.[6] Custis was less successful in fulfilling his wish to be inducted into the Maryland chapter of the prestigious Society of the Cincinnati, open only to male descendants of the Revolutionary War's Continental Army or Navy officers (and French counterparts). In November 1826, Custis wrote to presiding officer Nicholas Lloyd Rogers in Baltimore, enclosing a document from painter and war veteran John Trumbull "touching the service of my father on the General Staff of the Army of the Revolution." Having earlier lent the Maryland society the tent of Washington for its celebration of Lafayette's visit, Custis hoped his father Jacky's brief service as an aide de camp during the 1781 Battle of Yorktown would qualify him for the Cincinnati. "I have no merits of my own," he wrote, "but as a native of Maryland, I could hope to inherit the patriotic honours of my parent from the Society of my native state." His application was declined.[7]

A Memoir in Installments

Following the success of his "Conversations of Lafayette" essays published after the Marquis's visit in 1824–25, Custis embarked his personal recollections of the life and career of George Washington. They would not be published as a formal memoir until after Custis's death. But installments, as the spirit moved him, began appearing in 1825, the bulk in the Washington-based *National Intelligencer*.

Custis had a friend and cheering section in the paper's chief editor William Seaton, a Virginian who grew up knowing Patrick Henry and later became mayor of Washington, D.C.[8] The relationship was odd, however, because Seaton's *National Intelligencer,* with offices near the Capitol at 7th and D streets, was for its first two decades pro–Jefferson. It was in the 1820s, after its owners had won government printing contracts and opposed the rise of Andrew Jackson (whom Custis backed) that the paper became neutral enough to welcome writing from the patriotic Federalist Custis.[9]

Seaton and Custis were allies in the American Colonization Society and social friends. Inviting the cerebral Seaton for relaxation at his spring at Arlington House, Custis in 1825 wrote, "You will find the spring a comfortable place for aldermen to retire to from feasting and fagging in the toils of elections and great city affairs ... or for you laborers of the type; and if you are not 'worth of your hire,' 'tis not because the sweat of your brains is less than that of your brow."[10]

Seaton encouraged Custis to put down on paper his special memories of George Washington, and the editor prepared the reading public for their appearance decades before, as events unfolded, the main

William Seaton, Custis friend and editor of Washington, D.C.–based newspaper the *National Intelligencer* (Library of Congress).

volume's time.[11] They didn't always agree. On noticing Custis's impatience with efforts in the District of Columbia to erect a formal national monument to George Washington, Seaton in 1811 sought to assure "the first son" that the great chief on his own "will live on in hearts of countrymen."[12]

On Washington's birthday in 1828, the *National Intelligencer* published a dramatic installment titled "The Last Hours of Washington." It set the stage. "We understand that the publication of Recollections and Private Memoirs of the Life and Character of the Pater Patriae, which has been for some time expected by the American public, is delayed from the author not being as yet enabled to avail himself of the kind and paternal invitation of General Lafayette, to visit La Grange, where the valuable memoranda, to be obtained from the lips and papers of the general, have long since been tendered to the author's acceptance," the editors wrote. "We learn, however, that in the meantime, the Recollections are progressing, and that the work receives contributions from various and venerable sources, and consisting of details, anecdotes, and private memoirs, heretofore unpublished."[13]

That same year, the *Intelligencer* published Custis's biographical essay on Light-Horse Harry Lee, showcasing Custis's evolution as a storyteller with a quirky tale. "In very early life, [Lee] showed a disposition toward manliness, as appears from a ludicrous anecdote, probably still extant, in the village of Princeton," Custis wrote of the war hero whose son would soon marry into Custis's own family. "At that time of day, the village possessed but one Knight of the Strap, commonly called a barber, who mowed the chins & powdered the wigs of the 'grave, & reverend seigniors' of the faculty." Young Lee one day entered the shop & pompously called to the operator, "Shave me Sir." The waggish barber then played a trick on Lee, lathering him up but then walking outside. "Lee bore his situation for a while, with philosophic calmness, till his patience being exhausted he roared out, 'Why don't you come & shave me, Sir?' Because, replied the waggish tonsor, 'I am looking for your beard.'"[14]

After recounting Lee's exploits at the Battle of Cowpens in South Carolina and the 1794 Whiskey Rebellion in Western Pennsylvania, Custis asked, "But shall the biographer's task be complete, when the faults of his subject are not taken into account?" That was an elliptical reference to Lee's notorious debts that landed him in jail in Westmoreland County, Virginia. Custis avoided the sad details: "Let the faults of Lee be buried in his distant grave."[15]

If Custis couldn't afford the research trip to Lafayette's home in Paris, he could still deliver a flowery farewell tribute to the Frenchman a year after his death in 1834. Before the American Revolution was won, as the child of Mount Vernon recounted, Lafayette sailed back to France "again to plead our cause, again to prepare new armaments for our aid, when suddenly his faithful, generous and enthusiastic labors for us, and for ages yet unborn, are arrested by the sun of peace and independence, which, bursting through the dark mists of our long agony of privation and trial, sheds its benignant beams to brighten and to bless our land." Custis described the marquis's 1784 visit to Mount Vernon, when the younger general rushed "into the arms of the venerate chief, the modern Cincinnatus.... This touching interview, to which I look back through the vista of fifty years, was the first event to make enduring impress upon my childhood memory."[16]

Custis's byline had appeared earlier in the *Alexandria Gazette*. He wrote an obituary of District of Columbia militia officer William Allen Daingerfield, a Virginian hero of the Indian wars and the War of 1812. Daingerfield "was present at the victorious battles of 1794 which terminated the horrors of Indian warfare and gave peace and security to our suffering frontier," Custis wrote soon after the veteran died in 1821 in Prince George's County, Maryland, Custis's birthplace. "Daingerfield had become a doctor in Alexandria before retiring to pursue agriculture."[17] The *Gazette* also published Custis's description of Washington's own experiences in those Indian wars.

Other publications began carrying Custis's words. *The American Turf Register and Sporting Magazine* in September 1829 ran his patriotism-infused descriptions of George Washington's prowess as a hunter: "Washington, always superbly mounted, in true sporting costume, of blue coat, scarlet waistcoat, buckskin breeches, top boots, velvet cap, and whip with long thong, took the field at daybreak, with his huntsman, Will Lee, his friends and neighbors; and none rode more gallantly in the chase, nor with voice more cheerily awakened echo in the woodland, than he who was afterwards destined, by voice and example, to cheer his countrymen in the glorious struggle for independence and empire."[18]

In 1833, a publishing project titled the National Portrait Gallery, under James Longacre and James Herring of the New York–based American Academy of Fine Arts, invited Custis to write a biography of Martha Washington. This "little work of mine," as Custis called it proudly in a July 19 letter to his wife and daughter, showed off his knowledge of his ancestry, including the famous meeting of George Washington and the wealthy widow Custis at the Virginia White House plantation now owned by Custis himself.[19] "The young lady excelled in personal charms," he later wrote of his grandmother, "which, with pleasing manners, and a general amiability of demeanor, caused her to be distinguished among the fair ones who usually assembled at the court of Williamsburg."[20]

In 1840, Custis popularized the story of the mythical Molly Pitcher, the Continental Army's female gunner who became a legend at the Battle of Monmouth. The year before, the editors of the *Alexandria Gazette*

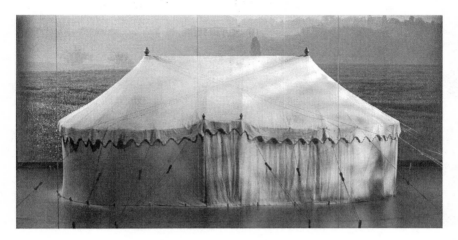

General George Washington's battlefield tent, portions of which Custis frequently displayed at special events (Museum of the American Revolution).

continued whetting the public's appetite for Custis's in-progress compendium. "The opinions and speeches of GWPC Esq.—the addresses delivered on several occasions by this gentleman, have been collected together. They will be published in a volume of about 250 pages, 12 months, which will be furnished in about six weeks to subscribers, at $1 per copy."[21] Those publishing plans in the coming decades would change.

Rescuing Washington's Landmarks

Following the War of 1812, Custis looked on as the nation entered a new era of monument-building. On July 4, 1815, citizens of Baltimore dedicated what, when completed in 1829, became a 178-foot column on downtown land donated by Revolutionary War hero John Eager Howard.[22] Custis, whose Arlington House was technically the first structure to honor Washington, that same year became disconcerted with the neglected state of Washington's birthplace, the site of the family home called Wakefield, on Popes Creek in Westmoreland County, Virginia. "The brick chimney is all that remains of the Washington mansion—the birthplace of General Washington—except the broken bricks which are scattered about over the spot where it was built," wrote Custis associate Bishop William Meade in his history of Virginia's elite families.[23]

In 1815 Custis explored the site ninety miles down the Potomac and located what he took to be the foundations, a "glorious old pile," he called it. So he made arrangements. The following year, on his ninety-ton topsail schooner *Lady of the Lake* returning from a visit to Smith's Island, Custis returned to Popes Creek. With him were two sons of Revolutionary War veterans, William Grymes and Samuel Lewis, the latter a Washington great-nephew.[24] They portaged a slab of freestone inscribed, using the old Julian calendar that pushed back Washington's birthday by eleven days, as follows: "Here the 11th of February, 1732, Washington Was Born." By happenstance, the crew encountered a fishing party in that remote area, persuading the strangers to lend a hand carting the heavy stone some three hundred yards inland to a wheat field.

There, they fashioned a crude pedestal from Wakefield's discarded bricks. A ceremony followed. After cannon fire and the unfurling of a flag, Custis read a declaration of the monument: "To the respect and protection of the American people in general, and the citizens of Westmoreland in particular." That object became known as the "first stone," or the first commemoration of a major American figure. Decades later, Custis attempted to encourage the Popes Creek birthplace as a devotees' destination, writing in the *Alexandria Gazette*, "Will not Wakefield, like Mount Vernon, in after time, be the resort of Patriotic Pilgrims?"[25]

Custis had less success with his involvement in the broad nineteenth-century movement to implement a 1799 congressional plan to transfer Washington's remains from his tomb at Mount Vernon to the crypt of the U.S. Capitol. When that debate resurfaced in the early 1830s on the centenary of Washington's birth, Custis was forced to take sides against fellow Virginians and other politicians from the South. In hints of the regional conflagration to come, southerners were pressing their rights to own slaves by seeking to nullify any federal legislation that would restrict them.[26] Possession of Washington's remains was for them a source of regional pride.

On February 13, 1832, both the House and Senate approved resolutions to move the body more than three decades after Washington's death. The proposal called for officials to seek permission from surviving executors of Washington's will, George Washington Parke Custis of Arlington House and, more important legally, John A. Washington II, the great-nephew of the great chief, who was now proprietor at Mount Vernon.

Previous efforts to fulfill Congress's intent, dating to 1816, had been blocked by Mount Vernon's then-owner, Bushrod Washington. The basement crypt in the Capitol remained vacant. In 1832, House members favoring the move warned that Mount Vernon, where the Virginian's tomb was in disarray, could one day be sold or "fall into unfeeling hands." Rep. Henry Dearborn of Massachusetts said that while the nation owes gratitude to Virginia for all its contributions, "those who were not citizens of Virginia wished the internment of those remains in common ground, which equally belongs to the whole United States."

Those opposed pointed out that the Capitol, already crowded with visitors, had been burned by the British in 1814, yet Mount Vernon remained safe. Washington himself had expressed a desire to be buried "without pomp" on his own beloved plantation, they noted. Rep. Richard Coke of Virginia proclaimed presciently, "There were at the present time, in the flag of the confederacy, the stars of twenty-four independent and sovereign states; but the time might arrive, when, at some distant period, those stars should be dimmed of their original brightness, and present to the view the twenty-four fragments of a great and powerful republic, warring that one with the other." Should Virginia, Coke continued, "in offering homage to the memory of the mighty dead, be forced to pay a pilgrimage to the remains of its own son, through scenes of blood, shed perhaps by kindred hands?"[27]

Custis, who would devote seven pages of his memoir to the issue, recalled that Martha Washington, who died two years after the general, had written to President John Adams saying she wished to be paired with her husband in death. Custis said she called him to her death bed to instruct him, "Remember, Washington [Custis], to have my remains placed in a leaden coffin, that they may be removed with those of the general at the command of the government."[28]

Custis in 1832 favored the move, which both houses of Congress approved later that February. He expressed embarrassment that visitors from foreign nations would behold such a quotidian tomb. "The ancient family vault having fallen into a state of decay, the chief surveyed and marked out a spot for a family burial place during the last days at Mount Vernon," he wrote. (Because of vandals and the threat of thievery, Custis in 1831 had helped his brother-in-law Lawrence Lewis build a new tomb enclosure near the original one, which Custis couldn't afford to help finance.)[29] "The new situation is peculiarly unfavorable and ill chosen, being a most unpleasant location for either the living or the dead," he said. Though the executors tried their best, Custis added diplomatically, Washington's own choice of the site resulted in the new tomb "being universally condemned as unfit for and unworthy of the purpose for which it was intended, while it serves as a matter of reproach to the crowds of pilgrims who resort thither to pay homage to the fame and memory of the Father of His Country."[30]

Scolding the southerners for contemplating a future secession, Custis wrote in his memoir, "No one state can appropriate to itself that which belongs to the whole."

In a February 14, 1832, letter to the "gentlemen" of Congress, Custis announced that "I give my most hearty consent to the removal of the remains, after the manner requested, and congratulate the Government

upon the approaching consummation of a great act of national gratitude."
Sister Nelly also favored the move.

But John Washington II felt differently. In a February 15 letter to the
Speaker and President of the Senate, he thanked Congress for the effort but
described a "struggle which it has produced in my mind between a sense of
duty to the highest authorities of my country, and private feelings, [which]
has been greatly embarrassing. But when I recollect that his will, in regard
to the disposition of his remains, has recently been carried into full effect,
and that they now repose in perfect tranquility, surrounded by those of
other endeared members of the family, I hope Congress will do justice to
the motives which seem to me require that I should not consent to their
separation."[31]

Thus John Washington II declined permission to transfer the great
chief. As Custis put it retrospectively in his memoir edited in the 1850s,
"This effort to have the remains of the illustrious citizen deposited beneath
the Capitol failed." He then proposed that the federal government buy
Mount Vernon and build on the tomb site "a dome of copper, surmounted
by an eagle in bronze, a bronze door, and for inscription two words ...
Pater Patriae." The key to such a sepulcher, said his modest proposal, would
always be kept by the current U.S. president.

But by then a new preservation society called the Mount Vernon
Ladies' Association had formed with the intent of purchasing Washington's
decaying home. "Now that Mount Vernon, through the efforts of patriotic
women, has become the property of the nation," Custis later wrote, "every
American should rejoice that the remains of Washington have not been
disturbed."[32] Those remains were left, he added in verse most flowery, "by
the verdant bank of that rushing river, where first they pillowed his mighty
head."

Mary Washington and the Tent

Custis's efforts to curate the Washington legacy extended to the cause
of the great chief's mother, Mary Ball Washington (1708–89). As early
as 1826, Custis had assembled and published family lore about both the
mother and her promising son as a boy. His account delivered detailed
anecdotes both about young George and his mother's own bravery, practical skills and pious charitable giving in her communities of Fredericksburg
and Lancaster, Virginia. "That distinguished woman," he wrote, "to whose
peculiar cast of character, and more than ancient discipline in the education of her illustrious son, himself ascribed the origin of his fortunes and
his fame."[33]

Three decades after her death in 1789, the remains of Mary Ball Washington lay in "a neglected grave" in a secluded area near the Potomac, Custis wrote in the *National Gazette*.[34] "Had she been of the older time, statues would have been erected to her memory in the capital, and she would have been called the Mother of Romans."

Responses came from around the country, and the Arlington House orator was able to persuade Samuel Gordon, the owner of Kenmore Plantation and the Fredericksburg-area land where her grave was located, to join other locals in planning an upgraded memorial. One New York newspaper proposed raising $2,000 to honor "Mary, the Mother of Washington."[35] But the effort flagged, and Custis became preoccupied with his work for the American Colonization Society, along with the national debate over reburying Washington.

Once Andrew Jackson was in the White House, the tide shifted. Custis had received a visit at Arlington House from the popular author and poet Lydia Sigourney, known as "the sweet singer of Hartford." They discussed Washington's mother, she being appalled at the pathetic gravesite covered with moss in an abandoned field. Her poem published in 1827 read, "Mother of him whose godlike fame; The good throughout the world revere; Ah! Why, without a stone, or name. Thus sleep'st thou unregarded here?"[36] In 1833, a wealthy New York merchant named Silas Burrows agreed to foot the bill for a monument to Mary, and Custis was able to attract the President Jackson himself to lay the cornerstone.

On May 7, 1833, the presidential party, which included Cabinet member and future Supreme Court Justice Roger Taney, traveled by schooner to Fredericksburg. Joining a procession were local dignitaries, including military officers, uniformed cavalry, city leaders, clergy, Masons, teachers, students, Burrows himself and 15,000 onlookers. President Jackson paid tribute to Mary's molding of the country's first war hero, telling the crowd: "This course of maternal discipline no doubt restrained the natural ardour of his temperament, and conferred upon him the power of self-command, which was one of the most remarkable traits of his character."[37] Sigourney penned a new poem (reprinted later in Custis's memoirs), saying, "But now we come; To do thee homage—Mother of our Chief!—Fit homage, such as honoreth him who pays."

Several days before, Custis had made special arrangements through the monument committee administrator George Washington Bassett. Custis would have "my man Philip" (his enslaved valet) pack up Washington's battlefield tent and ship it to Fredericksburg.[38] It takes "three men to assist pitching the tent," he told the planner. "With that assistance, it can be prepared for company in half an hour." The fading war relic was decorated,

Custis explained, with laurels and honeysuckle. The "draperies and curtains around the staffs; or uprights have most beautiful and picturesque effect," he said, regretting that there wasn't sufficient room in the ship for his "large equestrian picture of the great chief."[39]

The American public by then was familiar with the heirloom—purchased by a young Custis from his grandmother's estate. It had been displayed at Custis's discretion at events going back to his Arlington House sheep shearings in the century's first decade. He explained the object in detail in the May 18, 1855, *National Intelligencer*:

> There were two tents or rather marquees attached to the baggage of the Commander in Chief during the Revolutionary War. The larger that can dine about forty persons, formed the Banqueting Hall for the Grand Banquet given by Washington to the Officers of the Three Armies, immediately after the Surrender of Yorktown, when the victor made the feast and the vanquished were his guests.—
>
> The smaller, or sleeping tent, has a history of touching and peculiar interest attached to it, as related by Col. John Nicholas of Virginia, an Officer of the Life Guard. He said, 'Altho the headquarters were generally in a house, yet always pitched the smaller tent in the yard or immediately adjacent to the quarters, and to this tent the chief was in the constant habit of retiring to write his dispatches. His orders to the Officer of the Guard were, 'Let me not be disturbed when I have completed my dispatches I will come out myself.' Let the expresses be mounted, and in waiting.—
>
> Often would a courier arrive, bloody with spurring; and shouting, dispatches from General _____ to the Commander in Chief. Often the travel-soiled courier would have time to breathe a little after a desperate ride, till parting the door folds of the tent would appear the Man of mighty labours, the dispatches ready sealed in his hand.—
>
> From within those venerable canvas walls emanated the momentous dispatches that guided the destinies of the Struggle for Independence.— The tents were originally made in Philadelphia in August 1775, under the direction of Captain Moulder of the Revolutionary. They were first pitched on the Heights of Cambridge and in 1775, and are now preserved in the Portmanteau in which they were carried during the whole of the War of Independence.—[40]

It is doubtful Custis studied preservation skills for artifacts, even those considered advanced in his day. He frequently broke out the famous tent at events as a tribute to Washington that also advanced his own reputation.[41]* (He did, however, donate sections of the multi-part tent, one to the fledgling Washington Museum set up by Masons in Alexandria and another to

---

*Today, the dining tent is owned by the Smithsonian Institution, the office tent by the Museum of the American Revolution in Philadelphia, and the sleeping chamber by the Yorktown Battlefield Visitor Center run by the National Park Service.

the Grand Lodge of Boston.)* Later he would donate a part to the Smithsonian, and another to the Army. In February 1832, Custis had shipped portions to New York City, where they were pitched in front of City Hall by the First Division of the New York State Artillery unit. "Commissary Gen. Muir will furnish from the Arsenal such facilities of tent-poles etc. as may be necessary," read the order from the division inspector.[42]

Viewing the tent in 1833 was doubtless a thrill for that Fredericksburg crowd. But there was little follow-up to completing the Mary Washington monument. A sculptor was given a contract for a white marble obelisk, with the simple inscription, "Mary, The Mother of Washington." It would not be erected in Custis's lifetime.[43] In 1851, he was still complaining in letters to the *Alexandria Gazette* about a lack of respect for monuments to the nation's founding.[44]

Marking Bunker Hill

Custis's reputation as a history curator reached a crescendo with his well-publicized trip to Boston in summer 1845. Newspapers up the East Coast covered his first visit to New England since his youth, a long-envisioned pilgrimage prompted by a campaign to raise funds to better commemorate the Battle of Bunker Hill, for which a formal monument had been in the works since 1823. In announcing Custis's planned stop in New York City, that city's *Express* newspaper hailed his arrival "after an absence of more than 50 years." Arlington House was described as "one of the most eligibly suited estates in the vicinity of Washington." Custis himself was portrayed as "renowned, in the vicinity of his residence, for the high strain of eloquence" with which he addresses "assemblages of fellow citizens."[45]

New York's *Journal of Commerce* boasted, "Our citizens have been eager to testify their respect for one bred in the shades of Mount Vernon...." And this "gentleman, in the old Virginia sense of that term, has been greatly distinguished for his eloquence, and is perhaps more intimately acquainted with the men and the events of the last years of the great Father of the Republic, than any other living man," the paper said as Custis, his wife Molly, daughter Mary and her twelve-year-old son, George Washington Custis Lee, arrived. They settled in at the Astor House, New York's first luxury hotel.

---

*Though his hero George Washington was perhaps the most famous American member of the Masons, Custis never joined, organizational records show, despite donating numerous relics. One possible reason: his 1798 arrest for stealing spoons from an Alexandria tavern.

With Mayor William Havemeyer and hundreds of onlookers, Custis visited the site of President Washington's first home at Cherry and Franklin streets, City Hall and the Lenox Place home of former alderman John R. Peters. And the Virginian was introduced to Major William Popham, age ninety-three and a veteran of the war who had served as an aide to General George Clinton. He was wearing his diamond eagle badge identifying himself as president of the Society of the Cincinnati. Custis recited anecdotes of Washington, according to a news account. "On one occasion, a guard of soldiers who're about to escort General Washington to an event to which he had been invited. Washington stopped the commander and said, 'I shall not require your services; the best guard I can find may be found in the affections of the people.'" Next, when the old veteran and colleagues placed their hands on the head of Custis's grandson, Custis told the boy that day in New York, "There my son, you can have nothing better than that until you go up on high."[46]

Custis's party made their way to Boston and stayed at the historic Tremont House hotel. They visited the State House, Faneuil Hall, the Atheneum, "the city institutions at South Boston, and other places of general interest," wrote the *Evening Journal.* "He also made excursions to Concord and Lexington, Bunker Hill, and Dorchester Heights—classic spots—the scenes of important events in the history of the country. He also visited Lowell to examine the manufacturing establishments of that city, and expressed himself much gratified with his visit. While here, he was hospitably welcomed by our citizens, and renewed friendships with worthy men which time and distance and long since broken off."[47]

In his heart, however, Custis was disappointed that the battle site at Bunker Hill was not sufficiently memorialized. A granite monument had been dedicated just two years before Custis's arrival. But the hard-won funds were raised in part by selling nearby land to homebuilders.[48] "In vain, with patriotic pride, is the eye of the American cast around him from the Heights of Charlestown, seeking to rest upon some reminiscence of the past," Custis wrote months later in the *National Intelligencer.* "Not an inch of that soil, so venerable to liberty and dear to all Americans should have been desecrated by streets and houses."[49]

Custis was much more pleased with the preservation of the battle sites at Lexington and at Concord, where he was pleased to meet a living witness to the opening shots against the invading British. "These are as they should be, but little changed from the old days," Custis wrote.

His account of the trip at age sixty-four, which clearly stirred his patriotism, was garnished with a plea to the nation's schools. "While in our colleges and public schools of all sorts, the young Americans are literally *crammed* with everything that relates to other people and countries, they learn nothing touching their own," he complained to *Intelligencer* readers. "Not a history of the American Revolution is to be found in any school in the United States."

After Custis left Boston to return to Arlington House, he passed through Springfield, Hartford, and New Haven, and finally to Fort Hamilton, New York, where his daughter and son-in-law Robert E. Lee were stationed.[50]

The Custis Imprimatur

The decades-long national effort (private, and later public) to build the grandest Washington Monument in the center of the nation's capital did not officially involve Custis. He often pressed for such a project—even offering his own Arlington House property as a site in 1847.[51] His proposed "monument would be located on the domain of the American whom Washington adopted as a son, who from childhood to manhood was the cherished and happy object of his parental care and affection, and who is the sole male survivor of his domestic family," he wrote in a pitch to the Washington National Monument Society. But it was less his offer of Arlington House than his general reputation, openness to transferring George Washington's remains to the Capitol, and his long-time push for Washington celebrations, that impressed the project's advocates. In 1833, the Washington National Monument Society was formed with Chief Justice John Marshall and a succession of sitting presidents serving ex officio.[52] Construction didn't begin until 1848 (and would be interrupted by the Civil War). Custis didn't appear on the group's masthead, but he was invited to the laying of the cornerstone that July 4. "I hope you live to see it, complete in height, with your beloved Arlington," he was told by Society president Ellisha Whittlesey.[53] That June, the *National Intelligencer* reported spotting the "venerable Custis," at age sixty-seven, among those who helped push the twelve-ton Pennsylvania marble cornerstone from the freight yard across town.[54] At the big event inaugurating a building project that would transform the Washington, D.C., skyline, some 20,000 onlookers watched. Among them was President James Polk, Dolley Madison, Eliza Hamilton, and presidents-to-be James Buchanan, Abraham Lincoln, and Andrew Johnson.[55] Just over two years later, Custis, representing the Washington Light Infantry, presented to the District of Columbia mayor a block of Vermont marble to be applied to the incipient 555-foot monument that would be well visible from Arlington House.

In 1850, speaking alongside President Taylor at a July 4 ceremony at the monument construction site, Custis dedicated a stone from the citizens of the City of Washington placed at the 80-foot level of the structure.[56]

Erroneously, newspapers the previous year had reported that Custis had traveled to New York City to witness the October 1847 ground-breaking for its planned local memorial to George Washington (a tapered granite tower in Manhattan that in the end was never built).[57] "I did not go to New York to the great ceremonial laying of the cornerstone of Washington's Monument, although the papers said I was there and listed in the ceremonies afterward addressed for ... 100,000 people," Custis wrote in 1847 to his Pamunkey plantation caretaker. "I was too out of sorts, in health and spirits, to undertake the journey."[58] On July 4, 1851, Custis was present on the dais with President Millard Fillmore and others at the laying of cornerstone for the expanded U.S. Capitol, having attended the original in 1793.[59]

Custis also, during his final decade, continued to donate Washington artifacts to museums, distribute autographs and serve as a consultant to authors and painters presenting the Washington legacy.

President Franklin Pierce, on April 5, 1854, sent a dinner invitation to Custis, addressing him as "the sole surviving executor of Gen. Washington's estate." Pierce acknowledged "with great satisfaction" Custis's letter from Arlington House a week earlier, in which "you propose to present, through me to the Government of the United States, the standards taken from the enemy at the surrender of Yorktown and presented by General Washington by Revolutionary Congress of 1781...." These famous trophy flags captured from the British Army, which Pierce called "memorable memorials" of the father of his country, "cannot fail to awaken a fresh glow of gratitude for the great blessings we have enjoyed as a Nation for more than seventy years." The standards had been deposited earlier in the Alexandria Museum, but would now go, after a suitable ceremony, to the U.S. Patent Office.[60]

Another prize Washington artifact in Custis's care was his dress sword worn at the opening sessions of Congress. Late in his life, Custis discussed it in a February 1857 letter to Washington's great-grand nephew Lewis Washington, living in Jefferson County, Virginia.

Custis gave his version of the provenance of a Washington smallsword believed by some to have been sent to him by Frederick, King of Prussia. With its green scabbard and steel hilt, it was "brought by Col. [David] Humphreys soon after the Peace of 1783," Custis said. He quoted French Viscount de Mouaills, who paid tribute to Washington's military skill with the aphorism: "that the man was made for the sword, and not the sword for the man."* But the only Washington sword Custis owned, he told Lewis Washington, was "a cavalry sabre he gave me in 1798, when I was commissioned in the Last Army that he commanded. Too old to wield a sabre now, I have consigned the venerated relic to my son-in-law, Col. Robert Lee, to be foresworn by him for my grandson, Custis Lee, and officer of the Engineers, USA."[61]

In that same letter to Lewis, Custis teased his relative about how his share of the Washington family heritage lacked an image of Washington's mother, Mary Ball. If you "could have had a portrait of <u>The Spartan Mother</u> your collection would have been complete," Custis wrote, "but unfortunately, there is no portrait of this illustrious woman extant."

Another of Washington's personal artifacts handled by Custis was the miniature model of a Portsmouth, New Hampshire-built three-decker ship U.S.S. *America*. Sailing for France, that vessel that accommodated 74 guns was lost off of Cape Cod during the final days of the Revolution. The Viscount de Barras made the scale model as a gift to George Washington. It was bequeathed to Custis, who donated it to the Alexandria Masonic lodge room in 1812.[62]

Throughout his adult life, Custis provided advice and insight through correspondence that, in modern parlance, would have billed him as a consultant.

In 1838, after delivering a St. Patrick's Day talk, Custis was asked about the ornate carved marble mantle that graced the large dining room (called the New Room) at Mount Vernon. He proceeded to write to the children of Samuel Vaughn, whom he recalled as a British admirer of Washington, to confirm that Vaughn had donated the mantel in 1785. In those letters, Custis expressed regret that, at that time, Mount Vernon contained no archives.

Jared Sparks, the recently departed president of Harvard College and biographer of Washington, queried Custis in an 1855 letter as to why Washington chose buff and blue for the Continental Army's uniform, and whether a young Washington had worn those colors in the French and Indian War.[63] Sparks was editing a collection of Washington's letters, and Custis gave his permission to copy the famous Rembrandt Peale portrait of the chief. But he declined to risk shipping the original. Peale replied later, "I

---

*The sword reputed to be from King Frederick was with Lewis Washington in 1859 when he was kidnapped by abolitionist John Brown and his crew, who stole that Washington sword and carried it during their ill-fated raid on Harper's Ferry. Both were returned when Brown was apprehended—by Custis's son-in-law, Robert E. Lee. See Erik Goldstein, Stuart C. Mowbray and Brian Hendelson, *The Swords of Washington* (Woonsocket, R.I.: Morbray Publishing, 2016), 73–78.

can't blame you for not being willing to risk your portrait of Washington to the chances of the Railroad." So the painter asked his brother Titian Peale of the U.S. Patent Office "to go to your house to make a correct pencil tracing of the features of the portrait."[64]

Custis was willing earlier to send Sparks a Jean-Antoine Houdon bas-relief of Washington and the portrait by John Wollaston of Martha Washington.[65] Another author he helped was historian John Tyler Headley, who wrote on Washington's generals. "I have read nearly everything published on the Revolution, but there is a certain class of facts that I much am in need of," Headley wrote him. He specifically sought the "incidents, details things trivial in themselves [but] anecdotes familiarizing Washington's character—his transcendent greatness and his public character are well known—so are his private virtues and his moral excellence."[66]

Similarly, the prominent painter Emanuel Leutze, before executing his future-classic "Washington Crossing the Delaware," consulted Custis for detail. "Your precise and comprehensive descriptions have assisted me so much that the labor seemed pleasure," Leutze told him in thanks.[67]

As an old man, Custis gave a systematic explanation of his views on the varied and multiple portraits of his step-grandfather. In a series of letters in June and July of 1857 to New Yorker Thomas William Channing Moore, Custis welcomed coming donations of Moore's photographic copies of Washington images to his collection of "Washington Treasures" at Arlington House, where, he said, they must stay for safekeeping during his lifetime.

"There are so many likenesses of the Pater Patriae, some of very old date, that it is hard to estimate their genuineness," Custis wrote:

> It should be remembered that we had very few artists of merit in our olden times, & hence many of the portraits that have descended to modern days, should be received with caution. [Archibald] Robertson was the only miniature painter of eminence, say of sixty to sixty-five years ago, & resided I think in New York, his portraits of the chief and Mrs. (called Lady Washington in the Army) was taken in 1790 or 91. The engraving you saw from the National Gallery was engraved from a superb miniature in my possession by Field. As to the [Adolf Ulrik] Wermuller picture, it is in my opinion an imposition in toto, and so I told the Swedish ambassador who waited on me to get information respecting it. It is said to have been painted in 1795. Now I was not a day absent from the family of the Chief during 1795, & am sure that no such artist as Wertmuller had sitting of the great man during that period. The finest and purest likeness of the Chief, is the original picture in crayon by Sharples done in 1796, and with the original by [Charles Willson] Peale in 1772, of the Provincial Colonel, forms the first and last of the originals of Washington.

In sum, Custis opined, in calling for an official national portrait of Washington, the portrait by Gilbert "Stuart is the great original of the First

President of the U.S., Peale of the Colonial Officer, [James] Sharples of the man."[68]

In one stroke of historical irony, Custis in January 1856 received an inquiry from Army engineer and future wartime leader Montgomery Meigs of U.S. Capitol Extension, Post Office and Washington Aqueduct Office. Meigs, presiding over construction of the Capitol dome, informed Custis that the artist Constantino Brumidi, who created the famous historic frescoes for the great building, needed details on the uniform of the Virginia Calvary as Dragoons of the Revolution. The artists sought guidance on the "covering of the head, what form, material, color of helmet, of what material, iron or leather; —coat, breaches, waistcoat, boots, gloves," Meigs wrote. "Knowing the attention you have given to the Revolutionary subjects generally, and aware of the cheerfulness with which you have responded to the calls of your countrymen.... I have taken liberty of seeking from you, sir, the desired information."[69]

Eight years later, with Custis in his grave, Meigs, as the Union Army quartermaster general, would preside over an Arlington House confiscated from the family of Confederate General Robert E. Lee.

Custis, particularly during hard economic times, occasionally stepped down from his perch as eyewitness to history to participate in the budding American market for luminary autographs.

In 1834, he wrote to a man named Tefflt enclosing an autograph of Jackson administration Cabinet member Roger Taney and adding, "Give me in return a few hens."[70] In 1848, with his stock running out, he had to disappoint L.G. Lyon, a dealer on Broadway in New York City, writing, "I have no autographs to spare." Similarly, in 1849, he responded to an inquiry with a letter, "I regret it is not in my power to serve Mr. Boyd with an autographed letter of Washington."[71] Around that time, he received an inquiry, relayed through Bishop Meade, from Robert Bolton, a clergyman-historian from New Rochelle, New York, seeking an original letter from Washington. The Martha Washington engraving panel "you kindly sent me" the man wrote, "is nicely framed and glassed and ornaments my mantlepiece."[72]

In corresponding with collectors, Custis used some of his most flowery prose in praise of George Washington. In 1857, he sent to heraldry enthusiast J. Pickett, Esq. century-old fragments of letters and accounts "made by his hand," as Custis put it. "The fame & memory of that Greatest of Men forever ... is reflected in the bright and enduring beams from the hearts of mankind."[73] (Autographs from Custis himself would go on the market after his death. The *American Antiquarian* for August 1870 had a catalog with an asking price of $2 for a Custis signature, as compared with $200 for a rare Mary Washington autograph.[74])

"My autographs are exhausted," Custis wrote to Lewis Washington in

February 1857, stressing that "all my correspondence rests on one subject: the greatest and most beloved of all mankind." Custis's role as curator of all things George Washington had not flagged, and one of his interlocutors was a world-famous personage herself. The last autograph mentioned, Custis wrote, "derived from <u>paternal letters</u> written to me in 1796–7 when I was a lad at college, were sent to the Queen of England at her majesty's special request, she asking for nothing official but something of the heart. And directed to one whom the great man loved.... I am now cutting up scraps from old accounts of my father's and grandfather's estates of both of which Washington was guardian and administrator. Some of these are in 1762 or three years after his own marriage. These scraps are greedily sought-after."[75]

By this time Custis had a practice of authenticating Washington objects before donating or sending them out into the marketplace. From the pen of the "sole surviving executor of General George Washington," read one letter in June 1857 accompanying a cane and spy glass. "This is to certify" that these relics "were once the property of Washington and willed by himself to the relatives of the present proprietor," George Washington Parke Custis.[76]

During his final years, Custis was also thanked profusely for his donations to the Wisconsin Historical Society. Corresponding officer Lyman Draper wrote him saying, "It is a matter of real congratulation among the members of the society, that we are to have some personal memories of the Great Washington to preserve sacredly among our most precious collections."[77]

Recognition of his lifetime work, in part, came in the form of an invitation in November 1854 from Joseph Henry, the first secretary of the newly endowed Smithsonian Institution. Custis would have the honor of sharing his Washington memories as the first speaker at that Washington museum's new lecture hall.[78]

CHAPTER 7

Family Life at Arlington

A high-society marriage gives Custis an Army engineer as a son-in-law; daily life at Arlington impresses visitors; the family divides on religion; Custis makes his mark on local infrastructure and cherishes grandchildren named Lee.

Thursday, June 30, 1831, dawned a red-letter day for George Washington Parke Custis, his extended family, and, ultimately, the story of the United States. The wedding of daughter Mary Randolph Custis to well-born West Point engineering graduate Robert E. Lee assembled dozens from the Custis elite mid–Atlantic kin. It also shined a light on the Custis family aspirations to be generous as hosts (despite financial struggles) in the plantation community at Arlington House.

Mary had known Robert since childhood. Family tradition has it that the two were sweethearts, but they certainly played together as toddlers, likely at the home on Alexandria's Oronoco Street that Lee's father rented from her father, William Fitzhugh.[1] Mary and Robert were nearly the same age (he was born in 1807, she in 1808), both with Randolph family blood ties. They would likely have socialized during gatherings at Fitzhugh's Fairfax County estate of Ravensworth. Mary Custis in later life fondly repeated a memory that she and Lee as children planted a row of trees at Arlington House that grew into a lovely allée. She also told a friend she recalled beholding a uniformed Lee when they were teenagers, he as a junior marshal at the parade for the celebration when Lafayette came through Alexandria in 1824.[2]

The handsome Lee shows up in Mary Custis's correspondence as early as 1828, when she received a chatty letter from her Charlottesville, Virginia, friend Eliza Lewis Carter Tucker. "I assume he is still a worshipper at your shrine…. There is surely magic in that name,"[3] the friend gushed. Mary had been courted at Arlington House in 1825 by Congressman and future Texas Army hero Sam Houston. And so Custis's sister Eleanor would write to a friend in 1827 that Mary was "a charming daughter still unattached. There are few worthy of her, I think."[4] Mary's own mother, however, was on record criticizing her daughter as scatterbrained, unkempt and chronically late.[5]

In 1829, the twenty-two-year-old Lee was on his first Army assignment as a second lieutenant stationed on Fort Pulaski on Georgia's Cockspur Island. He began serious courtship. Mary Custis reported their engagement in an October 1830 letter to a friend, Hortensia Monroe Hay, grand-daughter of President Monroe), filled with religious thoughts. "Do not think I write this because I am sick of the world," Custis's daughter wrote. "For never was I surrounded with more of the joys of life than at this time—I am engaged to the one whom I have long been attached, Robert Lee. My father has not given a decided consent but I do not apprehend any opposition from him."[6]

In fact, Custis had reason to hesitate. True, Lee grew up to be a fellow admirer of George Washington (whose Virginia birthplace is just seven miles from Lee's). But despite Custis's decades of affection for the Lee family, the notion of his daughter becoming a peripatetic military wife rankled. (The future father-in-law annoyed young Lee by suggesting he quit the Army.) Custis knew well the disgrace of the betrothed's father, "Light-Horse Harry," the former congressman and Virginia governor who died in debt in 1818. And Custis's own finances were stretched as the 1830s began, an estimated $12,000 in the red.[7] Only weeks after the wedding, Custis begged a bank for forebearance. "My little note of $65 comes due today," he wrote the loan officer. "Being very short of cash at this time (a thing by no means unusual with me), I have to ask the favour of you, my dear sir, to let this small matter lay over in your hands a little while longer."[8]

But Lee was never deterred. "I am engaged to Miss Mary C.," he wrote his older brother in the spring of 1831. "Think of that … that is, she and her mother have given their consent. But the father has not yet made up his mind, though it is supposed [he] will not object."[9]

Lee's eagerness was revealed in an anecdote from a Washington, D.C., florist. "It was Mr. Lee's custom to ride out every afternoon for flowers for his sweetheart," the vendor named Pierce told a reporter. For a betrothed on a military salary, such gifts were expensive, particularly after Lee added flowers for cousins and friends staying at Arlington House with his intended. "It was hard to court three girls for one wife!" the florist said. One afternoon after several months of the routine he saw Lee ride up "pale and breathless, and cried out as he approached, 'Pierce, old boy, make me six bouquets, and don't spare pains or expense, for it's the last you'll get out of me! I'm going to be married on Thursday night, and then, by Jove, the girls must gather wild flowers.'"[10]

When the golden day arrived, the now-fully built Arlington House was decked out to show off its roses, jasmine and ivy. The family parlor was prepared by the enslaved domestics, and sleeping quarters for several days of celebrations were readied for members of the bridal and groom parties. Mary's six bridesmaids included Catharine Mason (a neighbor from nearby Analostan Island), as maid of honor; cousins Mary Goldsborough, Angela Lewis and Julia Calvert (daughter of Custis's Maryland aunt Rosalie Stier Calvert); and cousin Britannia, the daughter of Custis's older sister Martha and Thomas Peter of Tudor Place. Lee's groomsmen from West Point, wearing full dress, comprised: his brother Lt. Sydney Smith Lee: Lt. John P. Kennedy, Lt. James Chambers, Mr.

Army engineer Robert E. Lee, Custis' son-in-law, oil on canvas by William Edward West, 1838 (courtesy Washington and Lee University, Lexington, Virginia).

Richard Tilghman, Lt., James Prentiss, and his cousin Thomas Turner. Formal music was provided, family tradition had it, by Nelly Custis Lewis on the old Mount Vernon keyboard.

But sadly, it rained that day on the Potomac-side party. The officiant, the former rector of Christ Church Reuel Keith (and long affiliated with the nearby Virginia Episcopal Seminary), arrived late on horseback, sopping wet. How to outfit him with dry clothing for the ceremony? Only Custis himself possessed handy extra garments. The family would later recall with amusement that the clothes designed for the father's short stature were a poor fit on the tall, angular clergyman (even as Keith's embarrassment was partly covered by his surplice and cassock).[11]

The candle-lit ceremony under the parlor archway was moving. Bride Mary, "always a modest and affectionate girl, was never lovelier, and Robert Lee with his bright eyes and high color was the picture of the cavalier," recalled Custis cousin Marietta Turner. "The elegance and simplicity of the bride's parents, presiding over the feast, and the happiness of the grinning servants ... remain in my memory as a piece of Virginia life pleasant to recall."[12] After the service, all enjoyed a feast around the china punch bowl decorated with a ship that had been given to George Washington by French naval officers. Custis summoned the enslaved domestics to the parlor to play Virginia reels on fiddle and banjo.[13]

Lee himself seemed unsentimental about the event, which merited a three-line notice in the July 6 *Alexandria Gazette*. "You would have seen nothing strange, for there was neither fainting nor fighting, nor anything uncommon which could be twisted into an adventure," he wrote to his friend, the Army engineer Andrew Talcott, in July before taking his new post at Fort

Mary Custis Lee, 1830 oil portrait by Auguste Hervieu (courtesy George Washington Memorial Parkway).

Monroe, Virginia. "The parson had few words to say, though he dwelt upon them as if he had been reading my death warrant, and there was a tremulousness in the hand I held, that made me anxious for him to end."[14]

The Intimate Circle

The shared prominence of the scattered "children of Mount Vernon" meant that for decades the siblings exchanged visits to their elegant properties, with Custis and his three older sisters all conserving—and trading on—their treasures of George Washington's legacy. Custis's inner circle that gathered often at Arlington House also included many of the mid-Atlantic's cross-pollinated elite families—not without their eccentricities. They would meet for recreation at the baths in Berkeley Springs, Virginia, at Tudor Place, Woodlawn, and the Ravensworth and Hope Park estates. Custis was also fond of visiting Cedar Grove, the home sixty miles south on Chotank Creek where Custis' stepfather David Stuart was born. Custis told one correspondent that "some of the most pleasurable days of my life" were spent there.[15] Custis's circle no longer convened at the Mount Vernon homestead, owned for the first quarter of the nineteenth century by Bushrod Washington and, later, John Augustine Washington II and III.

No one had done more to expand the interlocked families than Custis's mother Eleanor. With her second husband, the politician and doctor David Stuart, she gave birth to at least a dozen children in addition to Custis and his three sisters from her marriage to Jacky. "What do you think of my sister-in-law Mrs. Stuart who, having eleven children alive and being grandmother to seven, is expecting a new addition to her family?" gossiped Custis's aunt Rosalie Stier Calvert to her sister.[16] But Eleanor's second marriage and prodigious mothering was appreciated by Custis's sister Eliza. Retrospectively, she envisioned her mother as a widow at age twenty-five as a "most captivating object," who "attracted admiration whenever she appeared, mounted on an elegant horse, which she rode well."[17] Neither Eleanor nor Custis' stepfather Stuart lived to see Arlington House completed. (She died in 1811, he in 1814.)

Custis' wife Molly lost her father William Fitzhugh in 1809. She inherited 2,000 pounds and sixteen slaves, while Custis assumed administration of the Ravensworth plantation until her brother, William Henry Fitzhugh, came of age. "The young Fitzhugh is not such a good match as you think," wrote Maryland cousin Rosalie Calvert just before the older Fitzhugh's death. "His father has dissipated a large part of his fortune in standing surety for his friends. However, the young man will have a fine fortune in land in Virginia which will produce a nice interest, if he manages it well."[18] That young Fitzhugh would grow up to be Custis's friend and ally in the American Colonization Society, and a political force in the state capital in Richmond. He also helped raise the young Robert E. Lee after Light-Horse Harry died in 1818. Fitzhugh would not live to see the Lee-Custis wedding, succumbing to injuries from a fall from a horse in May 1830. He left Ravensworth to his wife Anna Maria Sarah Goldsborough, of a prominent Maryland political family, with whom Custis would stay close.

Custis' oldest sister Eliza, back in 1804, had put the family through one of high society's rare divorces, moving from the Washington home she had shared with East India Company mogul and real estate speculator Thomas Law. "Mrs. Law and her husband separated amicably," Calvert gossiped to her mother. "I believe this is the most peculiar affair of this sort that has ever taken place. They don't accuse each other of anything except of not being able to get along together. You know he has always been a little bit crazy, and I think she is too."[19] (Law, it was publicly reported, compulsively carried a piece of cooking dough to manipulate in his hand, and he once embarrassed the ladies at Berkeley Springs by emerging on the promenade naked.[20]) The divorced Eliza went on to travel frequently and conduct romances. She corresponded affectionately with Lafayette. Unlike her

Federalist siblings, she maintained friendships with Republicans Thomas Jefferson and Dolley Madison, a reason, perhaps, that she became the most distant from her younger brother.

Custis was closer with his second oldest sister Martha. Presiding over her comfortable home at Tudor Place (nearly visible from Arlington House), she bore eight children, five of whom survived to adulthood. She and Thomas Peter bestowed patriotic names on three of them (Britannia, America, Columbia). Daughter Britannia would inherit the Georgetown property and maintain social ties across the Potomac with Robert and Mary Lee. It was only weeks before the Lee-Custis wedding that Custis joined with brother-in-law Peter in learning the outcome of their twelve-year legal battle over an aspect of George Washington's will (for which the two were among the executors). The case, which had gone all the way to the John Marshall–led Supreme Court, had begun in 1820. It involved a suit by Martha Washington's nephew John Dandridge claiming that he and other nephews were entitled to expenses for their education and professional training. Custis and Peter, represented by former Washington administration Attorney General Charles Lee, eventually lost, and were instructed in 1831 that Martha Washington's estate must pay nearly $1,000 to the nephews.[21]

Naturally, Custis maintained closest ties with his sister Nelly, the sharer of his Mount Vernon childhood. "My brother will have the pleasure of presenting his wife to you, and I will bespeak for her a share in your regard, for she is truly deserving of everyone's affection," Nelly wrote to a friend soon after Custis's marriage in 1804. "She is in great distress at present on her poor mother's account, who is confined in Philadelphia with a cancer."[22]

Correspondence reveals frequent carriage trips between Arlington and Woodlawn for relatives "anxious to change the scene," as Nelly wrote to her sister-in-law Molly in 1823.[23] "We returned yesterday from Arlington, where we left my dear sister [in-law] Mary, as well as usual, but her constitution is extremely delicate," Nelly wrote a few months later. "Her precious daughter Mary has chills and fever.... My brother has recovered, and exposes himself to the changes of weather as much as ever."[24]

Throughout their lives, Custis and Nelly traded intimate health reports, the brother in one letter in 1845 complaining of his bout with fever and diarrhea.[25] They collaborated with Molly in decorating the estate. While visiting their daughter in Fort Monroe in the 1830s, Molly wrote Custis with domestic contentment, "Will you let Eleanor take some of my butter money and get another breadth of the floor cloth as it is too narrow and another breadth will cover the little dining room?"[26] In the 1830s, Nelly and husband Lawrence Lewis moved from Woodlawn to Audley, a country home near Berryville, Virginia.

One of the few outsiders to frequent the Custis inner circle was religious reformer William Meade. The onetime rector of Alexandria's Christ Church helped found the Virginia Theological Seminary, later becoming Bishop of Virginia. He was close to Custis's wife, a cousin. Meade credited Molly for inviting him, as a half-hearted Princeton law graduate, to consult the library of books at Arlington House. There he encountered a folio edition of a widely circulated theological work that had belonged to George Washington. Published in England in 1782, it bore the verbose title "The Works of the Right Reverend Father in God Thomas Wilson, D.D. Fifty-eight Years Lord Bishop of Sodor and Man. With his Life Compiled from Authentic Papers by the Revd. C. Cruttwell."[27] So impressed was Meade that he committed to becoming a clergyman. Meade's visit there in 1809 was "a turning point, the instrument of withdrawing him from college, when she feared he was going 'blindfold into the ministry,'" as Molly put it. Mrs. Custis, wrote one nineteenth-century biographer, was for Meade an influence "whose personal piety diffused its fragrance in the gay atmosphere of her elegant home."[28]

Meade edited and published a new edition of those family prayers from Bishop Wilson, which circulated in Virginia and helped his career in reviving the stature of the Episcopal Church. Meade would also be active shaping alternative policies on slavery via the American Colonization Society, encouraging

Religious reformer Anglican Bishop William Meade, cousin and friend of Molly Custis (courtesy Fred Barr Collection, Stewart Bell, Jr., Archives Room, Handley Regional Library, Winchester-Frederick County Historical Society).

the religious Molly and her daughter Mary in their efforts to teach their enslaved domestics to read.[29] Mary's husband Robert was a lifelong admirer of Meade.

Molly Custis was more reflective on religion than her husband, and relied on her cousin Meade to hear her deepest thoughts. In an April 1819 letter recalling his college days a decade earlier, Mrs. Custis worried about Meade's ambitions and "self-righteousness." She confessed to him, "Ultimately, with tears and anxious desires for yourself, your ministry, and your mission, my soul was poured out in prayer. Unpossessed, however, with that assurance of faith, which many possessed, both for themselves and others, those tranquil emotions which succeed the unburdening of the heart to God, gave way once more to a trembling anxiety, which I have been subjected to on your account."[30]

Molly Custis would bequeath her religiosity to daughter Mary, whom she schooled at home while the girl was young. (As a teen, Mary received tutoring in French, Latin, Greek, history and science.) But it was only as an adult—indeed, with her engagement to Lee—that Mary had a spiritual awakening. The epiphany came soon after the death of her mother's brother Fitzhugh and as she suffered a serious illness. Mary would express the same doubts about faith as her mother. "I have communed today for the first time," she wrote after her confirmation at Alexandria's Christ Church on October 5, 1830. "I expect it would be a rejoicing time, but I was bowed down with a spirit of infirmity, a sense of unworthiness and ingratitude and did not enjoy it as much as I expected…. I knew I was a sinner."[31]

Custis kept his own counsel, and was less self-critical. He saw value in religion mostly as a social and organizing principle.[32] He did give a George Washington bible to Christ Church. He once joked in a letter to the Maryland Historical Society, "The old orator, you know, boasts of having two religions (most people have one but one and many none), while I have the Religion of Christianity and the Religion of the Revolution."[33] But give him credit for good works. He could summon the Christian ethic in his charitable giving and as a landlord. In 1841, Custis wrote to an overseer of the poor in the Virginia countryside noting the death of his tenant, Mary Ellis (Mortimer). "I direct James Scott to sell effects of said Mary," he instructed, "and devote the proceeds of sale ($218) wholly and solely to the use and benefit of the orphan children of said Mary."[34] On an earlier occasion, Custis's caretaker in Stafford County pulled at his heartstrings. "I believe your present tenants are nearly all bankrupt … they cling to the old leases, or rather it seems cruel to oust them."[35] When the old Mount Vernon coach fell into disrepair, Custis, after allowing grandchildren to use it as a playhouse, gave approval to have it broken up and made into snuff boxes, canes and picture frames—all to be sold to benefit charities.[36] In 1855, Custis donated to the Howard Society of Norfolk to help battle a yellow fever epidemic.[37]

That form of generosity permeated the family. His daughter in late life described Custis as "endowed with an even temper and remarkably buoyant spirit, and toward his family, his servants, his friends, and the world, there was a constant outflow of kindly feeling from his warm and generous heart."[38] But his personal approach to faith prompted his pious grand-niece Martha "Markie" Custis Williams to express concern for his secular soul. "I have this evening made a resolution to retire to my room every evening at twilight to pray especially for his conversion," she told her diary one Sunday in 1854. "It grieves my heart to see him going down to the grave without a saving belief in his Savior."[39]

Custis's private doubts did not prevent his taking pride in his wife's devotions. He would have agreed with a friend's public testimony in the 1850s that Molly "was familiarly acquainted with the best English literature…. But infinitely beyond all the writings of men, she valued the word of God."[40]

Custis balked at some of the puritanical tendencies of his wife, Meade and other clergy of the period to frown on drinking and leisure pursuits such as the theater, dancing, horse racing and card-playing. A burdened Custis once wrote to his wife, "I have made a great mental effort lately" in creative writings. "But I am sure that you and the bishop will think my energies might have been better employed."[41]

Yet the Custis's marriage endured, as did their friendship with Meade, who would end up an executor of Custis's will. Molly was philosophical on the "vicissitudes" of life and death, as revealed in an undated letter to Custis expressing delight at their "little epistolary" conversation and contentment with their hearth and home. "Heaven has bestowed on me everything necessary for the enjoyment of life," Molly declared. Among her many "invaluable gifts, it is a heart capable of sympathizing in the woes of my fellow creatures."[42]

The Daily Routine

When not hosting a wedding or a party, Custis tended to pass time alone. In his office mulling national and local issues and struggling with shaky finances, he wrote to his wife with the newlyweds in the summer of 1831, "A perfect solitude reigns with me, and suits well with the depression my pecuniary difficulties create in my mind. In better days, I shall be glad to take a peep at the world once more, [but] at present I am content to be a recluse."[43]

Custis's grand-niece Markie Williams recalled that he was "pretty regular in his movements. He reads and talks for some time after breakfast—then goes in his painting room where I generally go and sit with him some time," she wrote. "Then he goes to the farm and returns about 1 o'clock. After dinner, he takes his coffee goes into the painting room & then to the farm again. When he returns, he smokes a cigar and then comes in the parlor for the evening."[44]

When two ladies from Kentucky arrived at Arlington House by omnibus in 1845, they were astonished to be ushered into the first

Custis in 1848 by artist Junius Brutus Stearns (courtesy Washington and Lee University, Lexington, Virginia).

floor where "the wall of every room in the lower story, in addition to the hall, being covered with paintings and engravings."[45] they wrote. "There we stood, in the midst of a gallery of pictures, with the lord of the manor in his MacDonald plaid, rising from a lounge, where he had been taking a nap. 'Ha ha ha! A little more you would have caught me napping.'"

When the New England poet Lydia Sigourney visited, she found Molly "a woman of full character," but her husband "an oddity, an eccentric.... He showed us a handsome portrait of his ancestor Parke, a favorite of Queen Anne, who had given him her picture set in diamonds. 'Sly fellow,' said Mr. Custis. 'He kept the portrait but he sold the diamonds.'"[46]

Numerous relations and visitors noted Custis's cats. One, in a succession of pets, was named Tom Tita. A granddaughter later recalled his "gentleness to all within his household" and his tendency during evenings in front of a fire to "sit on the edge of his chair to allow Pussy undisputed possession."[47]

Custis's cousin reported that the sofa at Arlington House, "the one to the right, with its back to the window, is exclusively the seat of Mr. C and his cat. Mr. C is never without a pet in the way of a yellow brindled cat, called by him Tom, who returns affection, and gratitude for kindness shown, but who wears an air of dignified reserve as though he thought his place next in importance to his master's." With humor, she recalled that "one night when the prayers were longer than usual we all got up from our knees but Mr. C, who was asleep, with Tom on his back, also asleep. Our laugh awakened the sleepers."[48]

Son-in-law Lee ended one letter to Molly Custis, "Love to father of the puss."[49] (Years later, writing from his post in Mexico, Lee wrote playfully to his daughter, "I am glad to hear that your grandpa's cats are sleek and fat. But I should like to know, Annie, how they keep so fat, if they do not catch mice?"[50]) Custis himself often mentioned his cats in letters, in later life writing to sister-in-law Anna Goldsborough with details on spreading manure, visiting Ravensworth and improving his health. "I have fires at night and sit in my chamber til bedtime. Puss [is] asleep on the sofa," he wrote. "When cold arrives, [it] will drive it into the house."[51] Custis also owned a dog named "Royal E," considered a newsworthy item by the *Alexandria Gazette in* 1802.[52]

Family meals, as served by enslaved workers with produce from the kitchen gardens, were customarily formal. Lee, once ensconced in the household, "was very fond of gathering roses before breakfast and putting them on the plate of each lady," recalled his daughter Agnes Lee.[53] "Mrs. Custis, who is an early riser, is already there" for breakfast, recalled cousin Eliza Calvert. "She is tall of stature, is dressed with perfect simplicity, the lines of her skirt show no curve, or bend, but fall straight to her feet…. Mr. C now enters, soon the family are assembled; master and mistress, guests, children, and servants, all join more or less earnestly, according to the state of the heart, in the prayers so earnestly and lovingly uttered by Mrs. C."[54]

Formal repasts were served on the Washington family silver and china. One visitor was so impressed when touring the small dining room, she exclaimed, "Think of pouring out my own tea from the silver tea-pot which the honored mistress of Mount Vernon daily used?"[55]

The Host at Arlington Spring

Custis's desire for solitude did not mean he shunned the general public. One couldn't build a temple-like home on a bluff viewable from the nation's capital without implicitly inviting attention. During the War of 1812, the proprietor of the still-incomplete Arlington House received pleading letters from a Spanish diplomat. "Being a stranger, entirely unacquainted in the United States, to which country I was carried by an American privateer, who took from me my trunks, papers and money while on voyage from London," said his letter dated August 8, 1813. The desperate man, whose wife was expecting a child, said he was "imploring your protection for me and my wife until I could obtain gain again some relief from my country." El Marques de Monserrate, staying temporarily in downtown lodgings on F Street, had earlier crossed the bridge to present his case in person and to ask for Custis's advice on publishing. He interacted with Custis's "faithful waiter Ephraim." And he "saw the other day one of your yellow colour servant women, [who] informed me of her long sickness," he said, appealing to Custis as a "Christian-like" gentleman. Custis at one point did give the man money. The Spaniard's wife "spent that sum immediately on things for her future child," the desperate diplomat parried. But Monserrate needed more, for the first time in his life possessing neither money, friends, doctors or servants. He promised, "I will never trouble you again."[56]

Over the decades, the Arlington House doors would swing open for the Marquis de Lafayette, Henry Clay, Daniel Webster and Franklin Pierce.

Average citizens were also welcomed to what became a unique institution in the capital city—Arlington Spring. At a Potomac-side grove centered around a huge oak tree (site of the sheep shearings), Custis built a dock, kitchen, sixty-foot dining hall and an equally large dance pavilion alongside an ice house and cabins for the enslaved workforce. "Come over to the shades of Arlington, where peace and pleasurable breezes, good air, good water, and a tolerably good fellow will make you welcome," Custis wrote a friend.[57]

"No spiritous liquors were permitted to be sold there," Custis's daughter reported, "and visitors were not allowed there on the sabbath. All that he asked in return was good behavior, and a reciprocation of the kind feeling which made every class of respectable citizens cordially welcome."[58]

During warm weather, and especially on the Fourth of July, Arlington House hosted schoolchildren and picnic parties for as many as 300, or 20,000 for the season. Some arrived by commercial ferry, others by Custis's boat "The G.W.P. Custis." (His steamer called the *Arlington Belle* was destroyed by fire, and was replaced.[59]) An advertisement appeared in the *National Intelligencer* in 1852 reading, "The steamer G.W.P. Custis … can be engaged for excursions to Arlington or elsewhere by application to the captain on board or George Page, 7th St. wharf. $10 from Washington to Arlington, or 12½ per passenger.—Ellis L. Price, Captain."[60]

President Fillmore came on a vessel from the nearby Falcon Boat Club.[61] "After you entered the grounds, which were reached either by going over the Long Bridge or going across in rowboats, the road turned east and passed under the arched way that divided the public grounds from the gardens around the house," wrote Washington, D.C., memoirist Sarah E. Vedder, looking back decades. "A large spring flowed from the roots of an immense tree. That supplied water for any number of persons. Mr. Custis

The picnic pavilion at Arlington Spring, painting by Elizabeth Moore Reid, commissioned circa 1850 by Custis (courtesy George Washington Memorial Parkway).

had two or three pavilions built to accommodate the parties either to set the tables for dance. Frequently he would come down to the grounds and participate in their amusements. He has been known to take his violin and play for the dancers."[62] He also enjoyed dancing a pigeon wing in a reel.

Custis entertained patriotic societies, Sunday School classes, even military units, sometimes dressed shabbily in old-style knee britches and a ruffled shirt.[63] He allowed the militia called the Washington Guards to drill at Arlington Spring, served them dinner and awarded their best marksman a silver cup. One Fourth of July, he presented a silk flag to the Potomac Dragoons regiment.

On another occasion, Custis sent the visitors glasses of ice cream. The enslaved domestic who served the treat informed the guests that the silver tray he carried had belonged to George Washington. "The young ladies, as if actuated by one impulse," a correspondent reported, "immediately arose … and each, in turn, kissed the cold rim of the salver before touching the cream."[64]

Arlington Spring was also treasured by Custis relatives. Mary Lee's cousin Eleanor Calvert in 1845 penned a vivid portrait of her uncle's appearances at which he shared jokes and anecdotes. "While we are lingering at the spring, Mr. Custis comes to give us a friendly welcome, he may always be found at the spring when there is a picnic going on," she recalled. "He is fond of talking to the young people, and with the older ones, particularly those who are familiar with the events of his young manhood.... He plays some good old dancing times on the violin, with which he occasionally, when much urged, delights his visitors. He more willingly yields to the request for a speech, for he is the 'Old Man Eloquent.'"[65]

Near the end of Custis's life, on a sunny May afternoon in 1856, fifty students from Georgetown College came over to the spring in eight row-boats. (Custis, who spoke often on the campus, had been made an honorary member of Georgetown College's debating club, the Philodemic Society.) "Few had ever visited the place before, and were only acquainted with it as the residence of 'the old Orator,' and consequently, on their arrival, they regarded it with feelings akin to those attributed to the ancient Romans, on entering the Elysian Fields," the *Evening Star* reported. After play and a siesta, "They were agreeably surprised by a visit from the venerable Mr. Custis. He was soon engaged in relating anecdotes, etc. both interesting and instructive, to a circle of attentive hearers, many of whom soon imagined themselves in the presence of the illustrious Washington."[66]

Local Ties

As affluent members of the Federal City community, the Custis kin frequently crossed the Potomac to shop and sell wares. "I think it a happy day when we have permission to go to the 'Wash Market,'" wrote cousin Eleanor Calvert, repeating dialect of the enslaved help. "Passing many stalls, some displaying the substantial needs of meat, and fish, while others are piled with the beautiful green things that speak more pleasantly & more immediately, of the fields, and the sunshine: we reach, at last, the object of our coming; the stall rented by Mr. Custis of Arlington: and presided over by a gentlemen of color named Laurance, to whom we put the question, 'Can we go over in your boat, will you have room for us?' 'Yes, misses,' says Laurance, 'dare will be plenty.'"

Custis frequently took deliveries by schooner from the Port of Georgetown, and enjoyed carriage rides to Washington's Falcon Boat Club. Observers sometimes mocked his antiquated wardrobe, "gold-headed cane, and his old three-cornered hat and knee-breeches."[67]

He ordered bridles and saddles from Francis Alutz, Saddle Harness & Trunk Manufacturer, on Pennsylvania Avenue. He was a regular reader of newspapers and journals, even out-of-town publications such as the New York *Evening Post*. An 1842 letter survives in which Custis tells Frank Taylor of the *Albion,* a journal of news, politics and literature, to cease delivery. "An excellent periodical," Custis wrote, "but the precept is not suitable for the times."[68]

Most of the Custis family's social and commercial intercourse took place a six-mile carriage ride away in Alexandria. The family attended Christ Church, parking their carriage at Queen and Washington streets, and dined at Gadsby's Tavern. Invoices survive showing purchases of household tiles from the Dodge Brickyard. Another merchant patronized was Alexandria silversmith Adam Lynn (who executed the winner's cups for Custis's sheep shearings).[69]

Banking was done at an astonishing array of outlets: Farmers Bank and Bank of Potomac in Alexandria, the Metropole Bank and Bank of the Metropolis in the District of Columbia (and other Virginia banks in Winchester, Norfolk and Richmond). Custis's neighbor and friend John Mason headed the Bank of Columbia, but there's no sign Custis was a depositor. A downtown bank opened in 1854 under the name Arlington Bank, in honor of Custis's home. But the proprietor of Arlington House had a run-in with the Bank of the United States. "I have kept an account, … but not being accurate in such matters … have directed my agent in the South to make sales," he wrote to cashier Richard Smith, assuring him that he had kept upwards of $11,000 in the Bank of Washington for the previous four or five months. "It would be extremely painful to me that the bank should have to resort to any legal measure in regard to my limited dues; a very short time will suffice to prevent any such necessity and put matters again to rights."[70]

Custis frequented Alexandria bookstores and portrait studios. One of his most familiar portraits was executed by Charles Fevret de Saint-Memin, who set up a studio in Alexandria in spring 1805 at 113 N. Fairfax Street. That artists' new techniques in engraving were admired by Custis sisters Nelly and Eliza, too.[71]

Custis visited or spoke at the Free School on South Washington Street, the Alexandria Academy once supported by George Washington, as well as the St. John's Academy that stood at Duke and Columbus streets.[72] Custis also traded farming advice with famed local educator Benjamin Hallowell, who established a well-regarded boarding school and taught math to a teenage Robert E. Lee in an Oronoco Street building next to Lee's boyhood home.[73]

For household purchases, the Custis family were regulars at the Stabler-Leadbeater Apothecary, founded in 1792 near Alexandria's Market Square. (Stabler's customers also included Martha Washington and Nelly Custis.) "Please send three small ploughshares same as before … — also a good toothbrush neither too hard nor too soft," read a Custis order from June 3, 1846. "Those small and weak cigars suit one exactly." When an epidemic threatened, Custis on June 2, 1849, sent a note: "Please prepare the enclosed recipe for cholera mixture, as it is advisable to keep something of this sort as a family in these cholera times." On March 9, 1850, Custis asked William Stabler for seven papers of Flat Dutch cabbage seed. His daughter continued the patronage when Custis was in dotage, asking the shopkeeper in April 1857 to sell her messenger "spirit of alcohol and the same quantity of oil of sassafras, and of tincture of Arnica" to reduce muscle aches and inflammation.[74]

Custis also had a hand in Alexandria County's judicial system. He had been named a justice of the peace continually for decades by the likes of presidents Madison and Jackson. Custis collaborated with his newest estate manager, Robert Ball of the rural section of Alexandria, who doubled as a constable. One case involved handling warrants after a bar-room brawl. A magistrate had recommended directing a constable to "summon the Irishman who was knocked down by Harrison," as Custis wrote to Ball in August 1854, instructing him to "summon Griffin to attend court in the case of the fellow Edward, who struck him and tore his shirt."[75]

Ball became the owner of a local tavern and blacksmith shop purchased from the local Birch family. Molly Custis in 1837 wrote to daughter Mary with gossip about the sketchy characters she'd seen on the Ball tavern's porch.[76] Higher on the income scale among Custis's local associates was the wealthy neighbor James Roach, who had built Prospect House nearby in 1841. His business sold bricks, and he also served Custis as a contractor. Custis also made his mark in the future Arlington County by selling off lands in Washington Forest. A deed from March 24, 1837, shows that Custis and wife Mary received $400 from Nicholas Febrey for twenty acres on the border with Fairfax County. Febrey and his sons were some of county's most prosperous landowners.[77]

Neighborhood Intrastructure

By dint of his prominence, Custis exercised responsibilities in planning local development, particularly for two major infrastructure projects built on his own front yard.

In 1830, two years after construction began on the 184-mile Chesapeake and Ohio Canal connecting Western Maryland to Georgetown (planning for which had involved Custis since 1823), Congress chartered an extension. The Alexandria Canal would allow boats to traverse the Potomac atop the 1,000-foot engineering marvel called the Aqueduct Bridge, which linked Georgetown to what would become the Rosslyn section of Alexandria County. The mule-powered barges would then travel by canal seven miles to Alexandria City, where four locks would lower them to loading docks on the river for long-distance transport,[78] saving shippers much in labor costs.

Custis was the keynote speaker at the canal ground-breaking in Alexandria on July 3, 1831, just days after his daughter's wedding. A crowd assembled for a procession, an artillery salute and a ceremony at the town hall. The chairman of the newly formed Alexandria Canal Company presented a spade to Mayor John Roberts.[79] The city had raised capital for the mammoth undertaking (a ditch 45 feet wide at the surface) through private subscriptions, but with no federal appropriation. The company had to go to court to fight the citizens of Georgetown over cost sharing and rights to use the Potomac.

During construction, Custis also battled the Georgetowners, petitioning Congress in 1836 to be compensated for alleged damages to his riverside fishing grounds by the dredging machine used by the Corporation of Georgetown.[80] In 1839, he negotiated with the Alexandria Canal Company to give it right of way through his riverside land, later offering a foundry on his land as a setting for manufacturing. He also lent some of his Irish laborers for the construction. In a letter that year to his wife and daughter, Custis reported that "another Irish died, making six in all. They are [pressing] on with the canal, quick to [pinch] all the [help] I have to spare from the farm."[81]

The canal was completed in 1843, in time for new shipping technologies and the Morse telegraph. Even Army engineer Lee was impressed, though he worried that users would gain a view of the enslaved labor at Arlington. (Canal shipping, though interrupted by the Civil War, continued in and out of Alexandria until 1886.)

A second infrastructure project bearing Custis's imprint was Jackson City. This planned riverfront community on the Virginia side on the "Mason tract" near the Long Bridge was the brainchild of New York merchants and speculators. "A number of gentlemen of enterprise and capital, looking to the great increase of the commerce of the District of Columbia by the opening of the Chesapeake and Ohio Canal, have directed their inquiries as to the proper and probable point where this trade will concentrate," they wrote President Jackson in the fall of 1835. They flattered Old Hickory with comparisons to George Washington, declaring, "It has appeared to us also as peculiarly proper that the second man of the Union should have his name placed by the side of that of the first." Jackson was willing to lend his name and attend a cornerstone laying set for January 8, 1836 (the anniversary of the Battle of New Orleans twenty-one years earlier). "We will confess to a desire to shed over the destinies of this embryo a ray of reflected glory by identifying its birth with a great national anniversary," the businessmen said.[82]

But Jackson's willingness to participate did not mean Congress would help fund the planned suburban city of private homes and shops (it didn't). But Custis knew that prospects for developing Jackson City would boost the value of land near Arlington House. As he wrote to merchant Stabler, he was skeptical of trendy speculation, but retained hopes for a more-general economic surge for the Federal City. As it happened, foul weather postponed the laying of the cornerstone for three days. Finally, with cannon blasting, drums beating and a crowd of 7,000 watching in freezing wind, Custis, accompanied by his namesake grandson, stood on the dais with Jackson and dignitaries from Congress and the Cabinet. He managed to make his voice carry and share his own vision for the coming Washington Monument to be built downtown. And he welcomed his "northern brethren" bringing their "wealth, their industry, their spirit of enterprise."[83]

But a decade later, Jackson City was still a ghost town of a single home. Local Blacks were using the cornerstone to pound their hominy.[84] The development did attract residents and commerce after the Civil War, but deteriorated into a high-crime row of saloons and gambling dens.

Expanding Family

Custis's surprising admiration for the Democrat Jackson, at a time in the 1830s when Custis's adopted Whig Party was rising in opposition, was shared by many of his relatives. Son-in-law Robert Lee weighed in following the injurious assault Jackson endured during a stopover in Alexandria. On May 6, 1833, the president was returning on the steamer *Sydney* from his speech at the Custis-inspired dedication in Fredericksburg of the planned monument to Mary Washington. Though exhausted and ill, the 66-year-old Jackson agreed to receive visitors by the wharf. One who showed was Robert Beverly Randolph, a Virginia scion and Navy veteran with a long-held grievance against the Jackson administration over a debt he believed he was owed following a shipboard theft. Jackson earlier had ordered Randolph's dismissal. On this May afternoon, Randolph, boarded the Sydney and was ushered into Jackson's presence. But instead of opening a discussion, Randolph charged at the seated Jackson, grabbed him by the nose and wrenched it until he drew blood. In the confusion, the perpetrator escaped. The event later prompted a long legal battle over the unsuccessful prosecution of Randolph and politicized debate over the president's personal security.[85] "The disgraceful scene that occurred at Alexandria," noted Lee in a letter to Custis. "The poor old general's health I believe is fast breaking and that there is some appearance of his yielding the reins to the vice president."[86]

Lee and his new wife embarked on what would be three decades of a military lifestyle that would take them (or he alone) from the Virginia coast to Brooklyn, St. Louis, Mexico, Baltimore, West Point, and San Antonio, Texas. For the next decade and a half, the Custis and Lee family Bible would be filled with new inscriptions hailing the birth of Custis's seven grandchildren: George Washington Custis "Boo" Lee (1832); Mary Custis Lee (1835); William Henry Fitzhugh "Rooney" Lee (1837); Anne Carter Lee (1839); Eleanor Agnes Lee (1841); Robert E. Lee, Jr. (1843) and Mildred Childe Lee (1846). Lee was particularly joyful at the arrival of his first-born in September 1832, who was named after his father-in-law. "I have got me an heir to my Estates. Aye a boy!" he wrote to his brother Carter.[87] Mary Lee experienced severe health problems following the July 7, 1835, birth of Mary Custis Lee. So the Custises moved the recovering mother to fresher country air out at Ravensworth.[88] But over the years between Lee's postings, Arlington House became the sentimental home base for them all.

Lee corresponded intimately with his father-in-law, whom he addressed as "My Dear Major." In one early letter, he assured Custis that "your little grandson is growing finely, has three of his front teeth and is in perfect health."[89] The Lee children would eventually enjoy the playhouse made from the old carriage used at Mount Vernon. Grandmother Molly would take on duties as a home tutor for the Lee children under Robert's strict instructions. In one sign of the growing closeness between the in-laws, Custis hosted and entertained Lee's brothers and friends at Arlington House, playing music, pulling pranks and bestowing gifts of George Washington artifacts.[90] And Custis arranged for produce from his Pamunkey plantations to be shipped to Robert and Mary. Lee would later recall sentimentally the Christmas celebrations at Arlington House, for which Custis would carry in the Yule log and the enslaved domestics would decorate the mantles and windows with holly, myrtle, ivy, laurel and pine boughs.[91]

One of Lee's first duties to his in-laws was to undertake, from his post at Fort Monroe, a trip to evaluate the state of the Custis Eastern Shore property of Smith's Island. In a detailed letter of May 1832, Lee described the 2,600 storm-ravaged acres that were home to just four families, wild cattle, the sheep that Custis had made famous, and plenty of sea bird eggs and fish. "The soil of the glades is as rich as possible and covered with fine grass, that of the ridges contains a great deal of sand and is covered with pine," Lee wrote in his evaluation of business prospects. "But as the part of the island exposed to the ocean is wearing away, and the beach which used to protect the glades, has been in many places levelled, the water at common high tides finds its way into them and renders the pasturage not so good.... Timber is much wanted on the main [land] for ship and house building and I might make some arrangement with those," Lee wrote. But prospects for the sheep trade appeared bleak. "The number of sheep is not accurately known, but is supposed to be over 100. They are nearly as wild as the cattle and looked very ragged," he continued. "The shearing had not commenced, and I directed that they should then be counted and marked. I could learn of no one who wished to purchase, nor do I believe there is anyone who would give for it ¼ its value." Lee reported on the eviction from the island of certain residents for drunkenness. More cheerfully, he noted that "the keeper of the lighthouse and tenants were very kind and attentive to me, gave me plenty of milk, butter and eggs and fish."[92]

Mother-in-law Molly kept the military couple in touch with life back at Arlington. "I promise to be happy without you as I can," she wrote the Lees in St. Louis in 1837 from Woodlawn. "Your aunt Eleanor came down the evening of your departure ... unable to take [her weaning] child to Ravensworth without a nurse." Custis added a postscript: "I have only time, my son and daughter, [to] add my hopes that you are comfortably settled at the garrison and my prayers for your health and happiness."[93]

Lee wrote back two weeks later, saying he was sorry to hear that Molly was ill and giving details on the growth of the grandson Rooney. Lee encouraged Custis's hopes for the successful publication of his coming memoirs of Washington, noting that the Washington biography by Jared Sparks was selling well in Baltimore and Boston. "It speaks greatly in favor of the people, which I am sure you give them credit for," Lee wrote. He also wished Custis greater success in protecting his crops from drought. "I only wish I could spread two feet of this rich black earth over your farm and then with good cultivation nothing could hurt it."[94] Lee's affection for his home place at Arlington House was growing. "If we could and you would permit it," he wrote to his father-in-law in 1837, a time of financial strain, "we would locate ourselves at Arlington and I would have $20,000 a year to put everything in apple-pie order and make us all comfortable."[95]

Custis wrote sentimentally to his daughter, son-in-law and wife once when Molly was away visiting the Lees. He updated them on the free and enslaved workforce's progress on ploughing, spinning, washing and efforts to remove tall carrot weed from the gardens. "I have made a little improvement to surprise and pleasure my ... wife and daughter," he wrote his relations in St. Louis in 1839. "I have cleaned and scoured the parlour [and] whitewashed … nicely the woodwork a light cream color; will also finish the painting of the door frames and washboards in the hall."[96] Custis may have been teasing in demonstrating that he, as the Arlington House proprietor, was, not above pitching in on chores performed most often by the enslaved help.

CHAPTER 8

A Leisurely Creative Life

After glory and heartbreak as a patriotic playwright, Custis applies himself to painting historic battle scenes—to mixed reactions.

By invitation or by inspiration, George Washington Parke Custis carved out many hours at Arlington House in lone pursuit of the creative arts. He was not a master. But his outpourings in poetry, in paintings and in stage drama earned him a national reputation for their celebrations of patriotic history, if not for innate talent. Though his famous name and lineage may have invited opportunities, Custis stepped up to demonstrate "a quick and lively imagination," as his daughter later wrote in describing his "poetic effusions."[1] That required a fierce determination to press on when threatened by failure.

On May 10, 1842, Custis attended, by invitation from his Jesuit friends at Georgetown College, a special commemoration of the founding more than two centuries earlier of St. Mary's City, Maryland. It was a chance for Catholics to mark their own history in a young nation dominated by Protestants. Though he wasn't the main speaker at what he called "a happy pilgrimage" to the Eastern shore, Custis rose to the occasion by arriving with an original poem set to the tune of "The Star Spangled Banner." It began: "Oh, bright was the morn, and the spring breeze was sighing." It ended with "That Mary's fair land, be the land of the free."[2]

Custis was inspired by the event, at which he sang with Father George Fenwick of Georgetown along with a female descendant of prominent Maryland planter Charles Carroll, a signer of the Declaration of Independence. Three days later he enclosed a copy of his verse in a letter to the main orator, Irish Catholic celebrant William Read. "A Protestant citizen and a Catholic clergyman are singing together an ode in honor of the Catholic settlement of the colony of Maryland," Custis noted. "Being kindly received and encored, a charming and accomplished volunteer appears on the stage;

and then the trio consists of the grand-daughter of the venerable Carroll, a most respected ecclesiastic of one of the oldest families of the olden days, located near to the interesting scene of the landing of the Pilgrims, and the last male survivor of Washington's domestic family, in the gray-haired person of his adopted son."[3]

Custis's literary confidence—which blossomed during his adulthood despite his errant college years—was evident in all his lyrical odes to George Washington. To mark the centennial of Washington's birth, February 22, 1832, he wrote a poem, which he enclosed a year later in a letter to an autograph seeker. It began:

> A Century's gone by. All hail the Day
> An Infant Washington first saw the light.
> That beamed with pure & mild benignant ray
> on one who's course was destined to be bright
>
> And so it proved, for in his dawning youth
> The favour'd auspices of Life began.
> And Greybeards said that Courage, Wisdom, Truth
> Would form the promise of the future man.
>
> And now his Country calls her Warrior son
> To do her battle with the Savage Foe
> And soon the youthful Hero laurels won
> That might enwreathe a Veteran victor's brow....[4]

To the modern ear, the Custis rhetorical style seems stilted. He may have been influenced by childhood memories of diplomat, longtime Washington aide and biographer David Humphreys, who often recited verse in his stentorian voice. And Custis honored Washington by using the Latin he struggled with in school (but which Washington himself stressed as vital) in an all-purpose inscription:

> Pro novi orbis Libertate
> Decertabat juvenis
> stabilitam senex
> invenit.
>
> Donum libertatis optimum
> Fautori libertatis optimo.
>
> (When young, he struggled
> For the liberty of the new world;
> When old, he devised [its] stability.
> The best gift of liberty
> Is for the best patron/supporter of liberty.)[5]

As a lyricist, Custis made his mark in early 1829 with a poem to his friend, soon-to-be-inaugurated President Andrew Jackson. Titled *January 8*, it honored the anniversary of the Battle of New Orleans. Custis published its verses in the *U.S. Telegraph,* edited by teacher and Democratic politician Duff Green. A sample stanza:

> Comrades arouse! The dawning day
> Shews the proud Foe in full array—
> Soon we shall join in battle fray,
> Orleans, his grand emprize.

Custis revised the lyrics, and in 1836, after the National Theatre opened in Washington, D.C., they were sung publicly to "warmest enthusiasm," as a newspaper testified. Its final stanza:

> "But should a foe invade our land;
> Old Hick'ry will gain command;
> with trust in Heaven, and patriot band;
> And strike for victory."[6]

Taking to the Stage

Custis had proven himself a journalistic essayist with his "Conversations of Lafayette." Now in his forties, he took on the tougher challenge of dramaturgy.

The stage arts in this era drew disdain from the nation's pulpits and in some corners of high society, with a reputation for attracting low-life. But the theater had moved Custis since his boyhood exposure to first-class productions attended with the Washington family in New York and Philadelphia. In 1830, he may have been hoping to counter the scolds when he published recollections in the *National Intelligencer* detailing George Washington's night life at balls and in the audience at plays put on by the growing industry in New York. "The first president was partial to the amusements of the theatre, and attended some five or six times in a season, more especially when some public charity was to be benefitted by the performance," Custis recalled. "The house would be crowded from top to bottom, as many to see the hero as the play. Upon the president's entering the stage-box with his family, the orchestra would strike up 'The President's March' (now 'Hail Columbia'), composed by a German named [Phile]."[7]

In the recollections later edited by his daughter, Custis described the theater industry in Philadelphia in the 1790s, mentioning popular plays such as the British dramas "School for Scandal" and "Every One Has His Fault."* His ambitions four decades later would showcase his art in the venues on Philadelphia's Chestnut Street, Arch Street and Walnut Street.[8]

---

*In the twenty-first century, the Walnut remains America's longest-continually operating theater.

Custis was versed in Shakespeare and the nineteenth-century novels of Walter Scott. He read William Dunlap's *History of the American Theatre,* published in 1832. The work made clear how early American theater was dominated by the British, and Custis likely felt a need to boost a domestic form of the arts in the same way he viewed the value of stateside manufacturing. He would also select topics that, as part of his broader efforts to promote history and patriotic commemorations, celebrate the seminal role of his home state of Virginia.[9]

Custis artistic projects attracted lukewarm support from family. Daughter Mary wrote, with a hint of an arched eyebrow, to her brother-in-law, "The major ... devoted his leisure from agricultural pursuits to painting and tragedy."[10]

Custis's maiden effort in 1827 was, predictably, a drama about the heroics of Washington. But it also displayed sympathies for the threatened culture of the American Indian.[11] *The Indian Prophecy; or Visions of Glory* grew out of a legend from 1770 passed to Custis by Washington's physician James Craik.[12] That year Washington, with a young Craik, had returned to the area of the 1755 defeat of British General William Braddock by French and Indian forces at the Battle of the Monongahela (modern Pittsburgh). During their trip to the Kanawha River (modern-day West Virginia), Washington's canoe party encountered an Indian chief and veteran of that Braddock battle. This chief recounted, through an interpreter, his people's wondrous memory of the soldier behind Braddock who seemed immune to their weaponry. "The great spirit protects that man, and guides his destinies," said the chief. "He will become the chief of nations, and a people yet unborn, will hail him as the founder of a mighty empire!"

Having published the historical account in the Philadelphia-based *United States Gazette* (noting that the modest Washington never mentioned the prophecy), Custis wrote a play that, through connections and the strength of his name, was produced at Philadelphia's Old Drury. A *Democratic Press* review of *The Indian Prophecy* was scathing. "Absolutely destitute of plot, incident, character and stage effect ... trash," it sneered.[13] Still, the play went onto repeat productions, including for Custis's neighbors in Georgetown. The newly minted playwright approached orator-politician Edward Everett about staging it in Boston.

Custis is thought to have sought next to capitalize on the Indian theme with a play called *The Pawnee Chief or, Hero of the Prairie*, which premiered in 1832. And he mulled an idea for *Tecumseh, or the Last of the Braves*, but no text survives. More successfully, Custis took on the newest transformative technology of the day, the coming of the railroad. His 1828 offering, an operetta titled *The Rail Road*, was produced just as pioneer track was being laid for the Baltimore and Ohio. Using well-known actors, it broke dramaturgical ground by presenting, for the first time on stage, a full-size rendition of a "locomotive steam carriage." The prop was wheeled on to the whistling of "Yankee Doodle." The play would go on to more than one hundred performances in cities all over. The cast and crew of *The Rail Road* came to Washington, performing with an added theme mentioning the newly dug C&O Canal. At a show in Alexandria, the reception was reported as "rapturous."[14] Sample lyrics:

> Nine miles to the hour;
> With Thirty horsepower;
> by day time and night time,
> Arrive at the right time,
> Without rumble or jumble, or chance of a tumble,
> As in chaise, gig or whiskey, When horses are frisky.[15]

The election of Jackson in November 1828 prompted a Custis set piece titled, *The Eighth of January, or, Hurra for the Boys of the West!* One of a dozen known plays recalling the War of 1812, it too was staged in Washington and Alexandria.

By this time Custis had gained valuable contacts in the theater world. He boasted of his early success and sought editing help from celebrity performer John Howard Payne, who was collaborating with Washington Irving in translating plays from France.[16] In a shoptalk-filled letter in April 1829, Custis wrote to actor F.C. Wemyss proposing actors for a coming production of his latest, *Pocahontas; or, The Settlers of Virginia.* He assured the professional, who had complained to Custis brother-in-law Lawrence Lewis that the draft was too long, that he had "curtailed the dialog and soliloquies," rewriting the actions in red ink. "If, however, you think it advisable, you can further apply the pruning knife and make such alterations and amendments as you may deem proper," Custis offered. "I hope that time has arrived for American literature, if humble, like other American manufacturing, to meet with some portion of encouragement."[17]

The 1830 production of *Pocahontas* would become Custis's most successful offering. Staged with fancy sets and authentic costumes, it combined his Indian theme with the history of the Old Dominion, revisiting the well-worn tale of Captain John Smith being rescued by the Indian maiden who went on to marry John Rolfe. (The legendary event took place not far from Custis's Pamunkey River properties.) "Mr. Washington Custis," read the preface to the program at the Walnut Street Theatre,* "has fully proved his capability as an author. The plot keeps up lively interest, its

---

*Records show that *Pocahontas* was put on in Philadelphia fourteen times, with some one hundred productions continuing for six years, as far away as Charleston, South Carolina.

gradual development ... is at once natural and decidedly dramatic," the producers wrote. "We anticipate with pleasure his future productions, whether historical or otherwise."

Custis wrote confidently of his theater pursuits to his new in-law Carter Lee in 1831, a week after this Lee had seen *Pocahontas* at New York's Park Theater. "Your very kind letter with the enclosed playbill came duly to hand, and to afford me great satisfaction to learn that my favourite dramatic work went well, notwithstanding the disadvantage attending its first presentation," the playwright said. Custis knew he was pandering to popular demand. "What is a poor devil of an author to do?" he asked Lee. "Drama is all the go now," and in historical plays, "you must sprinkle, and pageant, a thing to please the senses, as well as their judgment." Custis expressed pride in the play's evocations of nationalist ambitions. "Now it only remains for us to say," he told the art-enthusiast, "that looking thro' the vista of futurity, to the time when these wild regions shall become the ancient and honor'd part of a great and glorious American Empire."[18] Custis was surely pleased when Lafayette wrote to his sister Nelly noting, "I have received a letter from your brother, who has produced two very good plays."[19]

His works' reception in the field, however, was not all warm. Theater historian Dunlap, writing in his diary in 1832, carped, "At tea I hear a most delectable critical conversation on plays and players. Geo. Washn Custis said to be over 50 and the author of several plays, all very bad."[20] The well-born playwright found himself begging for newspaper publicity from his old Alexandria friend Philip Richard Fendall, a politician who had edited the Washington publication *National Journal*. "Will you help out a poor author" by publishing a paragraph on the play *Eighth of January*? Custis asked, boasting that it had been performed three years earlier to acclaim in New York. "Your old friend, a farmer turned dramatic author," as the playwright billed himself, touted his successes with *The Indian Prophecy* and *The Rail Road*. Authors "labor hard for our amusement and ought not to starve in their vocation," he said. "Say something for us in Monday's journal."[21]

In 1836, Custis saw his *Pocahontas* performed at Washington's new National Theatre. The enthused reviewer from the *National Intelligencer* observed, "At the end of the piece the successful and respected author was loudly called for, and in a short time made his first appearance on the boards of any theatre!"[22]

Custis shared the joys and frustrations of playwriting with his wife. In 1833, Molly had written him to describe a trip through Fauquier County, Virginia, where she met Chief Justice John Marshall. "If you had written a little more in detail, I would have composed a fragment upon it, entitled 'A Scene in Fauquier,'" he wrote back playfully. "I had promised the poor rogues a play for the 12th Sept., the anniversary of the Battle of North Point; but, finding myself not *in the vein*, I wrote to them to defer it." The theater manager from Baltimore, however, pressured the playwright, saying Custis's promised output was worth another $600–$700 in the manager's pocket. "On Monday, not a line was finished," Custis told his wife in a remarkable boast. "At five o'clock I commenced, and wrote until twelve; rose the next morning at five, and by seven sent off by the *stages* a two-act piece, with two songs and a finale, called *North Point, or Baltimore Defended*, the whole completed in nine hours. It is to be played tonight. Tomorrow I shall hear of its success."[23]

North Point, a War of 1812 dramatization staged near Fort McHenry using actual fireworks, was a smash in Baltimore, with an audience that reached 2,300. "I have yielded them at least $1,000 more than $100 an hour," Custis told his wife. "I should sooner get out of debt by the labors of my brains than my ploughs at that rate."[24]

Following an attempt at another musical titled *The Launch of the Columbia, or, America's Blue Jackets Forever*, Custis in 1836 arranged the staging of a work from 1830 that was his only departure from themes of American glory. (He would return to George Washington with his 1839 finale *Monongahela, or, Washington on the First Great Field of His Fame.*) But late in the decade, particularly after the economic panic of 1837, America's urban theaters fell on hard times. In what would be his final moment center stage, Custis in 1836 won production of a six-year-old work titled *Montgomerie or, The Orphan of a Wreck*.

Performed in his hometown at the National Theatre on Pennsylvania Avenue, the drama set to music took the audience to 14th-century Scotland, with very European scenes in a castle and a prison. Though intended as a Jackson-era nod to the common man, it was a sharp change of scenery.[25] A reviewer from the Georgetown *Metropolitan* said the play, albeit lengthy, came across with "considerable éclat," enough to inspire the audience to call the author up to the stage.[26]

Less impressed with *Montgomerie* was the anti–Jackson *Washington Mirror*, whose critic fumed that "a more vapid, tedious, and uninteresting production never wearied the patience of an audience."[27]

The following September, Custis's allies editing the *National Intelligencer* published a letter from a theater fan offering some friendly criticism of *Montgomerie*. Could Custis, the writer asked, "find no subject worthy of his muse, in his own land? Our literature already has too much of the mockingbird character, and such a gifted writer as Mr. Custis should not be an echo of European writers."[28]

Custis was perhaps less thin-skinned than the average playwright, demonstrating a modicum of modesty. "I am most willing to hear and shall always estimate the judgment of my friends, and I hope to improve in my future dramatic efforts," he wrote to his in-law early in his playwright career.[29]

As late as 1855, Custis plays were still in demand, he having received a letter that year from actor and producer Edmund Law Rogers detailing plans to stage *Montgomerie* at the Bowery Theater in New York City.[30]

As a wordsmith, Custis was never completely washed up. And his historical enthusiasms for music were reciprocated by other artists. Two composers wove Arlington House into their works. John Hewitt of Baltimore in 1845 published "Arlington Waltzes: Composed and Dedicated as a Testimonial of Respect and Esteem to George Washington Parke Custis, Esq." And Hans Krummacher of Washington published sheet music in 1855 for his "Arlington Polka." Custis would have doubtless been pleased that members of the Washington-area Falcon Boat Club, who enjoyed many parties at Arlington Spring, left behind a song reported in 1848 with the final verse:

> For to us, so oft as the moonlight
> Shall flood the blue waters o're
> Will rise ever bright to our vision
> Our picnics to Arlington Shore.[31]

History in Brushstrokes

Custis deployed his status, insider contacts and leisure time to one other artistic endeavor. His late-life entries into the competitive field of historical painting (in an era before photography was commonplace) would meet with mixed success. What became eight large-scale canvases of Revolutionary War scenes created at Arlington House brought gratitude from some historians, but mockery from other corners.

Since his Mount Vernon childhood, Custis had mingled with well-established portrait artists, from Pine to Saint-Mémin. His ownership of invaluable Washington family paintings meant years of correspondence with luminaries from John Trumbull to Rembrandt Peale. Though Custis would later promote himself as "self-taught," there is evidence that around 1807 he studied in Alexandria with painter Cephas Thompson, who had done a portrait of Mrs. Custis. (See page 43.) George Washington's account books record that Custis was given a set of watercolor paints at the age of eight.[32] And as early as 1810, according to an *Alexandria Gazette* report, Custis supervised another painter's allegorical work displayed in the city's Caton's Hotel ballroom.[33] An 1810 Custis watercolor rendering of the principal entrance to his in-laws' Tudor Place mansion survives at the Georgetown hilltop location. And his more-abstract scene of an ocean-going ship is displayed at his sister Nelly's Woodlawn.

But the more-garish paintings with which Custis made his mark were executed in his studio from the late 1830s to the mid–1850s. In an August 14, 1838, letter to his daughter stationed with her husband Lee in St. Louis, Custis announced, "I am doing a picture of Gen. Washington for Mr. Bob."[34] Two months later, he was discussing the safety risks of shipping art with an agent in Buffalo, expressing hopes for "immediate pictorial renown."[35]

Custis worked with journalist-archivist Benson Lossing (future co-editor of Custis's memoirs) on the planning and marketing of his paintings. "I have an excellent studio fitted up in the South wing of this house, with a first-rate light, also a stove and everything comfortable," the artist wrote to Lossing in fall 1852. He also painted a self-portrait.[36]

Visitors could not miss the paintings, which the artist spent years retouching to achieve his desired lighting, fire and smoke effects. He was once seen staring at a sunset to absorb its patterns. The visit by the delegation of ladies from Kentucky in September 1845 allowed them to study Custis's paintings of General Hugh Mercer and Nassau Hall at the 1777 Battle of Princeton, the 1781 Battle of Yorktown, and the Escape of Sergeant Champe. (That last action scene depicts Continental Army Sergeant Major John Champe, who was picked by George Washington in 1780 to pose as a double agent to capture the traitor Benedict Arnold.)[37]

Entering Arlington House, "I went into the old gentleman's studio: You know he is quite an amateur artist," wrote family friend Augusta Blanche Berard after a visit in 1856. "The picture on which he is now at work is 'The Battle of Trenton.' It is almost finished and is very fine. … Mr. Custis hopes to begin another picture, 'The Battle of Monmouth.'"[38]

Custis's rendition of the 1778 action at Monmouth allowed him to portray Washington on horseback alongside the mythical Molly Pitcher, loading a cannon. He would also paint the Battle of Germantown (showing the Benjamin Chew family house near Philadelphia called Cliveden), Washington at Valley Forge in 1777 and Washington standing by his horse at Yorktown in 1781.

"I am now engaged in [a] magnum opus *The Surrender of Yorktown*, on a canvas 8 feet 6 inches by 6 feet 4 inches," he wrote Lossing at the end of 1852. "I have departed from the plan of dear old Trumbull's picture, which has always been considered kind of stiff."[39] Custis kept Lossing abreast of progress, promising to deliver despite the ailments of old age.

His family were only mildly supportive. "Considering the circumstances under which they were produced—painted without being first composed or drawn in outline, by an entirely self-taught hand more than threescore and ten years old—they are remarkable," daughter Mary, who

"The Battle of Monmouth," painting by G.W.P. Custis (courtesy George Washington Memorial Parkway).

helped her father research painting details, wrote after Custis's death. "In general conception and grouping, they are spirited and original. He was not disposed to devote the time or labor requisite to their careful execution, and therefore, as works of art merely, they have but little merit. Their chief value lies in their truthfulness to history in their delineation of events, incidents and costumes."[40] Custis's grand-daughter Mary Custis Lee pitched in by making leather framing for his works.[41]

Custis grew boastful as he drummed up an audience. "It would give me great pleasure to see you here, where I could show you many pictures, including some of my own performance, which I'm sure will interest you," he wrote to Lewis Washington, a distant relation. "I have just finished a large painting of the Battle of Trenton, 9' × 6', and I'm now engaged in a painting of the Battle of Monmouth, 12' by 8'. In this large picture, the figure of the Chief on a white charger, surrounded by his officers, has been particularly admired."[42] (Reproduction of the painting appears above.)

But by pushing to display his works in public buildings, Custis invited brickbats. After he arranged to have one painting, most likely his large-scale *Surrender of Yorktown* displayed early in his career in the Capitol Rotunda, several senators asked that it be removed.[43] Defensively, Custis protested in a letter to the Superintendent of Public Buildings: "A native subject, by a native artist, & one whose connections with the venerated individuals endeavored to be portrayed on the canvas, were so intimate, & endeared, might have hoped for charity from the public, toward the production of a self-taught artist," he wrote to Major William Noland. "A set of hired scrib-bler[s] who infest the Capitol, must abuse someone, or something.... I cer-tainly should not have presumed to place my humble work in the Rotunda, had I not respectfully asked permission to do, and that permission had been freely granted by the proper authority."

Facetiously Custis said he was asking his agent to remove the painting and "cast it from the bridge into the Potomac, that it may offend no more." He wasn't done with his defense. "Permit me to observe that this picture has undergone the scrutiny of some excellent artists, and candid, liberal men, and they have been pleased to say, that is had some good points, & some good painting in it," he said, "and that it was a considerable effort, for a self-taught artist, who never had one moment's instruction in the art...."[44] Custis's cousin Elizabeth Calvert later recalled seeing two enslaved workers carrying, as she quoted them in dialect, "out a large brown, greasy looking bundle. I found on inquiry, that it was 'Master big picture, he told us put it in the ribber, we is going to cut it up & make aprons wid it.'"[45]

Custis never gave up on recognition. One of his equestrian portraits of Washington was displayed at the National Hotel during the official dinner following the July 4, 1848, laying of the cornerstone of Washington monu-ment.[46] Six years later, he lobbied the District of Columbia Council: "Gen-tlemen," he wrote on August 4, 1854, "I have to solicit your permission to hang up my large historical and revolutionary painting of the *Surrender of Yorktown* in such part of the City Hall as you may be pleased to appoint. It has been for some time exhibited in the Capitol, and only requires a side light upon it in the new destination. From its size it is more especially cal-culated for a public building, and, if agreeable to you, to give it a berth in the City Hall for a short time...."[47] A New York publisher would later mar-ket steel engravings of the courtship of George and Martha Washington, advertising "drawings furnished the artist by the late George Washington Parke Custis, the adopted son of Washington."[48]

The damning with faint praise endured by the artist came even from his duty-bound son-in-law. "The major is busy farming. His cornfields not yet enclosed or ploughed, but he is rushing on all he knows," Robert E. Lee wrote to brother Carter Lee—with a tinge of mockery. Custis's play "*Mont-gomerie* failed," Lee wrote. "The 'big picture' has been exhibited in the Cap-itol, and attracted some severe animadversions from the critics, which he says were leveled at his politics!"[49]

After Custis's death, a Union soldier stationed at Arlington House admired the historical paintings, telling a newspaper "they are very spirited."[50] And the *Alexandria Gazette* would report in 1873 that "a handsome picture of General Washington painted by the late G.W.P. Custis is now undergoing repairs at the cabinet factory of the Green Brothers, and will be presented through them to the City Council by Mrs. General R.E. Lee."[51]

Custis kept the faith in his art. In a June 1854 letter to Lossing, he confessed to being "wretchedly depressed in spirits—not having mustered energy enough for my literary labour, I am engaged in painting all the time I can spare from my agricultural operations. My 'Surrender of Yorktown,' which is still in the Rotunda of the Capitol, has been well received and the horses [have] been particularly commended."[52]

CHAPTER 9

Of Two Minds on Slavery

Custis seeks a middle ground between the status quo and abolition, a family's condescending treatment, freedom for a special few, secret sexual exploitation.

"G.W.P. Custis, grandson of Gen. Washington, has freely offered his island, at the entrance to the Chesapeake, as a depot for captured blacks, until they can be sent back to Africa—and the president [Monroe] has ordered that all taken shall be conveyed there." So read a June 1819 dispatch published in the *Vermont Gazette* reporting on Custis's latest plans for his Virginia property of Smith's Island. "[Thirty] or 40 slaves lately seized in Georgia, are to be brought to the above island. There is to be a convenient establishment at the island, where the blacks are to be supported, instructed etc. under the care of the colonization society, til the colony in Africa is provided."[1]

Custis's very public handling of his inherited slavery interests would trail him throughout his life. The racism he shared with his privileged peers looms for modern Americans as his least appealing trait; his efforts to resolve the slavery issue among his most salient failures. Custis's slave holdings were never as large-scale or as dependent on brutality as were counterparts in the deep South. But the Custis family wealth put him, by one modern estimate, in the top five percent of American slave-owning families.[2] And like those of his anguished Virginia forebears Washington, Jefferson and Madison, Custis's ambivalent efforts at resolving the problem of the nation's peculiar institution, for the most part, failed.

"As a master of slaves, Washington was consistent," he recalled in his posthumously published memoir of his adoptive father. That betrayed a Custis pride that bordered on self-serving. At Mount Vernon during Custis's boyhood, enslaved workers, he claimed, "were comfortably lodged, fed and clothed, required to do a full and fair share of duty; well cared for in sickness and old age, and kept in strict and proper discipline. These, we

126

humbly conceive, comprise all the charities of slavery." Custis continued, "To [Washington's] old servants, where long and faithful services rendered them worthy, he was most kind."[3]

The memoir includes mixed accolades to Washington's treatment of his long-serving wartime enslaved aide William "Billy" Lee, who, injured and aging, was given a pension of thirty dollars a year. Custis spins a condescending tale of Lee's role during the 1780s as a Mount Vernon grounds "ambassador." A veteran officer under Washington, Colonel William Smith, went the tale, offended one of Washington's favorite hired hands at the mansion by appearing to flirt with his milkmaid daughter. To defuse the tension, the once-enslaved Billy Lee attempted diplomacy with high rhetoric.[4] Custis goes on to assert that the retired body-servant "became a spoiled child of fortune. He was quite intemperate at times," according to another enslaved man who knew him, "and finally *delirium tremens*, with all its horrors, seized him."

Custis displayed similar condescension in how he portrayed "Cully," a one hundred-year-old servant he interviewed seventy-five years after Washington's wedding. This man, he wrote, was a rude, "untutored negro" who still expressed awe at George Washington's presence as a horseman.[5]

Custis long maintained a belief in limits on the potential of enslaved Blacks once freed. "Although many of them," he wrote in his memoir, "with a view to their liberation, had been instructed in mechanic trades, ... they succeeded very badly as freemen: so true is the axiom, 'the hour which makes man a slave, takes half his worth away.'"[6]

Custis also learned, from his Mount Vernon days, the goal of efficiency in administering the enslaved. In later life, he praised Martha Washington's "admirable management of her servants and household, going through every department, or immediately after breakfast.... Her young female servants were gathered in her apartment to sew under her own supervision and they became beautiful seamstresses."[7]

It is a romantic, if sanitized view, of a situation of silent anguish. By the time Custis enjoyed status as proprietor of Arlington House, he would be well aware of the routine cruelty inflicted at the nationally prominent commercial slave market just seven miles away, at the office and pen on Alexandria's Duke Street, run from 1828 to 1836 by Franklin and Armfield.

At the time of his daughter's marriage to Robert E. Lee—who was destined to share Custis's struggles in treatment of the enslaved—Arlington House was home at any given time to sixty or seventy enslaved workers. Custis's original inheritance of a share of the "dower slaves" from the estate of Daniel Parke Custis had been augmented by the dowry of land, cash and sixteen enslaved workers his wife Molly inherited from her father in 1809.[8]

The Arlington field workers were housed in crowded, crude, mud-

floored cabins near the Potomac shore. They fired the bricks for the building of the house, maintained horses and carriages, hauled equipment and
manure, milked cows and tended to other livestock, sowed and harvested
wheat and cultivated gardens. The house servants, considered of higher status, resided in rough-hewn quarters behind the mansion. They prepared and
served meals, cleaned, kept the hearth fires burning, looked after children
and maintained the master family's clothing. Under the law, the enslaved
enjoyed no rights, could not enter into legally binding contracts, and, at a
moment's notice, could be permanently separated from their families. Mr.
and Mrs. Custis would give assignments calling most of them by their first
names—Daniel, Obadiah, Parkes.[9] To leave the Arlington House property
on assignment or by request, an enslaved worker had to ask the master for
a laissez-passer card with blanks to be filled in attesting that "belongs to the
Arlington estate and has permission to pass to…."[10] (See page 130.)

The cultivated public image of Arlington House invoked benign treatment of the human beings caught in the cruel institution. "Each slave had a
house apportioned him and bit of ground, the produce of which he owned
as securely as if his title to the land he occupied was duly recorded in the
records of the county courts," said one late-nineteenth-century guidebook. "The slaves were of course compelled to give a good portion of
their time to the master's service, but their work was not hard and they
were liberally provided for in decrepit old age as well as in sturdy youth.
Mr. Custis also respected the domestic relations of the negroes, and the
separation of mothers from their children and of wives from their hus-
bands was a practice in which he never indulged himself and abhorred in
others."[11]

Like Washington, Custis allowed his enslaved to kill ducks along the
Potomac for food.[12] The diet he imposed at Arlington House became the
subject of outsider study. In 1816, Custis friend David Baillie Warden wrote
a statistical portrait of the District of Columbia, which he dedicated to
Molly Custis. After examining the enslaved workers' food intake at Arlington House and the nearby Mason property on Analostan Island, he summarized a typical weekly diet as one peck (two dry gallons) of Indian meal, two
lbs. of salt meat weekly and a barrel of fish per year.[13]

More-exhausting work was extracted from Custis's enslaved persons
toiling under the scorching sun on the Pamunkey plantations. In October 1832, caretaker William Bromley reported to Custis from New Kent
Courthouse using a business practice routine then—but shocking to modern readers—combining the inventory of human captives with that for the
animals. Custis's White House holdings then consisted of 97 "negroes," 16
horses and mules, 2 colts, 47 cattle, 6 calves, 149 sheep, 94 hogs and 60 pigs.
Nearby Romancock, the manager tallied, contained 59 "negroes," 9 horses

and mules, 2 colts, 94 cattle, 11 calves, 145 sheep, 125 hogs and 50 pigs.[14] All of his caretakers updated Custis on "increases" and "decreases," again combining human property with livestock in itemizing illnesses and deaths. Only some had birthdates recorded. In 1825, the caretakers did list "names and ages of negroes" in the two Pamunkey plantations, names reminiscent of the Washington and Custis families: Fanny, Daniel, Dandridge, George, and Patsy, along with Elisha, Henry, Jemima, Dolly and Esther.[15] (See page 57.)

Up north by the Potomac, the individuality of the enslaved at Arlington House was more likely recorded for posterity, though unevenly. From Custis's Mount Vernon days this slave community included the elderly woman named Judy, known as "Mammy." There was cook George Clark (said to have married seven times and lived to be 110); Eleanor Harris, who had nursed Custis when he was an infant; Lawrence Parks, whose picture was drawn by a young Mary Custis (see page 140); a groomsman named Jim Connally; coachman Daniel; the valet and gardener Ephraim Derricks, with whom Custis enjoyed evening cigars; construction foreman and dining room steward Charles Syphax; a character cared for in old age called Uncle Gid (Gideon Lancaster); and Cassie, an enslaved woman Molly Custis lent to daughter Mary and son-in-law Robert at Fort Monroe. Perry Parks would be remembered for his daily routine of lighting and extinguishing candles, and performing a butler's task of announcing visitors.[16] Among those favored by Molly from her old Ravensworth plantation were a woman named Eleanor as well as children John, Charles, Edmund and Eliza, who were emancipated in 1818.[17]

Several individuals would leave a legacy richer in detail. "My old and favorite body servant, Philip Lee … is the nephew of Washington's celebrated Revolutionary follower, Will Lee," wrote Custis in an 1832 letter to a merchant. He was preparing him for Philip's help setting up the tent of Washington for a celebration in Fredericksburg. "Philip is a highly intelligent, nay, talented man, of gentlemanly manners, and worthy of every confidence and consideration. He will not be my slave much longer—he has been my friend for two and thirty years."[18] Philip Lee was also responsible on special occasions for the nighttime illumination of Arlington House. Having fathered children with a wife on another plantation, Philip in 1829 was permitted to raise money to purchase their freedom.[19]

But Philip Lee's loyalty had limits. While Custis was away on a trip to Philadelphia in 1832, the body servant appears to have escaped and was arrested. "Philip is very unhappy," Molly wrote to her husband. "He wishes to hear from you, from family, and to know what are the wishes of

Estate, and has permission to pass to   *belongs to the Arlington*
to
AGENT.

Estate, and has permission to pass to   *belongs to the Arlington*
to
AGENT.

Estate, and has permission to pass to   *belongs to the Arlington*
to
AGENT.

Estate, and has permission to pass to   *belongs to the Arlington*
to
AGENT.

Estate, and has permission to pass to   *belongs to the Arlington*
to
AGENT.

Estate, and has permission to pass to   *belongs to the Arlington*
to
AGENT.

Estate, and has permission to pass to   *belongs to the Arlington*
to
AGENT.

Estate, and has permission to pass to   *belongs to the Arlington*
to
AGENT.

Blank forms for laissez-passer required of enslaved persons to leave the Arlington House property (Virginia Museum of History & Culture).

his master. He evinces no disposition, that I can see to do wrong in any sense." Molly was negotiating with a Mr. Burrows about giving Philip $50–$60 and his freedom, or at least donating it on his behalf to the American Colonization Society. "I consider Philip the greatest sufferer … of his own responsibility and agency," she said. "All I want is that right should be done to all parties…. If you can come to a decision about that, my dear husband, it ought not to be delayed."[20] (It isn't known whether Philip was emancipated.)

Destined to be a favorite of Mary Custis Lee was the enslaved maid Selina Gray, born on the property as the daughter of Leonard and Sally Norris. Oral tradition has it that the Custises took the unusual step of permitting Selina and Thornton to be formally married in the parlor where the Lee wedding took place (the same story is told of other Custis slaves). Though blessed by the Episcopal Church, that union was without legal basis. Selina and Thornton Gray raised their eight children in quarters behind the mansion.

Court evidence survives showing that Custis did engage in the slave trade, but often with the goal of manumission. By one modern-day count, he sold twenty persons from 1803 to 1829, though the fate of most is unaccounted for. In the case of Louisa, daughter of Martha Washington's enslaved servant named Judith, she can be found on the August 18, 1802, list of Custis dower slaves. At the age of only two, the child was freed on March

Thornton Gray, left, with wife Selina Gray, one of the enslaved couples said to have been married in the Arlington House parlor (courtesy George Washington Memorial Parkway).

1, 1803.[21] Some he sold to Alexandria merchant Edward Stabler, knowing that the Quaker abolitionist would free them.

When handling adults, Custis exercised his belief that the enslaved could be more productive than paid laborers. While managing his earliest mill on Four Mile Run, he negotiated in 1812 a proposed sale of slaves to Alexandria merchant James Hooe for use at his Fairfax plantation. Custis's lessees, named Mason and Wiley, preferred to hire a white miller in place of the enslaved workers. So Custis offered Hooe a family that included an enslaved miller named Lewis, wife Fanny and two pre-teen girls for $600. "The girl Piety or Peg is 10 or 12 years old and very salable at $250," he wrote. "Fanny is surely worth very little, she is able to earn her living being a good spinner," Custis wrote. "Lewis is a good miller, a healthy slave.... For my own miller fully as old a man, and a much more infirm one, I have [been] offered $500 cash. I flatter myself you cannot but deem these terms reasonable. The miller is worth his price, I am assured, from the experience of my own mills, where I have [done] better with my own, than a hired man."[22]

Middle Ground on Emancipation?

In the Custis approach to slavery as a legal, philosophic and religious issue, human attachments were seldom the determining factor. His extended family's selective emancipations and Christianity-justified acts of charity were offset by a desire, as with all slave owners, to protect investments, minimize debt and respect enforcement of current law. The Custis and Lee families' ambivalence, and their mixed record on treatment of their enslaved, suggest a resignation to the belief that resolution of the slavery problem was a long way off. Custis naively deployed a common defense used by slave owners, arguing that the human beings he owned were more comfortable than working-class people in England. "To eat & drink & sleep are the only duties with [which the typical slave] has anything to do—with regard to most of them," he told grand-niece Markie Williams. "They have their comfortable homes, their families around them and nothing to do but to consult their own pleasure." Custis went further: "And truly in many instance[s] the master is the only slave."[23]

Just across the Potomac from Arlington House lay the headquarters of the American Colonization Society, which Custis, his wife and daughter would visit and help fund.[24] "The name of the venerable George Washington Parke Custis, the last member of the family of Washington, is also recorded as one of the most early, constant, and eloquent friends of the society," wrote its secretary, longtime Custis friend R.R. Gurley, in an annual report.[25] Founded in 1817 by Presbyterian minister Robert Finley, the society attracted major figures: Henry Clay, Bushrod Washington and Francis Scott Key, along with the presidents of the major colleges—Harvard, Yale, Princeton and Columbia. Its mission was to free American Blacks from slavery and then to charter ships and finance their voluntary transport to Africa to a new colony called Liberia. The group's annual meetings were held in prestigious locations—halls of Congress, the Supreme Court, churches. Its officers sought federal funding of their voluntary migration plan at a time when 1.6 million Blacks were enslaved in the American South. The motives were also financial; Society Secretary John H.B. Latrobe in 1827 encouraged southerners to consider that it is more economical to hire three white laborers and ten more seasonal ones than to raise thirteen slaves.[26]

Custis was passionate about this compromise between continued exploitation and immediate abolition. Slavery is "the mightiest serpent that ever infested the earth," he told the society's 1826 annual meeting. He characterized practice as a current burden created by men of the past.[27] But Custis couldn't abide the abolitionists, whose demands for quick emancipation frightened him. He and allies feared that quickly freed Blacks would sink into poverty and crime.[28] By the late 1820s and early 1830s, the abolitionist movement was gathering force with the formation of the American Anti-Slavery Society. Just as southern politicians began taking an ever-harder line in slavery's defense, Custis accelerated his support for colonization.

His rhetoric, to the modern ear, is a jarring mixture of prejudice and paternalism. "What right have the children of Africa to a homestead in the white man's country?" Custis asked the society in 1831. "Here there is no footing for the coloured man," he added two years later. "If he could be happy here, if he could be placed upon a level with the others here, he might stay, but here he can shine but by borrowed light."[29]

For the Blacks themselves, "Let us restore them to the land from whence they came," he continued. "There they may be masters; the land, the government will be theirs. Let them plough the ocean, till the soil, or explore the forest. Be it so. I shall envy not, but rather rejoice in their prosperity."

Having lived intimately with slavery his whole life, Custis in his fifties summoned pride in his version of reform. "I feel that the design of the Colonization Society must succeed, as strongly as I feel the force of any self-evident proposition," he told the 1833 meeting. "Reason and experience and principle are with us. The land of liberty is not a home for the slave. He perishes there. His mind and energies are withered."

The case he made for shipping American Blacks to Africa had a quasi-scientific tone, as he conjured an image of a climate in Africa hospitable to Blacks but not to whites. "While we should sicken and die [as] victims of that ardent clime, the native African, invigorated under the influence of a vertical sun, glories in its blaze and grapples with the lion of the desert," he counseled. "But expose the African to the keen rigours of our northern winter, and he shivers and dies, while the white man can bare his bosom to the blast."[30]

Custis took on his southern allies by appealing to their safety and self-interest. "Why, as in the slave colonies of other countries, you must have an army of troops to keep in awe this dangerous population?" Custis asked the Society's 1828 gathering. "What a sight this would be, in the land of liberty! The same breeze that fanned our harvests, that played among the leaves of the cane and the corn, would also rustle banners of war!"[31]

Custis the Federalist sought to balance his southern identity with fidelity to the Union. "Believe me, I am loyal to the South, aye 'every inch a Southron; in all her misfortunes, she is my country still,'" he told the group in 1830. "We groan, Sir, under the evil entailed upon us by our ancient rulers."[32]

Custis was joined in these views by wife Molly, her brother William Fitzhugh (the society's vice president), and Molly's cousin, Bishop Meade. Molly was interested enough to sit in on a Supreme Court hearing on recolonization. The Episcopal leader traveled extensively to raise funds from churches, to interview slaves and their owners and to implement the society's agenda. His agents in Richmond, as Meade informed Molly in 1825, sent a report "containing very favorable accounts from some few places in North Carolina which promise of themselves to send out a shipload this fall.... And now if Government will only do its part, how nobly should we go on realizing it at some of the many blessings which we have fondly hoped to derive from the successful operation of our Society."[33]

Abolitionists attacked, sometimes singling out Custis. The Anti-Slavery Society's publication *The Emancipator* in 1839 mocked British missionary efforts at Christianizing Zulus in Africa, facetiously suggesting "they could take a few lessons from the practical philanthropy from Mr. Henry Clay, and [Philadelphia philanthropist] Elliot Cresson, and George Washington Parke Custis!"[34]

The criticisms prompted the Arlington House master to declare to Gurley of the Colonization Society that "if the Abolitionists have sheltered themselves under my speeches, and 'marked me for their own,' it was time I should convince them to the contrary."[35]

William Lloyd Garrison, the righteous-toned editor of the *Liberator* newspaper, charged that the resettlement organization was founded on "persecution, falsehood, cowardice [and] infidelity."[36] Were the Colonization Society "bending its energies directly to the immediate abolition of slavery," he wrote in 1832, "seeking to enlighten and consolidate public opinion, on this momentous subject; faithfully exposing the awful guilt of the owners of slaves; manfully contending for the bestowal of equal rights upon our free colored population in this their native land; assiduously endeavoring to uproot the prejudices of society; and holding no fellowship with oppressors, my opposition to it would cease. It might continue, without censure, to bestow its charities upon such as spontaneously desire to remove to Africa, whether animated by religious considerations, or the hope of bettering their temporal condition," Garrison continued. "But, alas! its governing spirit and purpose are of an opposite character."[37] (Years later, fellow abolitionist and former slave Frederick Douglass would call the debate over colonization a "wrinkled old 'red herring,' ... a *ruse* to divert the attention of the people from the foul abomination."[38])

Custis thought immediate abolition to be impractical, given the poor prospects of American Blacks for earning a living. His daughter Mary would refer to abolitionists as "miscreants." Robert E. Lee professed a complex view that rejected both abolitionism and the putative middle ground of colonization in Africa. Slavery, he wrote his wife in 1856 (in a letter that fatefully raised the specter of a civil war), is "a moral and political evil in any country," and "is a greater evil to the white than to the black race." But his remedy was as self-serving as any other white slave owner's. "The blacks are immeasurably better off than in Africa, morally, socially and physically," Lee continued. "The painful discipline they are undergoing is necessary for their instruction as a race, & I hope will prepare & lead them to better things."[39]

One stalwart of the Custis clan countered the abolitionists even more forcefully. Nelly Custis Lewis, in a scathing letter in 1831 to her friend the Boston politician and businessman Harrison Gray Otis, called Garrison a "wretch." She blamed him for the deadly slave rebellion led by Nat Turner in southern Virginia two months previous. Her defense of slavery:

> Is not the Editor of the Liberator an incendiary of the very worst description?— He inculcates insurrection, murder, cruelty, & baseness, in every shape. The most lenient are as frequently the victims, as the most rigorous, & even more frequently; since nine times out of ten, a negro loves those best who are least indulgent— fear not principle governing the far greater part. Our whites unhappily evince too much fear of these wretches—they can never succeed in subjugating the Whites, but our young & lovely females, infant innocence, & helpless age will be their victims—.[40]

By the decline of its active years, just after the Civil War, the American Colonization Society had delivered an estimated 16,000 black migrants to Liberia (capital city Monrovia, named for President James Monroe). Many suffered in transit and struggled to relate to African culture. The bulk of them (mostly free Blacks from the north) traveled between 1848 and 1854 on fifty-four chartered ships.[41]

Among those sent to Liberia were the Burke family, enslaved at Arlington House. William and Rosabella Burke and their four children were selected for education and emancipation by Molly Custis and Mary Lee. William Burke was willing to migrate to Liberia, and on obtaining his freedom, he apprenticed with a Philadelphia blacksmith to prepare him with job skills. The ship sailed in November 1853. Once in Monrovia, Burke enrolled in a seminary to study Greek and Latin before becoming a minister. "Persons coming to Africa should expect to go through many hardships, such as are common to the first settlement in any new country," he wrote after five years in Africa. "I expect it, and was not disappointed or discouraged at anything I met with; and so far from being dissatisfied with the country, I bless the Lord that ever my lot was cast in this part of the earth."

Equally enthusiastic was his wife Rosabella, who wrote to Mary Custis Lee in February 1859, "I am at the time, and nearly all times, in the enjoyment of excellent health. My children are as fat as pigs.... They are all going to school and seem to learning quite fast. Little Martha does not go to school but is very fond of going to Sunday School.... In the morning I get up early to milk my cow, feed my chickens...." All things considered, Mrs. Burke assured Mrs. Lee, "I love Africa and would not exchange it for America."[42]

Reading and Church-Going

For the majority of the Custis enslaved remaining in Virginia, the repetitive daily toil was eased only by their unusual opportunities to gain literacy and to worship. Nationwide, only an estimated ten percent of the enslaved of the pre–Civil War period were permitted to learn to read.[43] Laws in both the District of Columbia (which applied to Arlington House until retrocession in 1847) and Virginia prohibited teaching literacy to slaves, enforced mostly by banning large gatherings (thought by whites to risk insurrections). Following the 1831 Nat Turner rebellion, those laws were toughened. Enforcement, however, focused more on the enslaved themselves than their high-status owners. Custis himself, as a justice of the peace, was aware of the risk. "Do you know," he asked half seriously of his companion Markie Williams as she helped with the teaching, "that it is my duty [to] confine you a month in jail, in accordance with the laws of the state?" But surely, he continued, "it can never be wrong to teach them that

Holy Book. No, Markie, I won't put you in jail. I want you here with me too much."[44] On other occasions, Custis appeared supportive. "I am much obliged by the African Education Society ... a praiseworthy institution," he wrote in 1831 to that society's secretary, the inventor and clergyman Isaac Orr.[45]

It was Molly Custis, who held twice-daily prayers and attended Alexandria's Christ Church, who took charge of teaching the Arlington House enslaved to read. She used the Bible and Sunday afternoon worship for context. Her daughter Mary would join her when she came of age, as would some in the next generation of Lees. "My mother devoted herself to the religious culture of the slaves," Mary Lee later said. "Her life was devoted to this work, with the hope of preparing them for freedom."[46] Custis himself was only mildly agreeable. "Teaching the colored children is not according to my notions, but it was my poor wife's plans," he told grand-niece Williams. "I wish things to go on just as she would desire. I have my own notions on those subjects, but she thought it was her duty to teach them and most faithfully did she perform it."[47]

As early as 1805, when Custis was soon to become a father, he had advertised a willingness to award a twenty-five-acre farm to the man who could build a schoolhouse at Arlington House "to educate a certain number of children on behalf of the proprietor."[48]

In the southwest corner of his property, about a mile from the mansion, Custis built circa 1825 a small "Chapel of Ease" that doubled as the schoolhouse. (Modern Arlingtonians would call it their county's first public place of worship.) White members of the public were invited as well as the enslaved, and sermons were delivered by students at nearby Virginia Theological Seminary. There was a baptismal font, and Custis relatives received communion. "The servants of all ages and all so attentive," recalled Markie's friend, the educator Augusta Blanche Berard, after a visit in which she also commented on the enslaved's "shiftlessness."[49] Custis himself wasn't always attentive. One of the seminarians who preached recalled the elderly proprietor falling asleep during services. And though perhaps not as dutiful as son-in-law Robert, Custis remained supportive. In November 1855, according to Markie Williams, Custis was preparing for Sunday service when the enslaved house worker Perry Parks ran into the mansion and shouted, "Master, your woods are on fire." Custis instructed the worker to tell the field slaves to put out the fire. "Afterward, Perry was to return to the house to saddle a horse for Markie to ride to church," she wrote in her diary. "With that, Mr. Custis calmly set out on foot for the chapel."[50]

Members of Arlington's enslaved community clearly would have welcomed the Sunday break from their labors. Markie Williams recalled "a troop of black boys" enthusiastically escorting her to services.[51] But whether they related to the Episcopal message at a time when that clergy was actively promoting colonization is questionable. Parish records at Alexandria's Christ Church for 1828–29 show baptisms of "slaves," "coloured" and "black" infants under the Rev. John P. McGuire.[52] Yet many of the Custis slaves organized instead to found the Alexandria Baptist Church.[53]

Condescending Treatment

America's slave-owning families in the nineteenth century took their cues from the ancestors as well as from popular etiquette. Custis's own memoirs note that his great-great grandfather Daniel Parke himself once counseled his daughter to "[b]e kind and good-natured to all your servants. It is much better to have them love you than fear you."[54] His grandfather Daniel Parke Custis had also allowed the enslaved to worship.[55]

Among whites, directing the enslaved domestics was a source of feminine pride. "The Virginia ladies, who are proverbially good managers, employ themselves, while their servants are eating, in washing the cups, glasses etc.; arranging the cruets, the mustard, salt-sellers, pickle vases, and all the apparatus for the dinner table," advised the popular book by the Custis cousin and author Mary Randolph. "This occupies but a short time, and the lady has the satisfaction of knowing they are in much better order than they would be if left to the servants."[56] Mrs. Custis and Mary did trade recipes with the enslaved cooks.[57] Mary painted a watercolor portrait of one enslaved girl.

It was common in Custis circles to assert that their treatment of the enslaved was humane. "The servants are all very well at this time & happy," Abby Nelson, the wife of his Pamunkey plantation overseer Francis Nelson, wrote to Custis's daughter Mary in May 1853. "At one time this spring several of the men were away several weeks. This seemed to throw a gloom over everything at the time, but they delivered themselves in Richmond, and since their return all things go as usual, and you may be satisfied in thinking Mr. Nelson will do all in his power to make them comfortable and happy, just as much (I know) as if they were his own. They have every comfort in eating & clothing an abundant plantation affords, even to furnishing them tobacco, & when they are sick Mr. Nelson attends them more closely than he does his children."[58]

The masters' condescending attitudes show up in the memoirs of Custis's grand-niece Markie, who while gardening ordered an enslaved black boy to shade her with an umbrella.[59] Both the enslaved and the master family members were often affectionate (children of both races played together). But such intimacy had obvious limits. Markie offered differing views on the elderly women known as "Mammy" and Aunt Ellenor ("Old Nurse" from Mount Vernon days). Ellenor, she opined, was "the personification of pomposity" whereas Mammy was "the picture of humility and meekness." Nurse was a "privileged character and always prided herself on her superior wisdom and the right she possessed of speaking just as she chose to any of the family," Markie declared. "The Queen of Ethiopia could not display more pompous dignity in her mien than did said 'Nurse.'"[60]

A similar recollection was recorded by Custis's granddaughter Agnes Lee, who recalled life at Arlington House sentimentally: "Just on the edge of the groves, under a spreading tree, was my own little garden, a white lilac in one corner & violets forming the borders of the beds. Harry Washington Gray, a small darkey, was my head gardener, and much fonder of play than work."[61] Agnes expressed gratitude toward an enslaved groomsman named Austin who reunited her with her runaway horse.[62] Former slaves recalled gently scolding Mrs. Custis, "You should not be outside in this weather."[63] And granddaughter Mary Custis Lee recalled that the famous Arlington House rose gardens cultivated by Molly and daughter Mary were actually the work of "Old George, little George, Uncle Ephraim, Billy, and swarms of small Ethiopians."[64] The Lee girls also depended on "Nurse" and "Old Mammy" to manufacture the rose water and pomade they used to groom their hair.

Several who were enslaved at Arlington House later discussed their treatment in interviews after the Civil War and emancipation. They "tell of their extraordinary well being 'befo' the wah," wrote an unnamed female correspondent for *Harper's Weekly*, quoting one in 1886 in period dialect. Custis "was fond of the chase, and believed himself clever at depicting it," the reporter learned. As she visited the "ivy-grown servants quarters to the rear of the house," the writer described answers she received from "one tall mulatto bending over his trowel." The now-freed worker explained, "What I know 'bout did yere place? Waal, dar's not much I don't know, I reckon. Bo'n an' raised on it. My mother she died two months back. She was old Missy Custis's maid, an' my father was Mas'r Custis's body servant." The reporter gave the man a quarter to continue speaking. "Member ole Mas'r Custis? 'Deed I do, missy. An' a fine-appearin' old gentleman he was. Right tall an' stoutish, an' mighty fine-mannered, an' kind to his slaves when he was old,' but dey do say he was 'clined to be rude to 'em in his young days'"[65]

More detail would come from Jim Parks, who, though born in slavery in 1843 (to Lawrence Parks and Patsy Clark), stayed on as an Arlington House employee well into the twentieth century. Recalling Custis playing the fiddle at Arlington Spring pavilion, Parks gave an account summarized in dialect by an *Evening Star* writer in 1928. It made Custis appear relatively kind, if patronizing:

Lawrence Parks, born into slavery, drawing by Mary Custis Lee (courtesy George Washington Memorial Parkway).

He had always been well treated and knew nothing to the contrary with respect to the other slaves. According to "Uncle Jim" no one was allowed to "tech airy one of Maj. Custis' ni**ers, 'thout gitten' into trouble, no suh." Then he told me how every negro leaving the plantation had to have a pass or he might get taken up by the "patterolles," meaning patrols, I gathered, or anyone, perchance, thinking to earn a few dollars by intercepting some runaway slave for whose capture a reward would be offered by the master. Apparently, such passes were not hard to obtain from "Major Custis" at Arlington. Frequently when some slave wanted to leave the place for a few days, perhaps to make a visit, and asked for permission and a pass, Mr. Custis would pretend at first to deny the favor, but always yielded and wrote the pass, or ordered it issued. The recipient of the pass almost invariably discovered that he had been granted leave for more time than requested, sometimes twice the amount. That they presumed upon the old gentleman's kind heart and good is fairly certain, Because, relates "Uncle Jim," when any of them thus wanted to be away for a week or a few days, they always needed a little money, which they seldom had. After securing the necessary pass, the next request would be for some money to provide for their meager wants. To this Mr. Custis would say, "Money, I haven't any money. I don't work; what do you want with money?" The explanation being furnished, he would usually write out an order and direct that it be presented to "Miss Mary" at the big house. "Miss Mary" was Mrs. Robert E. Lee, Mr. Custis' only child: and when the order was exchanged for money it was usually discovered to be double the amount coaxed from the master.[66]

Others freed from Arlington House mentioned the existence of a whipping post, though no documentation survives detailing its use.[67]

Custis displayed some humanitarian concern for the enslaved outdoor workers down south on Virginia's Pamunkey River, who earned him his best profits. In 1823 correspondence from his overseer John Walden, Custis

Twentieth-century photograph of former enslaved worker James Parks, who continued on the property as a lifetime employee, *The Evening Star*, 1929 (courtesy George Washington Memorial Parkway).

received an updated inventory highly personalized details on the health and marriage status of the adults and their children. "At White House there are three: 2 boys, twin children of Caesar and Dolly, and one girl, daughter of carpenter Billy and Dinah," the manager wrote. "At Old Quarter, there are two, a boy, son of Paul and Peggy, and another, a girl, daughter of Jack and Juliana. Juliana is a daughter of Chloe ... and went from White House after marrying." Walden recommended that Custis supply them with cotton cloth for pantaloons, "which is nearly as warm, and will last much longer than wool."[68]

Custis often instructed his managers to make sure clothing and medical care for the enslaved arrived safely. In June 1849, he wrote to Francis Nelson that "the object of this letter is to prepare you for the cholera, which I find is getting among the plantations on the James River, and also a few cases in Gloucester and York River. Phials of camphor to each overseer, keep the ones at the Mansion House. At the first appearance of cramps or spasms of the stomach or bowels or diarrhea, give 5 drops and a little water, or water and sugar and repeat the dose every 10 minutes."[69]

In January 1857 Custis was feuding with Nelson. He instructed new caretaker William Winston that, "to get the negroes comfortably housed and provided with clothes and blankets," the manager should begin selling off belongings. "But am greatly pained, disappointed and mortified to hear that you have found any of my affairs so dilapidated, and out of sorts, more especially in the want of houses and other deprivations of ... unfair literate negroes, it ought not to be so," the frustrated 76-year-old Custis wrote from his office. "My negroes have been heavier worked there than any of my slaves in Virginia, so much that anonymous neighbors have complained. 'I am not to blame.' I have been so in ignorance of the state of my affairs that I might as well as lived in the Sandwich Islands."[70]

When an enslaved person attempted escape, Custis generally sided with the law. In 1829, he offered a $50 reward for the capture of a runaway named Eleanor.[71] And his name appears in an 1836 advertisement in the *Daily National Intelligencer* taken out by a neighbor. "'One Hundred Dollars Reward' for runaway from last month; Mary Dodson, about 23 year of age, about five feet 2 or 3 inches high, black complexion, bushy head and is easily confused when spoke to," the ad said, noting the runaway took two female children. "The above has a husband belonging to G.W.P. Custis Esq. of Arlington, who calls himself Daniel Dodson, who, there is no doubt, effected her escape, with an intention of following her. It is quite likely she will endeavor to make her way to the North."[72] Also that year, Jane Steiner, "spinster," was accused of abetting the escape of one of Custis's enslaved females. But Custis gained a reputation for declining to pursue runaways. "'Let 'em go,' he used to say," according to an account in a Manchester, New

Hampshire, newspaper after Custis's death, "a slave that will run away is not worth having."[73]

In a letter to his daughter, Custis in 1839 coupled his report on his rheumatism with observations on an apparently returned runaway. "He will be closely watched," Custis wrote with a routine air. "As it is not likely that he may have had it in his own contemplation to go again to take a lady with him. I have learned nothing of his adventures as yet."[74]

The Custis attitude toward the enslaved would be repeated in the shifting homes of Army officer Robert and Mary Custis Lee. Robert, of course, maintained attitudes toward slavery that were destined for national impact, and he had grown up living with a small contingent of enslaved domestics. Despite the travels necessitated by his military career, he also maintained a strong identity as a Virginian. He would have seen eye-to-eye with his wife on the Christian commitment to allow the enslaved to read and worship. But as an Army man, he was not at liberty to embrace the Colonization Society. Neither, however, did he back abolitionism. On reading a news account of a New York Anti-Slavery Society event (probably during his New York posting in the 1840s), Lee sent Custis the clipping and commented on "what extent some men are carried by their evil passions—which indeed is calculated to excite some apprehensions in the peace & prosperity of the country." Lee suggested that his father-in-law see "that they contend for the ruin of the present American Church & the destruction of the present Union. That the pulpit is denounced as the great stronghold of slavery. The founders of the Constitution & fathers of the Revolution *Swindlers*, in accomplishing that which after fifty years trial is found to be a *curse* and not a blessing."[75]

The Lees were capable of the same Custis condescension. One enslaved domestic whom the Custises sent to St. Louis to serve the Lees prompted Mary to write her mother of her disappointment. The servant was never previously "balky" or not sufficiently "cheerful." But her husband had said that if this worker couldn't behave better, he might send him to the White House plantation "if you don't want him" at Arlington House.[76] Of another servant, Mary Lee wrote to her mother in the 1850s, "I wish indeed I could find a purchaser for her in order & she deserves no favours."[77]

On other occasions, the sincerity of the Custis and Lees' commitment to elevating their enslaved came through. After vacating Arlington House for good once the war started, Mary wrote to the occupying Union general to reveal that her gardener Ephraim Derricks had a wife in downtown Washington with whom he was permitted to spend weekends.[78]

Both Mary Lee and Molly Custis joined in helping an enslaved woman named Rose celebrate her wedding, outfitting her with a bonnet.[79] And in the mid–1840s during their stay at Fort Hamilton, New York, Mary is recorded to have been apprised that a freed former slave woman named Cassy, the daughter of Old Nurse who had helped raise her father at Mount Vernon, lived nearby. The worker, now a laundress, and her husband had fallen on hard times. Mary Lee contacted Cassy and invited her to Fort Hamilton on a steamboat. She offered her paid work if she would return to Arlington House. "She says I must tell her Mammy she does not wish all the servants to know they are not in prosperity," Mary wrote her husband. "I gave her a little money & some few things, as many as she could carry back with her." Cassy remained in the north.[80]

Hidden Interracial Sex

Surviving down through the decades are credible reports that the owner of Arlington House, like other white male American slave owners, carried on sexual relations with the enslaved. Though the Custis cases never garnered the modern-day attention that Thomas Jefferson's have, they are persistent and multi-faceted enough to require honest examination.

George Washington himself in modern times became the subject of now-disproven claims that he fathered a mixed-race child named West Ford, a Westmoreland County enslaved laborer brought to Mount Vernon after Washington's death and freed circa 1805.[81] And Washington's stepson Jacky, Custis's own father, stands accused of fathering a mixed-race son named William Costin born in 1780. (As a prominent adult living in Washington with his black and mixed-race children, Costin maintained steady friendships with George Washington Parke Custis and his sisters, which encouraged rumors that they were half-siblings.[82] A check that Custis made out to Costin survives at Tudor Place,[83] and his sister Nelly Custis wrote in a letter that she had paid Molly Custis for the transportation services of her "friend Billy" Costin.[84])

Closer to the private life of G.W.P. Custis is the story of Eugenia and Sarah, grandchildren of Caroline Branham, the elderly Arlington House domestic who was Martha Washington's maid. The claim from a white family's oral tradition comes from a 1920s reminiscence of an historian of Alexandria named Mary Gregory Powell (1847–1928). Being the daughter of a Scottish Alexandria hardware merchant, Powell wrote up a startling childhood memory:

> My father bought from George Washington Parke Custis of Arlington a family of negroes. He liberated the mother Lucy Harrison and her infant son Charles, apprenticed Walter and kept the two younger girls, Eugenia and Sarah, mulattos

of 12 & 14 as nurses for his children. By the time of the purchase, these girls were to be set free at age 20. These girls were the grandchildren of Caroline Branham, Mrs. Washington's maid who appears in the well-known engraving of Washington's death bed, standing at the foot of the bed…. And it was generally believed that Lucy, the mother of Eugenia and Sarah who was lawfully married to a respectable mulatto named Harrison, was the daughter of (George) Parke Custis and Caroline. She bore a very strong resemblance to his daughter, Mary Custis, who married Gen. Robert E. Lee. These children might easily have passed for white.[85]

(Branham, who had been present at the 1799 death of George Washington, in the late 1820s was interviewed by Jared Sparks for his Washington biography. Custis brought the author to Branham's cabin, and she agreed to recall the death scene on condition that Custis free her enslaved grandson, Robert Robinson. Custis did, and he later arranged for her burial in Alexandria.[86])

The most jarring and enduring story of Custis's illicit fatherhood revolves around the Syphax family, the best known and most carefully studied family enslaved at Arlington House. The telltale event was the birth circa 1803 of a mixed-race child to an enslaved maid named Arianna Carter (1776–1880). The father is believed to have been Custis, for several reasons. The child was called Maria Carter (1803–1886) and grew up at Arlington. In 1821, she married Charles Syphax (1791–1869), who had come to Arlington House from Mount Vernon and was assigned to help construct the mansion. He was also said to be the de facto leader of the enslaved community there. In 1821, the Custises are said to have granted this couple the rare privilege of a wedding in the family parlor. In 1826, Custis implicitly admitted paternity. Maria herself is the central source for this historic claim, having stated it to a journalist who visited Arlington House in 1888. "I am General Custis's daughter. He told me so face to face," the bedridden Maria said while being interviewed in a stone hut behind Arlington House. (The title "General" was an honorific.) "He was kind to me and made me my sister's maid. So, you see, I love the Lee family. I went everywhere that Mary Lee went and was faithful to her. I love to think of those old days, but they are long gone by."[87]

Modern students of the issue see a resemblance between Custis's acknowledged daughter Mary Custis Lee, and Maria and (see photo, page 146). Other mixed-race children were visible at Arlington House—the 1860 census showed that half the enslaved and all of the freed Blacks had mixed blood.[88]

Another clue is the fact Custis emancipated Maria (though, curiously, not her husband Charles) via Edward Stabler and gave her an unheard-of seventeen acres of his land at the southwest corner of the Arlington estate.

Twentieth-century analysis of court records for enslaved persons freed by Custis suggest a pattern of favoring young females.[89] And rumors of his overactive sex life drew scandalized comment in newspaper coverage shortly after his death, suggesting that he fathered fifteen or as many as forty mixed-race children who were now living in the area, several working for the government.[90] "Is not the South full of such cases?" the writer asked. "Is not amalgamation [race mixing] one of the settled kindred principles and effects of slavery?"[91]

The Syhax's "white cottage was surrounded by tall trees and pleasant stretches of grassland and the place was beautiful as well as homelike," recalled later descendants.[92] The couple raised ten children there.

Maria Carter Syphax, the enslaved secret daughter of Custis emancipated in 1826. The rare daguerreotype has chemically faded with age, despite the best preservation efforts at Arlington House (courtesy George Washington Memorial Parkway).

After the federal government confiscated her land during Civil War, Maria and her freed son William (who became a messenger for federal agencies and a pioneer in Black education) lobbied Congress for its return.[93] Though she had no official deed, Congress determined that her years of residency sufficed. "Mr. Custis, at the time she married about 40 years ago, feeling an interest in the woman, something perhaps akin to a paternal interest ... gave her this piece of land," New York Senator Ira Harris said, as recorded in *The Congressional Globe*. "It has been set apart for her and it has been occupied by her and her family for 40 years. Under the circumstances, the committee thought it no more than just, the government having acquired title to this property under a sale for taxes, that this title should be confirmed to her."[94] On June 11, 1866, Congress passed the Relief for Maria Syphax bill. It was signed by President Andrew Johnson, ordinarily a fierce opponent of rights for free Blacks.

CHAPTER 10

Dotage, Debt and Death

A fading Custis struggles with finances, continues public appearances, leans on younger relatives, bids farewell to family, and leaves one "unpleasant legacy."

As Custis entered his seventies, his image as the last "child of Mount Vernon" helped retain his fame, prestige and (shaky) finances. Invitations to speak and correspondence remained steady. His leisure time at Arlington was enlivened by the company of grandchildren and other affectionate young relations. And his efforts at maintaining profitability of his Virginia properties engaged him—even when his health declined and economic disaster threatened.

"There is one person living who has attended the inauguration of all our presidents, from Washington to Pierce—who has been a witness of the changes at the White House," wrote the *Cleveland Herald* early in 1853. "We allude to George Washington Parke Custis, Esq., of Arlington, Virginia, grandson of Mrs. Washington. He has formerly favored the public with many of his reminiscences of the days of Washington, and still, we believe, retains his memory and other faculties of mind."[1]

Custis's health "continues remarkably good, and his cheerful buoyancy of spirit has suffered no abatement," added the *Washington Weekly Union* the next year. "Often it was our privilege to sit under the 'music of his lips' orations" on George Washington.[2] A new financial house for "gentlemen of wealth and distinction" called the Arlington Bank opened near Pennsylvania Avenue the summer of 1854, the name, *Alexandria Gazette* opined, "in compliment, we presume, of George Washington Parke Custis Esq. of Arlington."[3]

The dark clouds on the horizon came from the Pamunkey River plantations, where Custis's caretaker was delivering a series of letters bearing, with a few exceptions, bad news.

In the late 1840s, Custis's expectations were riding high, particularly with his new caretaker at Romancock and White House, Francis Nelson. Writing from Arlington House, Custis reminded Nelson after a good wheat harvest, "I make nothing here, all my reserves are derived from my estates in the South."[4] In 1847, Custis noted that the success of oyster shells as fertilizer could "transform the Pamunkey River lands."[5] And when directing Nelson to purchase fishing mesh, he predicted that "fishing landing [s] are about to become the most valuable property in the United States."[6]

During his final decade Custis monitored prices for corn and other produce in Richmond, Baltimore—even in Europe—occasionally asking his caretaker for cash advances to tide him over. They traded technical advice: "Use hickory ashes to protect corn from insects," Custis directed. Buy guano, clove and plantains. "Don't sell the 1,000 barrels of corn at 80 cents a bushel as one can get $10 a barrel in Europe, 95 cents in New York, $1 in Baltimore."[7]

Custis tried to stay current on transportation technology. "I perceive by the papers that the counties of New Kent, Hanover and King William are waking up on the subject of steam navigation of the York River and its branches," he wrote Nelson in 1850. "It's a very important move and if carried out may be of much benefit to those overseeing property on the aforesaid rivers."[8] Another potential development to keep an eye on, he added, was the laying of a plank road from nearby West Point, Virginia, to Richmond.

Dabbling in stereotypes of Jewish Americans, Custis, in bed with a fever, praised Nelson for rejecting a demand by Jewish merchants to receive corn cargo for credit rather than cash. "The conduct of the Jews in Richmond exceeds anything I've ever known. You did right in resisting such abominable imposition," Custis wrote as a warning. He directed Nelson in the future to ship corn to Baltimore, where cash sales are made "within the hour that it reaches the wharf." Custis then pleaded poverty. "I am trying to improve my land here. I have spent all the money I had. I have succeeded in my improvements but not left myself a horse to ride."[9] Seven years later, Custis again complained to his caretaker about pressure on Virginia farmers to accept IOUs. "The Richmond market is the only one where the grain is sold on credit and this is unjust and unfair to the farmers who get cash in all other markets," Custis argued.[10]

The next year, Custis confessed that his spirits were "very wretched" because he had to reject the advice of his publishing partner Benson Lossing that he take his first and only voyage to Europe, where he might have visited Paris to examine the papers of Lafayette. The aging Custis told Nelson, "I do not wish to embark on such a tour with scarcely a hope that I may ever return to my native land without first having made a perfect arrangement and settlement of my affairs at home."[11] Custis reminisced with his caretaker about his sheep-shearing parties a half century earlier. And, speaking as a vice president of the U.S. Agriculture Society, Custis assured Nelson in 1853 that he had made "honorable mention" of the caretaker's great service.[12]

The following year he shipped Nelson "a fine Durham bull calf" and exulted in a bumper corn crop: "If I get $2 [per unit], I shall be well satisfied to have by far the largest income I have ever had from my estates in 52 years!" Custis wrote.[13] He apparently succeeded. In July 1855, Custis reported that his neighbor and brick contractor James Roach "just returned from … White House and brings me the most flattering account of the fat crops he says exceed everything he had ever had an idea of [in] corn productivity."[14]

But nerve-wracking farm market vicissitudes and some miscommunication soured Custis and Nelson's relationship. The patron had vented his frustration early, telling Nelson in 1844 that "the herring fishery on the Potomac proved to be an almost total failure" and that the price of corn had plummeted. "This is a cruel remuneration to the poor farmer for the toil and expense of making a crop of corn."[15]

Custis also confided in Nelson his frustration that his flour mill, built in the mid–1830s on Four Mile Run, "has not yet yielded me a single cent because it is unfinished, and is only employed grinding for this estate to my little country work. If finished for manufacturing purposes, it would support the estate."[16]

The 1850s brought two new factors to Custis's thinking: The widely anticipated coming of the railroads and son-in-law Lee's gradual takeover of his plantation accounts. "My health is much the usual, my spirits much depressed," Custis told Nelson in April 1855 while informing the caretaker of a land sale. "Col. Lee having accepted his new commission, [and] finding it out of his power to look over the acres, they have been put into the hands of two gentlemen every way capable of examining and settling them to the perfect justice of all parties," he wrote, citing an Alexandria lawyer and a banker with Farmer's Bank of Virginia.[17] The following February, Custis reported that Lee had examined the accounts of the Custis property in Hanover County, adding that "fish has increased in value by 500 percent."[18]

Credit Custis for anticipating the arrival of the railroad in southern Virginia—more than two decades after the pioneering Baltimore and Ohio track was laid. In May 1854, he reported to Nelson that the commercial investors, bridge builders and government right-of-way planners indicated that a "railroad will run through Romancoke* to West Point," and that he

---

*As he took over Custis's affairs, Lee changed the name of Romancock to the more tasteful Romancoke.

hoped to "get good compensation in cash." Months earlier he had specu-
lated that "the difference in sending my crops would be as 30 miles to 300,
five hours to six days."[19] Custis noted that railroad work paid well, which
would attract local laborers. He empowered Nelson to represent him at a
meeting in King William County with the Richmond & York River Rail
Road Company.[20] That entity, which had been approved and financed in
part by the Virginia General Assembly, "must pay cash," Custis insisted, "as
is done in every market in the United States but Richmond."[21]

There were continual delays, as Custis watched rail ties going down
linking the District of Columbia, Alexandria and points south. He wanted
"just compensation" for sale of his land. But Custis wanted "no more negro
property," of which he already owned $100,000 worth, "to be bought with
proceeds."[22] He never intended to part with large parcels. "I intend to leave
my old patrimonial acres to my grandchildren," he wrote Nelson, "hoping
they will make them more happy than they have made their grandfather."

His relationship with Nelson was fraying in part due to letters that got
lost or were ignored. "Answering a letter is the floor *civilite* that is observed
between man and man in all parts of the civilized world," Custis scolded in
a December 1854 complaint about his sixth letter in three months with no
reply. Though being "treated with marked contempt," Custis signed the letter, "I remain faithfully yours."[23]

By June 1856, with the thirty-nine-mile regional railroad under construction, Custis had had enough of Nelson. "As the time of year is near at
hand when it is customary in Virginia to give notice of the discontinuance
of employment, I take the opportunity to say that I shall change the management of my estates now under your case at the close of the present year,"
Custis wrote gently. "I do so with pain and regret, and shall probably be a
loser in regard to my interests—by the change." Nelson was "a manager of
great ability," the patron continued. "In the meantime, for the half year that
we shall continue the connections that have so long existed between us, and
I feel assured that you will do the best for my interests."[24]

Nelson, however, had submitted an eye-popping invoice for his
eleven years in Custis's employ. Lee was stunned, but he counseled his
father-in-law not to challenge it. "By economy, & good management," Lee
said, "you can soon pay it off, & then all will be right again."[25]

Still "Old Man Eloquent"

Up north on the Potomac, "the farmer of Arlington" aged with continued celebrity. Photographer Mathew Brady in the late 1840s took a portrait of the last child of Mount Vernon. Alexandrians thrilled at the sight of

his coach arriving at the Lyceum for a speech. "Old Man eloquent is really one of the few Americans of his age whose hearts, souls and minds keep pace with the ideas of the times in which he now lives," opined the *Evening Star* when Custis addressed the U.S. Agricultural Society in February 1855.[26] At the society's gathering the previous year, "Mr. Custis compared the products of his farm with what it was in former times, when for forty years one of his farms with 100 hands working on it, only served to starve him. Now from seven thousand to nine thousand bushels of wheat per year, with a prospect of fifteen to twenty thousand, was the state of his affairs," he boasted.[27] Suggesting this might be his last appearance to the group at age 73, Custis nodded to current regional strife by declaring tactfully that he "loved his country, and though a southerner, ... loved the true Yankee."[28] It was to that society that Custis in 1853 had proposed creation of an experimental model farm (a project the government would actualize in the early twentieth century on Custis's own land).[29]

He continued to travel to farmers' gatherings. In Philadelphia in 1856, fifty thousand at the National Agricultural Fair listened to him "with profound attention," the *Alexandria Gazette* reported. At the Montgomery County (Maryland) Agricultural Society in September 1850, Custis "delivered an address that drew forth the oft-repeated plaudits of the immense company," according to the *Port Tobacco Times and Charles County Advertiser*.[30]

Custis delivered extemporaneous remarks on George Washington as a farmer at an 1850 exhibition by the Fairfax Historical Society—as a last-minute substitute. He warmed the audience by saying, "Fairfax was the home of his infancy and that the happiest days of his life were spent therein," according to the Alexandria *Gazette*.[31]

"With his ruffled wristbands and rich old-fashioned vest and polished address, he carries us back to the very life of the time which he so eloquently describes," recalled an impressed visitor from New England.[32]

On St. Patrick's Day 1851,

An elderly Custis in 1852, pencil sketch by I. Kaylor (courtesy Mount Vernon Ladies' Association).

Custis was cheered by Irish Americans packing Washington's King's Hotel. "I thank God, my friends and friends of Ireland, that I have been spared once more to address you in behalf of a much injured, much enduring land," said the rhetorician. "In this the seventy-third year of my poor services in the cause of unhappy Ireland, I am proud to say you find your old orator at his post, and whom, though worn by time, neither time, age nor circumstance can over change from being the firm, unflinching advocate of a just and righteous cause."[33] The following October, two Irish officials from Baltimore presented Custis with resolutions honoring him "handsomely printed on satin paper and neatly framed," according to the *Alexandria Gazette*; the gesture caused a temporarily speechless Custis to shed a tear.[34]

For Washington's birthday in 1852 at the downtown Willard Hotel, Custis presented a flag to the Continental Guards militia. In August he was toasted as the guest of honor at District of Columbia city government dinner, in which the Board of Aldermen president praised him as "our venerable and esteemed friend.... May he long live to enjoy the affection and regard of those whom his liberality and kindness so often rendered happy."[35] Custis addressed an art exhibition by the private Maryland Institute and continued his support for Irish immigrants and veterans. And he called on Congress to raise the sunken ship HMS *Jersey* and commission a monument to the eleven thousand American troops who died on British prison ships from 1776 to 1783 in New York. Custis proposed the adage, "This is what liberty costs."[36]*

In 1854, Custis traveled to Mount Vernon with Alexandria military groups to "welcome to the soil of Virginia" the "Old Defenders" of Baltimore, who fought in the War of 1812, and veterans of the Mexican War, who came down the Potomac on the steamer *George Page*.[37]

Patriotic demand for a glimpse of Washington's battlefield tent had not abated by Custis's years of dotage. In May 1855, he gave a military group permission to pitch the tent for their ball at a Washington theater. "I send you the praetorium of the revolution," he wrote to a Colonel Riley. "I had to surrender to the earnest solicitations of so many younger soldiers than myself, more especially when led by the request of a son of a soldier of the revolution. Your greatest and best care will be in regard to the lights," Custis cautioned, "as the old canvass, now eighty years old, is very combustible, and would kindle in an instant."[38]

Custis's talks on Washington's birthday were lavish as ever. At an Alexandria banquet in February 1855, one hundred diners enjoyed oysters in

---

*Such a monument was finally dedicated in Brooklyn in 1908.

sauce, baked shad, red currant tarts, mutton, tongue, and filet of beef. "The cry was then for 'Custis! Custis!' and the venerable man arose and responded," *The Evening Star* reported. He proclaimed that he had "seen the country in prosperity and in adversity, but that he had never seen it dishonored." Custis then warned against a "spirit of sectionalism rampant in other parts of the country ... in the name of Washington, as they had renounced allegiance to his counsel. The only name under heaven or among men whereby the country could be saved from those evils was the name of Washington," he thundered, "and the only power that could effect it was that of the principles contained in his farewell address."[39]

Perhaps Custis's most lofty sentiments—encapsulating his entire life— came in a May 13, 1854, celebration of the Jamestown Society of Washington, held to honor Captain John Smith and the original English colony in Virginia. "It is almost time that I should give place to a younger and better man," said the veteran orator, according to a newspaper account:

> But so long as my countrymen do me the honor to call me out on occasions like the present, so long I shall be at their service.... (Cheers). Now, my friends, when you look around you and see how free, how happy you are, oh, let your minds go back to the days of trial through which our fathers passed. ... In my humble career on very many occasions, when my friends and fellow citizens have done me the honor to call me out to address them, I always say to them, no matter what they have met for, whether for social or political purposes, whether to advance agriculture or promote temperance, whenever a body of Americans are together, their country is the subject that should be uppermost in the heart. ... Now, reasoning by the rule of three, I ask Americans: What shall we be in sixty years more! I will tell you. We shall be the master power of the world ... [and] Teach other nations the value of liberty.... Tell me not of foreign wars, tell me not of that power that can shake this government.... As old John Adams said, a little war is occasionally useful; it is like the agitations of the human system; it takes off a good many people who can very well be spared, and besides it produces a variety. (great Laughter) ... Young people come to me and ask me, "Did you ever see Washington?" "Yes," I answer, "I saw him when I was a boy." It is good for Americans to have this feeling. ... Then you impress upon young men the value of the history of their native country. Now they are taught the histories of Greece and Rome, while you forget to put into their hands the history of their native land.... I will tell my son, and my grandson to recollect Jamestown and the old days of Virginia.[40]

Custis's own relatives were impressed with his late-life performances. On March 4, 1853, he braved a sleet storm to attend the outdoor inauguration of President Franklin Pierce.[41] After accompanying Custis to a Washington's birthday talk at Liberty Hall in Alexandria in 1853, his granddaughter Agnes Lee testified, "All called for 'Custis.' Grandpa came forward, made a polite bow. I was so tired or I should have liked to have listened as his [speech] was not long, but I could not. I counted almost a hundred times they clapped."[42]

Grand-niece Markie Williams praised his dignity as she helped Custis prepare for an Arlington Spring picnic. It was "astonishing" that at age 70 he retained "so much relish for amusement," the twenty six year old wrote in her journal. "Uncle shaved, put on a clean shirt—which is always my special province to button just before he goes away—and even changed his coat. From these extraordinary arrangements we all knew that it was a *high day* with him. I reminded him to put on his cravat which else I am afraid would have been regarded as superfluous—and put on his chin myself a piece of coat-plaster to hide a gash which had been made in shaving. An old brown cloth coat and a buff vest which I remember to have seen for many years on the premises, formed his best attire. I wonder what the fashionable modern belles thought of his costume. But with all of Uncle's eccentricity of dress, he always looks the intelligent gentleman."[43]

Granddaughters Agnes and Mildred reminisced that as children they had loved hearing old Custis at the piano singing Revolutionary War songs. He tolerated their playing Indians on stick horses in his drawing room amid his paintings. And he scolded them when their clothes got dirty, recalling that Martha Washington "always wore one white gown a week, and when she took it off it was as spotless as the day she put it on."[44]

From his office at Arlington House, the graying Custis continued to receive prominent visitors. His family members were thrilled when luminary novelist Washington Irving, preparing his own biography of George Washington, arrived in 1857 to examine pictures, books and furniture from his subject's household. Irving, as Custis himself marveled, was equally excited and took "the steps three at a time," and the two shared personal recollections of being in Washington's presence.[45] Arlington House also greeted the journalist Benjamin Perley Poore, who had written a biography of Napoleon, when he came to quiz Custis on the Revolutionary War.[46] After the celebrated authoress C.M. Kirkland arrived to research a George Washington article for *Putnam's Magazine*, Custis showed that he wasn't too doddering for a flirtation. He confessed later to his friend the editor William Seaton, "I was charmed. What a fine, handsome woman! I am not, therefore, surprised that you, my dear sir, a 'squire of dames,' should be so eloquent in her favor."[47]

Custis was still in demand as a consultant on artistic representations of his step-grandfather. An aspiring biographer of Washington came to Arlington in 1852 to regale Custis with details of his visit to Washington's ancestral home in England.[48] A portrait of Washington based on Gilbert Stuart's original was marketed as an engraving by Thomas B. Welch in Boston in 1853, its advertisement quoting Custis's endorsement as "a faithful representation of the celebrated original."[49] Custis's authority was invoked the following year in a letter to Washington's *Daily Globe* in which a reader disagreed with a critic of the famous Jean-Antoine Houdon statue of Washington, quoting Custis saying, "The statue of Houdon is, and must ever be, the *standard statue* of the beloved Washington."[50] His never-ending duties as an executor of George Washington's will continued. In a September 1852 letter to John Augustine Washington III, the last private owner of Mount Vernon, Custis urged appointment of an attorney to move quickly to finalize the disposition. "The life of an old man of 72 is very uncertain that there is no calculating upon it," Custis wrote, expressing skepticism about a report that Washington's estate had neglected to bequeath all of his lands in western Virginia.[51]

At a time of life colored by nostalgia, Custis was visited by a former Arlington House employee in what became a dramatic reunion in the summer of 1850. Thirty years earlier, a carpenter named Edward Byrne had come to Custis's home seeking work, as reported later in the *Evening Star*. The man was alcoholic, and because he had trouble supporting his wife and children, Custis counseled the worker and arranged for his wages to be sent directly to his family. "You shall never see me again if I do not entirely, and forever, give up strong drink," Byrne told his patron. He then departed for shipyard work in Baltimore. Fifteen years passed, the *Star* quoted Custis recalling. One day Custis was lolling under the prized Arlington House oak when a man approached. Custis didn't recognize him. "Is it possible that you do not know me? said the stranger.... Have you forgotten Ned Byrne— your drunken Ned, who built these houses, and made the very bench on which you are now sitting?" "I recollect him well," Custis said, tearing up. Custis seized the man's hands and welcomed him, asking, "How's business now?" The guest's reply: "A minister of the gospel," the Rev. Edward Byrne.[52]

Custis's prominence in his local community also continued during his final years. In 1855, a man posing as the owner of the steamboat *George Washington Parke Custis* (which offered passage from Alexandria to New York City) was arrested for insurance fraud.[53] (That steamer went on during the Civil War to become the first water vessel used to launch a surveillance balloon.) Custis monitored plans for railroads in Northern Virginia, working with Arlington House farm manager Robert Ball. "I am anxious to hear what you think of my chance of selling the land on Four Mile Run, 40-acre lots where the Rail Road will be laid out," he wrote to Ball from West Point, New York, in 1854, eager to protect his mill.[54] The two also shared tasks stemming from Custis's role as a justice of the peace. "I am still weak from my late attack and able to do but little," Custis wrote the same year. He described to Ball an Alexandria court case involving an assault. A magistrate had recommended a warrant to have a constable "summon the

Irishman who was knocked down by Harrison," who struck him and tore his shirt, the letter said. "I mention these things to you as our constable is a new hand and requires some little attending to."[55]

Family Farewells

Custis's relationship with son-in-law Lee was maturing. Success in the U.S. Army had put to rest any talk of Lee de-enlisting to become a farmer. In 1851, Molly Custis had written to her grandson Custis Lee speculating that his father Robert might have been happier early on with such a career change. But "your grandpa says when I tell him so 'He would not then have gained so much glory.' But I think happiness is better than glory," said a reflective Mrs. Custis.[56] In 1852, Lee was made Superintendent of West Point.

From afar, Lee was becoming more active in helping improve the physical plant at Arlington House, adding marble mantles, a new roof on the stable, a new furnace and repairs to the Arlington Mill. "You will hardly know the old place when you get back," Molly wrote her grandson Custis Lee.[57] Lee advised Custis as he struggled to afford a new pair of oxen and a set of waist tiles for repairing the mansion's portico.

Lee asked for Custis's help in rebutting an old assertion from Alexander Hamilton's family that George Washington had help from Hamilton in drafting his farewell address. Lee worried the claim would detract from Washington's glory.[58] Custis's response isn't recorded, and later scholarship confirmed some role by Hamilton.[59] But Lee and his father-in-law had bonded in their admiration for Washington.

The decade for children of Mount Vernon and all the Custis-Lee clan would bring several deaths that ended an era. On July 15, 1852, Custis's childhood companion and sister Nelly died, at age seventy-three in her rural Virginia home Audley. She had suffered a stroke two days earlier. A hearse and single carriage brought her and her grandsons to Mount Vernon, to lie in the same room in which she'd been married in 1799. Custis attended her service and burial near the tomb of the *Pater Patriae* and grandmother Martha.[60] A few years later, Custis would fondly recall memories of childhood with Nelly in correspondence with District of Columbia official and collector Samuel Yorke Atlee. He had sent Custis excerpts from a new book titled *Republican Court, or American Society in the Days of Washington,* asking that he verify some facts. The book quoted an English merchant who seventy years earlier had taken breakfast with the first family at the presidential mansion in Philadelphia. Custis confirmed his detail that young Nelly was forced to practice the harpsichord. "The poor

girl would play and cry, and cry and play, for long hours under the immediate eye of her grandmother, a rigid disciplinarian in all things," Custis
recalled. He quibbled over the author's detail alleging a blemish on the dining room's wall, but tore into him for his suggestion that Nelly talked politics. No Federalist, but only a "filthy Democrat" would conduct himself in
such a manner, the teenage Nelly is alleged to have said of an unnamed personage. Custis found the anecdote "absurd," avowing that Martha Washington would never tolerate political language at table.[61]

On July 13, 1854, Custis's older sister, Martha Parke Custis Peter, died
in her Georgetown home, Tudor Place, of heart disease. Mary Custis Lee
attended her during the final days. "She was grandpa's last surviving whole
sister—that the last of them may be spared to us a little longer," wrote Custis's worried granddaughter Agnes Lee.[62]

But between those two deaths came the most intimate tragedy for Custis: the demise of his wife of forty-nine years. "Your grandmother is passing into the decline of life and has not a vigorous old age," Mary Lee had
recently written to a Custis
grandson. Molly is "busy with
domestic cares and often sick
and weakened from the effects
of sickness even writing is too
much for her."[63]

Mary Lee Fitzhugh Custis
died of a stroke at age sixty-five
on April 23, 1853. A doc-
tor had diagnosed her with a
mere headache. Grandchildren
Annie and Agnes Lee, along
with niece Britannia Peter, were
at her side. Agnes would recall
that her grandmother Molly
recited the Lord's Prayer amid
worry over how her daughter
Mary, up at West Point, would
handle her loss. Custis himself was near collapse. "Poor
grandpa. I can hardly think
of his agony," Agnes wrote.
"He knelt by her bedside, and
implored God to spare her....
He is almost heartbroken & is
quite sick."[64]

**Mary Custis in old age, Daguerreotype
(Virginia Museum of History & Culture).**

The funeral in the mansion was conducted by the Rev. Charles Dana of Christ Church, Alexandria. Her coffin was carried by four enslaved men— Austin, Lawrence, Daniel and Ephraim. The burial was on a site in the front park selected by Mary Lee. Molly Custis's death made several newspapers, among them one as far afield as Sandusky, Ohio, whose dispatch reported her as being "of the family Randolph, a name conspicuous in the annals of Virginia. She married Mr. Custis in early life, and her associates were in the leading circles of the tidewater counties of Virginia.... She was inclined to favor the emancipation of slaves as opportunities were presented, and her husband's views in promoting the objects of the Colonization Society, it is believed, met with her cordial approbation."[65] Indeed, daughter Mary soon told her diary, "In looking over my poor mother's papers, the great desire of her soul was that all our slaves should be enabled to emigrate to Africa— For years this has been the subject of her hopes and prayers not only for their own benefit but that they might aid in the mighty work of carrying light & Christianity to the dark heathen countries."[66]

That view aligned with those of Molly Custis's admirer, Bishop Meade, who recalled of her, "Scarcely is there a Christian lady in our land more honored than she was, and none more loved and esteemed. For good sense, prudence, sincerity, benevolence, unaffected piety, disinterested zeal in every good work, deep humility, and retiring modesty, I have never known her superior."[67]

From New York, Lee helped the grieving Custis arrange for a banker and attorney to settle the estate.[68] He recommended a simple monument, eventually settling on a five-foot tapered pylon on a plinth carved by Robert Lauintz of New York. The front read: "Mary L. Custis Born April 22, 1788 Died April 23, 1853." The reverse read: "Blessed are the pure in heart, for they shall see God."[69]

Lee wrote to comfort his grieving wife and the new widower, saying, "I hope he will go on mending rapidly & have many days of peace and happiness in the quiet evening of his life."[70] Mary Lee consoled herself in part by arranging for publication in the *National Intelligencer* an adoring tribute to her mother from an unnamed friend who for thirty years admired Molly's Christian devotions. "She dedicated herself to those gentle offices, quiet duties, and daily graceful ministries of love, so becoming to her station and her sex," the friend wrote. Custis she described as "a gentleman whose genius, taste, eloquence, and courtesy, have attracted multitudes from this and far distant lands to that mansion, where, alas, he now sits in sorrow and darkness."[71]

Molly's death had a profound effect on the religious sentiments of the Lees. The Army officer on July 17, 1853, at age forty-six, joined his daughters at Alexandria's Christ Church and knelt to be confirmed as an Episcopalian.

Custis that December wrote to sister-in-law Anna Maria Sarah Goldsborough Fitzhugh to say he appreciated that the "kindness and affections of my friends has been a balm to my crushed feelings and saddened soul." But, he added, "my health mends very slowly, under the defrayed state of my spirits. I cannot expect to recover my health very soon."[72]

Custis spoke publicly of his wife's death the following February, when he was honored at a Washington's birthday procession at Alexandria's City Hotel, followed by a dinner at Carlyle House. "Will Custis be here?" a member of the gathered asked, according to the *Mercury* newspaper. "For celebration of Washington's birthday without Custis would be like performing the play Hamlet with Hamlet left out. Taking his hat in his hand, which he always does on such occasions, and walking to the platform, [he] dropped a slow, deliberate, and graceful bow to the assembly, to which they responded with deafening applause." Speaking of his late wife, Custis confessed, "I am not what I once was." But he assured the crowd that "his heart greeted with undiminished ardor the recollections inspired by the return of this day."[73]

Still, Custis felt weakened enough to delay, on doctor's orders, a trip to the grander West Point on the Hudson River, which his son-in-law Lee had encouraged. And he was eager for Lee to take over the management of his properties. "His arrival will be of great service to me," Custis wrote to the Pamunkey plantation manager Nelson a few weeks after Molly's death. "He is a thorough man of business, a first-rate accountant, and much better qualified to manage the affairs of this world, than I am."[74]

It wasn't until August 1854 that Custis summoned the energy to travel north to West Point. He left Arlington House farm manager Ball instructions on cattle feeding, noting that because of wet weather, "Fodder will be valuable this year on account of the hay being scarce [and] badly cured."[75] The busy Lee took time to take his father-in-law on a pleasure trip to Niagara Falls. But while Custis's spirits rose, Lee sensed that he missed Arlington. "You will be pleased to learn, I know, that his health is quite restored," Lee wrote to Custis's grand-niece Markie Williams at Tudor Place, "and that he seems cheered and interested by the new scenes around him. I fear, however, that he will soon tire of the monotony of our life and wish to return to his home. I cannot bear the idea of his living there alone and yet I can do nothing to remedy it."[76]

The result: Markie, just back from a European trip, agreed to move to Arlington House to keep Custis company. "I feel it my duty to stay with dear uncle if he desires it, though it entirely frustrates my plans for this winter," she told her diary, giving up on plans for painting lessons.[77] But by October she was meeting her uncle's carriage at a Washington bookstore, shedding tears on regaining Arlington House.

Custis's own long-desired return home (traveling alone) revived his motivation to maintain his properties. He wrote to Nelson with optimistic plans to renew the soil fertility at Romancoke. And he made a point of carrying the keys to the Arlington House facilities to perform chores, as his grand-daughter Agnes noted. The company of Markie was also of solace, though he rejected her invitation to join her in religious rituals. "Uncle," she said in 1854, "I miss our morning & evening prayers—won't you have prayers as we used to have? He sighed and said, 'Ah, my dear, I do not feel like doing anything of that kind. I'm in no spirits for that—or anything else—but, I have no objection to your having them.'"[78] Markie also played go-between in receiving a letter from Lee in which he confided his affection for his father-in-law. "I cannot let this day pass, devoted as it is to friendship, without offering to you … my sincere regard and true affection," Lee wrote. "Those feelings always strong are now much deepened by your kindness and consideration for your venerable uncle, whose affections I experienced in boyhood, who since has been to me all a father could, and whom I shall never cease fondly to regard and love as such."[79]

The following year, Lee encouraged his wife to bring her father and servant cooks to his planned posting at Jefferson Barracks in St. Louis, where the Army could treat her father to a taste of rural life in Indian country.

But the aging Custis remained home-bound. "Being on the verge of my seventy-sixth year, I rarely go from home, although I have great inducement to do so, as I receive the most encouraging and cordial kindness and attentions from my countrymen," Custis told his nephew Lewis Washington. The "last relic of the domestic family of the Beloved Chief is made welcome everywhere. God bless my countrymen—their universal kinship makes pleasant an old man's passage to the grave."[80]

Bad news loomed. Though he had recently enjoyed a rich wheat and corn harvest from the Pamunkey River plantations (White House more than Romancoke), Custis grew angry when he received results of Lee's 1855 inspection trip to the tidewater properties. The cashiered caretaker Nelson, he learned, had not built the new slave quarters Lee had assigned. An enslaved man at White House had attempted to murder a steward. And Nelson, it was revealed, had been speculating with proceeds from the property and hadn't kept records for two years.[81] The situation would only worsen. Custis responded by reluctantly hiring a new, nonresident overseer, William O. Winston, which prompted the overstretched Lee, on learning of the appointment, to instruct his wife with resignation to "tell your father he must do as he thinks best."[82]

At Arlington, the senior keeper of Washington relics immersed himself in voluminous correspondence, mostly with the well-connected. In January 1855, he received an inquiry from Washington biographer Jared

Sparks on the origins of the Continental Army's blue and buff uniforms.[83] And in a March 1856 letter, Custis assured Washington Museum curator John Varden that he had "placed the model of the Bastille in the Alexandria Museum for safekeeping."[84]

In October of that year Custis sent a letter proposing to rent Smith's Island to politician Henry Wise from the Virginia Eastern Shore county of Accomack. "Col. Lee can handle terms," he said, touting it as a site for ocean bathing comparable to Cape May, New Jersey or Newport, Rhode Island.[85] (The deal never occurred. Custis deeded six acres on the island to the federal government for a lighthouse, and Smith Island would be sold for back taxes by the government in 1864.)

In December 1856, Custis received a letter from New York Senator Hamilton Fish thanking him for setting him straight on George Washington's feelings about the controversial Society of the Cincinnati. Critics of the elite group were simply envious of patriotic ancestry, said Fish, whose own family became a New York political dynasty. Plus, John Marshall's biography of Washington said the father of the country had cherished the society. "You were kind enough on the occasion on which I have referred," Fish wrote, "to maintain several incidents within your personal recollection of his interest in the society, down to the late period of his life."[86]

Painter and professor of design Robert Weir wrote to Custis in April 1857 of his "distress" of having lost his copy of his manuscript on George Washington that he had shown to Custis during the Virginian's visit to West Point, New York. Weir confessed he had passed it to Washington Irving, who mislaid it.[87] Custis's correspondence with other major painters included one to Rembrandt Peale, to whom he acknowledged while arranging a pencil sketch of one of Custis's Washington portraits, "I am myself no chicken, having entered my 77th year."[88] In his role as consultant, he gave a New York businessman his views on which artists had best captured the elusive Washington in the original. "Trumbull for the figure; Stuart the head: & Sharples the expression and you have all you can have of the portraiture of Washington," Custis wrote.[89] And he continued responding to letters from children by forwarding them scraps of Washington's handwriting that he kept in the general's eighteenth-century trunk. "Sir: I have read the Life of Washington and wish I could be like him," read one sent July 4, 1857. Custis replied: "Surely the fame and memory of the *Pater Patriae* must be rife in the hearts of his countrymen when children of less than ten years' growth covet anything the Patriot Father's eye hath ever seen or his hand has ever touched."[90]

Two significant proposals came to Custis during this late-life correspondence. A Maryland entrepreneur named J. Augustus Johnson sent him an oddly prescient proposal that the U.S. government buy Arlington House to make it a national tourist site called Washington Park. "Water could be forced up from Potomac with steam power and elevated sufficiently to have in various parts of the park *jets de eau* and them conveyed into basis and pools ... [with] a variety of fish," the man envisioned in April 1857. He supplied Custis with comparable costs of such parks in England: Greenwich Park, Hyde Park and Buckingham Palace.[91]

That same month, Custis received an advance invitation from Ann Pamela Cunningham, the South Carolina matron who led the nationwide campaign to rescue George Washington's home from decay. He was to be a special guest at a ceremony to take place in February 1858 at the Capitol marking the purchase of the estate by the newly formed Mount Vernon Ladies' Association. (Custis himself in his final year had served on a committee of the U.S. Agricultural Society exploring the idea of buying Mount Vernon.[92])

Handling those stacks of mail took its toll. The decline in Custis's cognition and energy didn't escape the notice of his companion Markie Williams, who began volunteering as a ghostwriter and "amanuensis." When he finally relented, she wrote in her journal, "As many many times, as I have offered my services in this line & been refused! In this admission of physical inability, what a sad record is written. It speaks more than his tottering steps, even, of how much he is failing, for it a point he has never before yielded!"[93]

Daughter Mary noted that "Father is ... so engrossed now with the [Arlington] Spring, nothing seems to trouble him much," as she wrote in springtime 1857.[94] Custis was slowing to enjoy leisure time, touch up his paintings, and sort the Washington relics. "You might see him on the grounds in an old straw hat and in common dress, and you would with difficulty be convinced that he was the adopted son of Washington," said a visitor.[95] Custis's long-standing hopes for taking a trip to Louisville, Kentucky, for the annual meeting of the U.S. Agricultural Society were dashed when his daughter determined he was too frail. "Courage was not wanting but strength was," Custis wrote in September to Colonel Anthony Kimmel of the Maryland militia.[96] "I hope that we shall meet at the annual meeting of the Society of Washington."

The End Nears

The most vital correspondence comprised exchanges over the past several years with Benson Lossing, the author, artist and archivist who would shape Custis's legacy. Since 1850, Custis had been trading materials with the avid researcher—who had written on the history of the Revolution and published in *Harper's* magazine. When Lossing toured Arlington House, Custis certified him to make exclusive drawings of the Washington treasures.[97] The result: a major illustrated profile of the man, the house and the American Revolution in the September 1853 issue of *Harper's New Monthly Magazine* titled, "Arlington House: the Estate of G.W.P. Custis, Esq." Also in 1853, Custis began what would be final arrangements for publication of his long-accumulated essays on George Washington. "I will employ a litterateur to arrange the work, and I hope to send you a presentation copy before a great while," Custis informed his friend William Seaton of the *National Intelligencer*. He thanked that editor of the journal "that has published me for so long and so well, and diffused my humble works through all parts of the literary world." Custis's installment "The Last Days at Mount Vernon," delivered on February 20, "will probably be the finale," Custis announced, "as I am hard pressed by some of the men in our country … to bring out the work entire in book form; and as a man of 72, if he has anything to do should do it as a beefsteak should be broiled—quickly."[98] He told Lossing he hoped to "tell a tale of history far more enduring in the record than brass and marble."[99]

But Custis also assured Lossing that he was "untiring and untirable as a speaker but dreadfully annoyed by penmanship." To escape, he included the archivist in his late-life bid to enlist admiration for his historical paintings (Lossing would later call them useful but "poor specimens of art."[100]) Custis also discussed long-standing plans for a new sepulcher for Washington's tomb. Once cast in the role of editor of his recollections of Washington, Lossing was inspired by circumstances to humor Custis, gently nudging him to keep up editorial progress. "I rejoiced to find you in the enjoyment of such a degree of health, and I earnestly hope you will be spared to your friends many long years," Lossing wrote him in December 1856 after a visit. "You are in the valley of old age and hold in your hands the key to the treasures pertaining to the Great Chief."

Benson Lossing, who edited Custis' memoirs and profiled him in *Harper's* (courtesy New York Public Library).

Urging him to "lay aside your brush and pallet and maulstick this winter," the eager archivist reminded him, "Posterity loves details; and in regard to Washington, you, alone, can gratify posterity."[101]

In reply, Custis preferred to describe his efforts at lighting effects in his paintings. And he sent an essay on music, describing the Presidential March "Hail Columbia," penned by German immigrant Philip Phile and heard at the 1789 first inauguration. As for the coming manuscript, Custis cautioned that the publication would be a "delicate affair." There is risk that his beloved Washington could "soon be swept from memory by the stream of oblivion." With a pinch of hyperbole, he characterized the project as a remedy that "if exposed to the full glare of truth & revelation, would exhibit the beloved Washington in the unequalled purity and pride of character that belonged to the foremost man that ever lived in the history of time."[102]

Custis would not live to see his final recollections in print. In October 1857, after he contracted influenza, his family summoned a doctor, who diagnosed "a minor bilious complaint." It was followed by pneumonia. "God have mercy on me in my last moments," the 76 year old mumbled, according to granddaughter Agnes. "I am so thankful I leave a pious family. Lay me beside my blessed wife."[103] The patient asked after Robert Lee and his son Custis Lee, both away on military assignments. "Though almost from the commencement of his brief illness [he was] convinced he must die," his daughter Mary Lee recalled, "yet no feeling of terms betrayed itself—with a heart overflowing with affection to all around him patient, gentle, humbly as a little child did … sure all felt that ministering angels were around that death."[104]

When the Reverend Dana of Christ Church arrived, the irreligious Custis took his final communion, rejecting the clergyman's offer of brandy. "You know I never liked spirits," he said. At noon on Saturday, October 10, 1857, the last surviving child of Mount Vernon died.[105] The event marked the end of Virginia's prestigious Custis line.

The funeral and burial service, conducted by Dana, included a casket carried by six loyal neighbors: William Seaton, Philip Fendall, Cassius Lee, Bushrod Hunter, Henry Daingerfield, and William Randolph.[106] Thousands would descend on Arlington House, among them the Washington Light Infantry, of which Custis was an honorary member, noted the *Evening Star*. Members of the Association of the War of 1812 of the District of Columbia gathered that Monday morning at City Hall. "The attendance from this city, of all classes of people, promises to be unusually large," the *Star* forecast, "and all the routes in the direction of Arlington—by water, by the Long Bridge, and by the aqueduct, are fully occupied. Not the least affecting incident of the day is the sorrow evinced by the colored people, who, at the expense of a long and painful walk, have started in numbers to be present at the funeral of one who was always to them the kindest of friends."[107]

The pallbearers took Custis to the hillside plot alongside the existing marker for his late wife. It would later be marked by an eight-foot marble obelisk atop a base with a block-like plinth. A plaque was carved with the words: "George Washington Parke Custis; Born April 30, 1781; Died October 10, 1857." On the reverse of the plinth is the Biblical verse: "Blessed are the merciful for they shall obtain mercy."

Custis in uniform as field cornet, 1804 by Robert Field (Virginia Museum of History & Culture).

Obituaries for Custis were telegraphed from newspaper to newspaper nationwide. "The last member of Washington's family is dead," reported the Albany (New York) *Evening Journal*, on Monday, October 12, from "whose recollections the world owes most its knowledge of Washington's private life."[108]

The "old orator of Ireland—as he delighted to term himself— ... sleeps the sleep that knows no waking," wrote the *Irish American* from New York. "Mr. Custis was an American in the noblest meaning of the word. Gifted with a fine presence, brilliant talents, and a fascinating address, his personal influence was great; and it was never abused."[109]

The tribute in *Harper's Weekly* summarized how at Arlington House "he gathered together many precious mementos of the great man with whom he was so intimately connected, as well as his own direct ancestors. And here he devoted himself to the studies he most loved, and to the generous hospitalities for which he was long celebrated."[110]

At Georgetown College, where Custis frequently spoke, the Philodemic Society approved a memorial resolution "expressing the feeling of the society at the melancholy event," sending it to the family survivors and numerous newspapers.[111]

Other Custis-favored organizations followed suit. The U.S. Agricultural Society at its annual meeting the following January bemoaned the loss of "the farmer of Arlington" who had done so much to develop the nation's natural resources.[112] And the American Colonization Society in its annual report included a proclamation from secretary R.R. Gurley that "the name of the venerable George Washington Parke Custis, the last member of the family of Washington, is also recorded as one of the most early, constant, and eloquent friends of the society."[113]

Writing privately to Custis's daughter, Gurley expressed more-personal feelings towards his friend of three decades: "He was warm and constant in friendship, had a high sense of what is due (in conversation) to absent acquaintances, and was very reluctant to attend to remarks disparaging or injurious to others. He sympathized quickly with distress, and the poor found in him a ready and liberal benefactor."[114]

Colonel Lee received the dark news by telegram on October 21, at his post in San Antonio, Texas. His reaction, as recorded in his diary: "The shock was as unexpected as afflicting. Determined to go immediately to my wife to give her all the comfort & aid in my power."[115] Two and a half weeks later, having obtained an Army furlough, he rode up to Arlington House at 1:00 p.m. Doubtless recalling the loss of his own parents at an early age, Lee "found all sad suffering and sick," he wrote to his wife. "I miss every moment him that always received me with the kindness and affection of a father, and I grieve to find his chair empty and his place vacant."[116]

That image was echoed by granddaughter Agnes, who wrote, "Everything around us reminds us so forcibly of him who has left us forever. Even his cat wanders around the hearth as if it misses the familiar figure in the armchair."[117] More formally, Agnes told her journal, "What is Arlington without its master? None can ever fill his place. So kind he was, so indulgent, loving us so fondly, humouring our childish caprices, grateful for our little kindnesses."[118]

The newly orphaned Mary Lee, suffering from arthritis along with her grief, received one condolence note that was especially fateful. "The *Telegraph* this morning brings us intelligence of the death of your dear father," wrote Benson Lossing from New York. After reminiscing about his visits with Custis, the archivist-author got right to the point—rescuing the incomplete memoirs. "Excuse me for alluding to the subject now," he told Mrs. Lee. "My plea is, the great anxiety I feel that historical matters, so truly valuable, shall not be lost to our literature."[119]

The Grand Recollections

Six weeks after her father's death, Mary Lee replied, apologizing for her delay. "I was overwhelmed with many cares after the death of my dear

The Custis Lineage

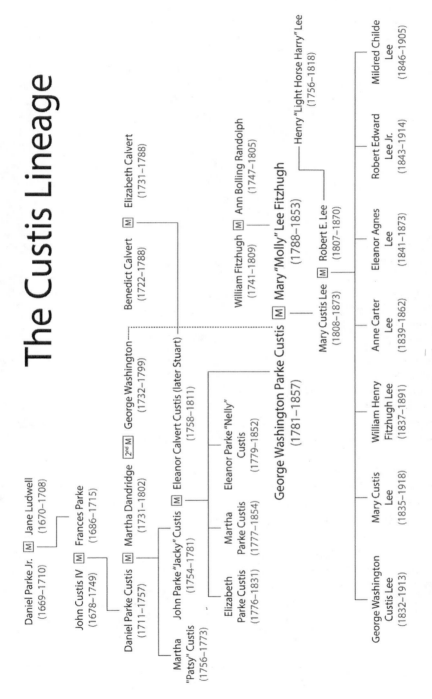

Family Tree

Daniel Parke Jr. (1669–1710) M Jane Ludwell (1670–1708)

John Custis IV (1678–1749) M Frances Parke (1686–1715)

Daniel Parke Custis (1711–1757) M Martha Dandridge (1731–1802) 2nd M George Washington (1732–1799)

Benedict Calvert (1722–1788) M Elizabeth Calvert (1731–1788)

Martha "Patsy" Custis (1756–1773)

John Parke "Jacky" Custis (1754–1781) M Eleanor Calvert Custis (later Stuart) (1758–1811)

Elizabeth Parke Custis (1776–1831)

Martha Parke Custis (1777–1854)

Eleanor Parke "Nelly" Custis (1779–1852)

George Washington Parke Custis (1781–1857)

William Fitzhugh (1741–1809) M Ann Bolling Randolph (1747–1805)

Mary "Molly" Lee Fitzhugh (1788–1853)

Mary Custis Lee (1808–1873) M Robert E. Lee (1807–1870)

Henry "Light Horse Harry" Lee (1756–1818)

George Washington Custis Lee (1832–1913)

Mary Custis Lee (1835–1918)

William Henry Fitzhugh Lee (1837–1891)

Anne Carter Lee (1839–1862)

Eleanor Agnes Lee (1841–1873)

Robert Edward Lee Jr. (1843–1914)

Mildred Childe Lee (1846–1905)

father, who you may know was not very methodical in the management of his affairs," she wrote Lossing, praising her father's gentle bravery during his last moments. Now her "purpose is to command the time to make [an examination] of all his papers to see what materials I can collect for his memoirs of Washington…. I shall be truly most truly indebted to you for your advice and perseverance from your long experience and success as an author and your friendship with my father."[120] Mary was "actuated by filial affection," she would explain in the work's introduction, "and a feeling that these recollections of the Father of the Country, by his adopted son, should not be lost—that leaves so precious should not be scattered to the winds—I have undertaken to perform what he left undone."[121]

For the next three years, the two teamed up to prepare the unique manuscript, assembling primary sources. "The writings you, Madam, are about to publish," wrote Colonization Society Secretary Gurley to Mary Lee in October 1858, "will be welcomed by the people of the United States as historical papers of great value."[122]

The 644-page result, printed in 1860 by the New York firm of Derby & Jackson (with editions in Philadelphia and Washington), bore the run-on title *Recollections and Private Memoirs of Washington, by his Adopted Son, George Washington Parke Custis, with A memoir of the Author by His Daughter, and Illustrative and Explanatory Notes, by Benson J. Lossing.* An advertisement in a Virginia newspaper for April 27, 1860, had it priced in cloth-bound in at $2.50, $3 in sheepskin or library style, and $4 in half calfskin. "The publishers feel confident that a work like this," the notice read, "containing the minute details of much of Washington's private life, as well as his public career (which general history does not reveal), and related, too, by a member of Washington's own family—one who lived with him from his infancy until his 19th year—will be peculiarly acceptable to the American public."[123]

Custis's amalgamation of Washington facts both large and small was an oddly organized, a chronological hodgepodge. The book delivered chapters on major Revolutionary War battles as well as profiles of Washington's luminary associates—Light-Horse Harry Lee, Daniel Morgan, Robert Morris, Thomas Nelson and Alexander Hamilton. But Custis's own essays—most of which had been published years earlier in the *Alexandria Gazette* and the *National Intelligencer*—and his personal letters were not always distinguishable from the commentary and footnotes by Mary Lee and Benson Lossing. The book contained rich material on Custis's notable ancestors, and intimate correspondence between Custis, when an errant student, and the *Pater Patraie.* But the minutiae for which the public likely hungered lay in Custis's exclusive authoritative, close-up observations in chapters titled "Washington's Home and Household," the "Personal Appearance of Washington" and "Washington as a Sportsman."

Readers of *Recollections* learn that "Washington was remarkably fond of fish." He "could throw a stone from the bed of the stream to the top of the Natural Bridge; another over the Palisades into the Hudson, and yet another across the Rappahannock, at Fredericksburg."

Did Washington ever swear? Custis gives the answer. "Yes once," said an inveterate swearer named General Charles Scott. "It was at Monmouth, and on a day that would have made any man swear," Scott said, alluding to Washington's confrontation with General Charles Lee on that New Jersey battlefield.[124] Did Washington really look like the familiar paintings and sculptures? "While several original pictures and sculptures are excellent likenesses of his physiognomy, in various stages of life, there has been a general failure in the delineation of his figure," Custis wrote. "His manliness has been misrepresented by bulkiness, while his vigorous, elastic frame, in which so many graces combined, has been drawn from the model of Ajax, when its true personification should be that of Achilles."[125]

Missing from the work were any substantive reflections on Custis's activism on the slavery issue, which had been a dominant theme of his essays on Lafayette back in the 1820s.

One of the "scoops" was a fleshed-out portrait of Washington's long-time body servant William Lee,[126] as well as a mystery left unanswered. The book explains how Washington, retired at Mount Vernon in 1798, had hired, on the advice of his friend General Alexander Spotswood, a clerk from Caroline County named Albin Rawlins. His job was to be the copyist of the chief's voluminous correspondence, to place record copies in books. The letters, or "passages, personal and explanatory, in the Life and Correspondence of George Washington," were not official business. They were intended, perhaps, for a Washington personal memoir never written. (Washington had rejected most requests for cooperation on a biography, the exception being an effort by David Humphreys that would sit unpublished until the twentieth century.[127]) But the letters were of a "delicate character" and could affect reputations. They "shed more light on the true character of the men and things of that distinguished period than any letters or pages that were even written and published," the *Recollections* volume declared. Somehow, Rawlins' copybook was lost. Though Custis was only a teenager when the drama unfolded, in his seventies he still felt the pain from "the Lost Letters of the Rawlins' Book." His present readers, he nonetheless declared, "may rest assured that there is not a line, nay, a word, in the lost letters that Washington wrote, that, were he living, he would wish to revoke or blot out, but would readily, fearlessly submit to the perusal and decision of his countrymen and the world."[128]

Most reviews of Custis's *Recollections* were favorable. "This is a most interesting book, one that will be highly praised by all who would study the private life and character and become familiar with the virtues of Washington," opined the *Boston Evening Transcript*. "A highly interesting feature in the work is the correspondence between Washington and Custis, which was never before published, and which shows both the wisdom and paternal kindness of Washington in the education of his adopted son."[129]

Author and poet Lydia Sigourney called the book "delightful," though she had wanted more material about Mrs. Custis. *National Intelligencer* editor Seaton called it "a splendid memorial to Washington" that is "clear, concise, and interesting."[130] But British publications were less warm. *Saturday Review* dismissed it as "a pile of biography" that was "turgid and bombastic." The *Athenaeum* called it "bulky and uninteresting."[131]

Still, the U.S. publisher ordered a second printing, and Mary Lee took upon herself to boost sales by touting her father's fine memory and insider's view of Washington. Son-in-law Lee collected clippings for a scrapbook. "It would have been very easy to have said more," Lee wrote to his wife, the co-editor. "But it is difficult to draw the line between what would be pleasing and interesting to friends and that to the general public. A man engaged in public affairs, the events in which he participated, lends interest to his history," wrote the Army officer who would soon become seriously engaged in public affairs. "But one who has passed his days in retirement and shone in domestic scenes, is without the same means of eliciting general interest."[132]

Custis's *Recollections* would draw wide interest among modern-day researchers, who mined it for immediacy in the nation's inaugural first family but challenged some passages on factual grounds.*[133]

Mary Lee herself was embarrassed by the work's missing words, repetition and factual mistakes. "Several little things are omitted that I had proposed to put in," she wrote to Lossing on January 6, 1860, just after copies had been distributed. "Among others are the line I so much admired which I cannot correctly repeat but which run [like]: this 'the great, the best, The Cincinnatus of the West.... Nor do I find ... the notice of Mrs. Washington's having given from her private fortune $20,000 to supply the wants of the soldier in their hour of need. I wrote you about it & think it was in the times of the Valley Forge affair," Mary said. "It was probably an act of generosity that she did not make known to the world but it is duly recorded in

---

*Two examples: Highly ranked Washington biographer Douglas Southall Freeman, writing in the 1940s, called Custis's treatment of the first meeting of George Washington and Martha Dandridge Custis "florid" and "somewhat overwritten." And he expressed skepticism that Custis, writing four decades after his time with Martha, should be the final authority on the iffy question of the exact date in 1758 the couple met. More recently, Craig Shirley's biography of Mary Washington asserts that Custis misstated the chronology of when the first president and his mother were reunited.

Washington's daybook ... & is an interesting fact which may now be published without wounding the delicacy of any of the family." Mary told the professional editor, "I can correct a few slight inaccuracies ... should you bring out another edition." She then complimented Lossing on his recent 1859 illustrated book *Mount Vernon & Its Associations*, "which I think is the most finished of all your productions & some of the illustrations are admirable."[134]

Mary Lee would renew correspondence with Lossing after the bitterness of the Civil War. In a February 1866 letter from Lexington, Virginia, she told the New York editor that her copy of *Recollections* was "one of the few which are not utterly destroyed" by the Union troops that occupied Arlington House. "The graves of my beloved parents now ravaged, desecrated, the fine oak, which has been cherished for 50 years and more, leveled to the ground & the graves of those who have [caused] our ruin planted up to our very door," she complained. She then asked Lossing's advice on a proposal from a Philadelphia publisher for a new edition of the memoir. She suggested that Lossing "resign all interest," as the re-release was not likely to produce much income. "Then I would feel at liberty to make any disposal of it I thought best," Mary said.[135]

The Contested Will

The death of Custis left both Mary and Robert E. Lee in a new era—with a load of added responsibilities. With help from their son Custis Lee, they invested in improvements at the Arlington Mill, and new fertilizing techniques using oyster shells and guano. But Lee, even though his military obligations had not subsided, felt duty-bound to tackle the decaying state of Arlington House personally rather than leave it to his son Custis. "I fear [Custis] could not support his [grandfather's] name and place as he desired," he wrote to Anna Fitzhugh in November 1857. "Everything is in ruins and will have to be rebuilt. I feel more familiar with the military operations of a campaign than the details of a farm."[136] The Lees hired a new overseer for Arlington House, William Moore.[137] Lee also sought, by popular demand, to continue and even improve the entertainment offerings at Arlington Spring, which still attracted thousands for the Fourth of July. The heir leased it to a concessionaire who advertised German music festivals, picnics, even a jousting tournament.

For her part, Mary was growing wary of slave behavior and the rising influence of abolitionists. "Scarcely had my father been laid in his tomb when two men were constantly lurking about here tampering with the servants and telling them they had a right to their freedom immediately and that if they would unite and demand it, they would obtain it," she wrote to editor and publisher W.G. Webster (son of Noah Webster) on February 17, 1858. "The merciful hand of a kind providence & their own inertness, I suppose, prevented an outbreak," she said, cursing the "idle and thankless dependents." Mary added facetiously, "We should be most deeply indebted to their *kind friends* the Abolitionists if they would come forward & purchase their time & let them enjoy the comforts of freedom at once."[138]

In February 1858, Colonel Lee took more time off from official duties and journeyed to the Pamunkey plantations. Three enslaved workers had recently escaped from Arlington House and were dispatched to those dusty fields of Romancoke and White House. Lee found the White House crops in decent shape, and the enslaved workforce productive under new overseer Winston. But the buildings were dilapidated and Romancoke even worse, "with no funds, no corn." "Nothing looking well," he wrote home.[139] A second visit in April 1858 saw the situation improved. But Lee was also informed that Custis's debt to Nelson was $1,200 higher than thought.[140] It was a harbinger of grimmer problems.

The last will and testament of George Washington Parke Custis, dated March 26, 1855, was filed in Alexandria Courthouse. It contained a booby trap. The resulting drama would haunt his extended family for nearly a decade.

Will of G.W.P. Custis

In the name of God, amen. I, George Washington Parke Custis, of Arlington House, in the county of Alexandria and State of Virginia, being sound in body and mind, do make and ordain this instrument of writing as my last will and testament, revoking all other wills and testaments whatever. I give and bequeath to my dearly beloved daughter and only child, Mary Ann Randolph Lee, my Arlington House estate, in the county of Alexandria and State of Virginia, containing eleven hundred acres, more or less, and my mill on Four-Mile Run, in the county of Alexandria, and the lands of mine adjacent to said mill, in the counties of Alexandria and Fairfax, in the State of Virginia, the use and benefit of all just mentioned during the term of her natural life, together with my horses and carriages, furniture, pictures, and plate, during the term of her natural life.

On the death of my daughter, Mary Ann Randolph Lee, all the property left to her during the term of her natural life I give and bequeath to my eldest grandson, George Washington Custis Lee, to him and his heirs forever, he, my said eldest grandson, taking my name and arms.

I leave and bequeath to my four granddaughters, Mary, Ann, Agnes, and Mildred Lee, to each ten thousand dollars. I give and bequeath to my second grandson, William Henry Fitzhugh Lee, when he shall be of age, my estate called the White House, in the county of New Kent and the State of Virginia, containing four thousand acres, more or less, to him and his heirs forever.

I give and bequeath to my third and youngest grandson, Robert Edward Lee, when he is of age, my estate in the county of King William and State of Virginia, called Romancock, containing four thousand acres, more or less, to him and his heirs forever.

My estate of Smith's Island, at the capes of Virginia, and in the county of Northampton, I leave to be sold to assist in paying my granddaughters' legacies, to be sold in such manner as may be deemed by my executors most expedient.

Any and all lands that I may possess in the counties of Stafford, Richmond, and Westmoreland, I leave to be sold to aid in paying my granddaughters' legacies.

I give and bequeath my lot in square No. 21, Washington city, to my son-in-law, Lieut. Col. Robert E. Lee, to him and his heirs forever. My daughter, Mary A.R. Lee, has the privilege, by this will, of dividing my family plate among my grandchildren, but the Mt. Vernon altogether, and every article I possess relating to Washington and that came from Mt. Vernon is to remain with my daughter at Arlington House during said daughter's life, and at her death to go to my eldest grandson, George Washington Custis Lee, and to descend from him entire and unchanged to my latest posterity.

My estates of the White House, in the county of New Kent, and Romancock, in the county of King William, both being in the State of Virginia, together with Smith's Island, and the lands I may possess in the counties of Stafford, Richmond, and Westmoreland counties are charged with the payment of the legacies of my granddaughters.

Smith's Island and the aforesaid lands in Stafford, Richmond, and Westmoreland only are to be sold, the lands of the White House and Romancock to be worked to raise the aforesaid legacies to my four granddaughters.

And upon the legacies to my four granddaughters being paid, and my estates that are required to pay the said legacies being clear of debt, then I give freedom to my slaves, the said slaves to be emancipated by my executors in such manner as to my executors may seem most expedient and proper, the said emancipation to be accomplished in not exceeding five years from the time of my decease.

And I do constitute and appoint as my executors Lieut. Col. Robert Edward Lee, Robert Lee Randolph, of Eastern View, the Rt. Rev. Bishop Meade, and George Washington Peter.

This will, written by my hand, is signed, sealed, and executed the twenty-sixth day of March, eighteen hundred and fifty-five.

> *George Washington Parke Custis.*
> *26th March 1855*
> *Witness:*
> *Martha Custis Williams.*
> *M. Eugene Webster.**

Its bequests constituted a male-centered investment in the future. Arlington House (and its relics) and the Four Mile Run land, after Mary Lee's death, would go to grandson Custis Lee. White House would go to Rooney, Romancoke to Robert Lee, Jr. Each of the Lee's four daughters were to

---

*Text from Encyclopedia Virginia.

receive $10,000, derived from an expected sale of Smith's Island and other properties. Most vital: all the Custis slaves would be freed—within five years. By awaiting until his own death to take the financially ruinous step of manumitting his enslaved persons, Custis was repeating the behavior of his *Pater Patriae*.

Lee, on Army duty in Texas, was the only one among the executors to qualify in Alexandria court. He dutifully produced a detailed inventory of Custis's estate, itemizing sixty-three enslaved persons by name, as well as the remaining livestock and farm equipment, both at Arlington and on the Pamunkey, as certified by the overseers. But Lee immediately ran into obstacles. He was unable to locate the referenced lands in Richmond and Stafford and Westmoreland counties. The Washington square 21 he had to abandon to the whims of District of Columbia law. Most ominously, Lee soon estimated that, with the Arlington Mill contractors' demand for back wages, the estate was in debt of $10,000.[141] On visiting the Pamunkey, Lee was angered to discover that caretaker Nelson had neglected to build new quarters. "But this is not the worst of his behavior," Lee wrote to his son in California. "Suffice it to say he failed to account for wheat crops of 1855, as far as I can ascertain, rendered no accounts at all for the year 1855 ... and left the place before the arrival of Mr. Winston, leaving no inventories of the property." Putting those properties in order would require about $10,000, Lee said.[142]

The departed father-in-law "has left me an unpleasant legacy," Lee wrote to his son Custis in 1859.[143] And his private troubles were about to become public, as the abolitionist movement took notice of the Custis legacy. Newspaper coverage came as far north as Manchester, New Hampshire, where the local weekly reported in December 1857 that Custis's will was admitted to probate court "for the December term of the Alexandria County (Va.) court, and by it he directs that all of his slaves, some three hundred in number, be emancipated within five years, leaving it to his executors to provide funds for removing them from the Commonwealth. These slaves are mostly directly descended from those left to his grandmother by her second husband, George Washington. The families at 'Arlington' (his estate across the river from this city) are mulattoes," the reporter wrote, "some of them very light, but those on his lower Virginia plantations are black enough. Several of the Arlington slaves have within a few years past gone North by the underground line."[144]

Northern newspapers took to mocking Custis, the *Chicago Tribune* belittling him as "the inevitable" after-dinner speaker, unworthy of George Washington's company and whose wife Mary in later life allegedly avoided him in reaction to his "licentiousness, which was strictly Virginian in its impartiality for color."[145]

Down south, by contrast, the *Charleston Mercury* styled "the emancipation, by will, of the slaves of the late George Washington Parke Custis 'a death bed folly' and 'a wanton destruction of property,'" the paper wrote at the end of 1857. "As a large proportion of these slaves are Mr. Custis's own children, it seems to us that the 'folly' of his death-bed will hardly more than compensate for the follies of his living bed, and the 'wonton destruction of property' for the 'wanton' creation of it. If he was only 'quits' with his conscience, the *Mercury,* nor anyone else has any just ground for complaint."[146]

The Lees soon discovered that the enslaved workers, long familiar faces in their household but now under their direct authority, expected freedom sooner than the will's five-year time frame. Not surprisingly, their productivity declined. Mary betrayed signs of frustration when on February 10, 1858, she wrote a friend to note that "it is very unsatisfactory work for the servants here have been so long accustomed to do little or nothing that they cannot be convinced of the necessity now of exerting themselves," in order to speed up the accomplishment of the promise of freedom in the will. "Unless there is a mighty change wrought in them, I do not know" what good they will do themselves, "but at any rate we shall be relieved from the care of them which will be an immense burden taken from our shoulders."[147]

Some of the Arlington House enslaved workers Lee hired out in Alexandria. But their efforts were deemed insufficient by the boss. One such worker, Reuben Parks, prompted Lee to call him "a great rogue and rascal whom I must get rid of in some way."[148] Several others did run away, and the stricter Lee, after they were apprehended, sent them to the Pamunkey plantations.

The larger community of Custis's enslaved persons, egged on by the abolitionist press, had the clear impression that Custis had promised them immediate freedom. In December 1857, a newspaper called the *Boston Traveler* published an astonishing set of claims by its Washington correspondent, reprinted in the widely circulated *New York Times.* "The emancipation of the slaves left by the late Geo. W.P. Custis, of Arlington, will, it is feared, be much retarded, if not wholly prevented, by the heirs, chief among them stands John Washington," it said. "All attempts to see the will of Mr. Custis have proved abortive. After much inquiry, it has been admitted by the heirs that the slaves are to be set free in five years. The poor darkies tell a different story. They of the Arlington House say that they were called into the room, and stood by the deathbed of their master, and that after taking leave of each of them personally, he told them that he had left them, and all his servants, their freedom.... It is well known that the old gentleman always said that he intended to free his slaves at his death. I have frequently heard him say as much, though not in exact terms. Unfortunately, when this declaration was made to the house servants of Arlington, *no white man* was in the room, and the testimony of negroes will not be taken in court."[149]

Reading a reprint in his local *Alexandria Gazette*, Lee in January 1858 published a rebuttal. He denied that Custis's will was secret, that he was selling Custis slaves or that "foul play" was distorting the execution of the will. John Washington III "is not one of the heirs, has no interest in Mr. Custis' estate, and so far as my knowledge extends, is ignorant of the provisions of his will," which was probated on December at Fairfax County Court, Lee said. "There on record in his own handwriting, open to inspection. There is no desire on the part of the heirs to prevent the execution of its provision in reference to the slaves, nor is there any truth, or the least foundation for the assertion, that they are being sold South. What Mr. Custis is said to have stated to the Washington correspondent of the *Boston Traveler*, or to his assembled slaves, on his death-bed, is not known to any member of his family. But it is well known that during the brief days of his last illness he was constantly attended by his daughter, granddaughters, and niece, and faithfully visited by his physician and pastor. So rapid was the progress of his disease, after its symptoms became alarming, that there was no assembling of his servants, and he took leave of but one, who was present, when he bade farewell to his family."

But with storm clouds of Civil War gathering, neither the enslaved workers of Custis's estate nor the abolitionists would let the matter drop. On June 24, 1859, The *New York Tribune* published a letter signed by "a citizen" that launched more scandalous charges against Lee:

> Sir: I live one mile from the plantation of George Washington P. Custis, now Col. Lee's, as Custis willed it to Lee. All the slaves on this estate, as I understand, were set free at the death of Custis, but are now held in bondage by Lee. I have inquired concerning the will, but can get no satisfaction. Custis had fifteen children by his slave women. I see his grandchildren every day; they are of a dark yellow. Last week three of the slaves ran away; an officer was sent after them, overtook them nine miles this side of Pennsylvania, and brought them back. Col. Lee ordered them whipped. They were two men and one woman. The officer whipped the two men, and said he would not whip the woman, and Col. Lee stripped her and whipped her himself. These are facts as I learn from near relatives of the men whipped. After being whipped, he sent them to Richmond and hired them out as good farm hands.[150]

Other newspapers,[151] some after Lee had left the Union to fight for the Confederacy, added details of Lee's alleged cruelty, including that he lacerated the enslaved woman's skin and applied brine.

The accusations after the Civil War were repeated credibly by an actual slave, Wesley Norris, born at Arlington House, whose testimony was published in 1866 in the *National Anti-Slavery Standard*:

It was the general impression among the slaves of Mr. Custis that on his death they should be forever free; in fact this statement had been made to them by Mr. C. years before; at his death we were informed by Gen. Lee that by the conditions of the will we must remain slaves for five years; I remained with Gen. Lee for about seventeen months, when my sister Mary, a cousin of ours, and I determined to run away, which we did in the year 1859; we had already reached Westminster, in Maryland, on our way to the North, when we were apprehended and thrown into prison, and Gen. Lee notified of our arrest; we remained in prison fifteen days, when we were sent back to Arlington; we were immediately taken before Gen. Lee, who demanded the reason why we ran away; we frankly told him that we considered ourselves free; he then told us he would teach us a lesson we never would forget; he then ordered us to the barn, where, in his presence, we were tied firmly to posts by a Mr. Gwin, our overseer, who was ordered by Gen. Lee to strip us to the waist and give us fifty lashes each, excepting my sister, who received but twenty; we were accordingly stripped to the skin by the overseer, who, however, had sufficient humanity to decline whipping us; accordingly Dick Williams, a county constable, was called in, who gave us the number of lashes ordered; Gen. Lee, in the meantime, stood by, and frequently enjoined Williams to lay it on well, an injunction which he did not fail to heed; not satisfied with simply lacerating our naked flesh, Gen. Lee then ordered the overseer to thoroughly wash our backs with brine, which was done. After this my cousin and myself were sent to Hanover Court-House jail, my sister being sent to Richmond to an agent to be hired; we remained in jail about a week, when we were sent to Nelson County, where we were hired out by Gen. Lee's agent to work on the Orange and Alexander Railroad.[152]

Lee continued to deny such accusations, but largely declined to answer publicly. He felt duty-bound to delay freeing the enslaved until he could produce the cash for Custis's heirs as dictated by the will. He wrote to Colonel L. Thomas at Army HQ in New York City in June 1859 arranging an extension of his leave of absence to sell the Pamunkey lands. "Mr. Custis directed that his slaves should be emancipated as soon as his debts & certain legacies could be paid," Lee wrote. "Justice to the negroes requires that this should be accomplished as soon as possible."[153]

To his eldest son, however, Lee confided that he "can now see little prospect of fulfilling the provisions of your grandfather's will within the space of five years, which seems to be the time, with which he expected it to be accomplished, and his people liberated."[154] He also asserted that "the condition of political affairs in this country will … militate against the sale of Smith's Island."[155] So Lee the executor took the case to Alexandria Circuit Court to argue for more time, while the enslaved persons, doubtless aided by abolitionists, argued that Custis's will did not require awaiting five years. They asked for ten acres for each of the children at Arlington House.[156] On April 9, 1861, three days before the attack on Fort Sumter, South Carolina, that opened the Civil War, the *Alexandria Gazette* reported that the

Supreme Court of Appeals in Virginia heard the case from the lower court. Then, in 1862, the highest state court ruled against Lee. But the question was truly settled only when Army of Northern Virginia General Lee, on December 29, 1862, in Central Virginia after the Battle of the Fredericksburg, signed the manumission papers (three days before President Lincoln's Emancipation Proclamation took effect). He listed the freed persons by name.

***

Could Custis himself have imagined the forces he had unleashed? (We moderns can only imagine the sting if he had lived to see his son-in-law leading southern troops in the Civil War.) It is no surprise that Custis would mimic his hero George Washington in freeing his enslaved people only after his own death. He may also have presumed—self-servingly—that Lee as his executor would work miracles in paying for the emancipations by heightening profitability at the plantations.

Custis's relative leniency toward his enslaved workers, and his ill-fated enthusiasm for the deportation strategies of the American Colonization Society, were likely overshadowed in his mind by where his heart lay. That being the central theme of his life: a patriot's perpetuation of the fame and memory of George Washington as "a sun that never sets."[157]

To the end of his days, Custis preserved a patriotic optimism, one that leaped from his orations and writings, but that was perhaps out of step with the times during the days when a great national crisis loomed. "Having lived to see my beloved country attain its present condition, having witnessed the first day of our constitutional government, and seen it in all its changes, from that time to this—a period of more than sixty years—I assure you, the improvement, the rise, the progress, and the grandeur of our country appear to me as a romance," the first son told the Jamestown Society in one of his final speeches. "If, in the wildest days, the wildest man that ever was born of woman had been told 'that the United States of America, in the short period of some three score years, would become one of the leading powers of the world, and would be, in a short time, the mistress of the world,' he would have pronounced the prophecy an idle dream."[158]

Singing such lyrics to Washington and to America was, for Custis, a role thrust upon him, yet one he embraced.

Afterword

BY MATTHEW PENROD

George Washington Parke Custis in the 21st Century

G.W.P. Custis lived a life of conditional superlatives. He was the first presidential son in American history though he was technically a step-grandson. He was one of the most famous boys in the world. His image adorns the Rotunda of the U.S. Capitol. In adulthood he befriended presidents, congressmen and senators. When he died, obituaries appeared in newspapers all over the country. His home became one of the most visited in the United States with over half a million people from all over the world touring the mansion every year. Yet, if you quizzed an average person today, would they know his name? Having worked at Custis's home, Arlington House, for twenty-eight years as a National Park Service ranger (now retired), I had the pleasure of introducing Custis to millions of people. Their most common response: "Oh, I had no idea."

Custis served a higher cause, as he saw it, and fashioned his life around it. He didn't believe in wasting a minute of any day. His influence on American history and culture was profound. So, why has he largely been forgotten?

When that man of twenty-one stood on that most conspicuous of bluffs on his most prized property just a cannon shot from the White House, he could hardly have imagined what the world would become or that his legacy might fade. Certainly, he had intended to be remembered just as he had intended for his mansion to be the first and foremost shrine to his step-grandfather, the Father of the Country. George Washington's ghost was to inhabit every inch of its thousands of square feet, and Custis was to be its caretaker. That was his public service and duty to his country. He was to devote every second of his life to it: his entire 55 years of adulthood.

Some houses are historic because someone important lived there or some significant events occurred within their walls. Few houses are built to be historic. Arlington House was one such place. Every part of its design was crafted to send a message across the Potomac to the leaders of the nation. Who was sitting in the White House when Custis chose his architect, George Hadfield? None other than Thomas Jefferson, who represented the antithesis of almost everything Washington had stood for. Jefferson's love for architecture was well established, especially his passion for Roman design with its domes. He reviled Greek architecture as coarse and ugly. So, what style did Custis choose for the most prominent part of his mansion—the massive portico? Greek. Custis never wrote that it was in defiance of Jefferson, but given his attention to symbolism, it's not surprising that many historians have taken that leap.

Such was Custis's personality: provocative and adamant.

What are we to make of him?

That was an easy question to answer when I first started working at Arlington House in 1990. Custis was to me such a dynamic figure. His role as the first presidential son and his life-long devotion to George Washington captivated me. Of course, the intent of the National Park Service was to focus everything on Robert E. Lee. It was a national memorial to honor him, after all. I was trained to relate all of the site's history to Lee. All well and good, but it seemed to me that it should have all been related to Custis. He was so much more of a prominent figure than Lee was during the historic period before the Civil War to which the house and grounds are restored. Plus, he was so much more interesting than Lee. Here was a man who crafted a public persona of being the primary caretaker and spokesperson of Washington's legacy. He made himself the gatekeeper of the public memory of the Father of the Country and, in so doing, put himself at the forefront of the public creation of the American identity. He prolifically wrote, orated, playwrighted, and painted a uniquely vivid concept of what this new national being was that was in its infancy. I'd never met anyone else like him in my studies. Part serious historian, part P.T. Barnum, Custis was a character. So, I formed my interpretation of the site that put Custis at the head of a generational transformation of the country that mirrored his own development from childhood, to adolescence, to manhood, to middle age, to dotage, then death. He was born six months before the British surrender at Yorktown and died just three and a half years before the death of the first incarnation of the American republic through secession and civil war. By framing it that way, I came to realize how representative he truly was of what it meant to be American in all of its complexities through that time. The making of America was messy, often ugly and full of hypocrisy, but just as often a dream of an ideal of virtue and aspiration. Through it, Custis used what he learned from the Father to teach and instill in his countrymen the vision and fortitude to bear through the morass and strive for that ideal future.

Custis didn't arrive at Arlington fully formed, of course, and neither did I. Like Custis, I was in my twenties and had yet to learn many lessons still to be taught. And the culture of the country was so different in 1990. Symbols of our racist past were not so discredited, and you didn't have to talk about slavery if you didn't want to. I was trained to refer to the historic slave quarters as servants' quarters. The memory of slavery was there if you looked, but few people cared to. The longer I worked there and the more I studied the history, the more I believed how unfortunate that was and how it needed to change.

A question was asked in this volume's introduction: "Do we need another book on a white male American slaveowner?" To which I answer, it depends on the slave owner. We've entered a period in our culture when the need has become even greater to understand the minds of those who had the compunction to own other humans; to know what drove them and what it says about our country. In many, if not most cases simple greed and White supremacy were to blame. Not Custis. It's too easy to lose him in the forest of other slave owners but we need to examine him. His involvement with slavery as Washington's step-grandson, his many schemes to rid himself of it, his public pronouncements about its evils, and his lifelong inability to divest himself of the burden and responsibility are all very meaningful. This was a man openly struggling with the horrific original sin of our nation and fighting to understand then explain how it affected our identity as Americans. He never quite figured it out. But he offered many ideas to study.

Custis the slave owner seemed not to know how exactly to think about the institution. He lamented in letters and public speeches being born into a culture that legitimized the ownership of millions of humans based on race while not hesitating to benefit from and exploit the labor and lives of those he himself owned. And he owned quite a few. In 1802, when Custis inherited his estates and human property, the average American slaveholder owned fewer than ten slaves. By 1860, three years after Custis's death and the height of slave ownership in the United States, only one percent of families owned more than forty slaves. One tenth of one percent owned as many as one hundred people. Custis owned nearly two hundred people at any given time, over three hundred people total during his seventy-six years. Yet he denounced slavery as "the mightiest serpent that ever infested the Earth."

Was this just another case of the hypocrisy of that culture or was it a true moral struggle?

As in all things, Custis studied Washington's life for guidance.

Generational enslavement was lucrative and fundamentally All-

American. It was a gold-plated apple cart that could only be upset if the masters themselves got ideas. During the American Revolution and his subsequent presidency, George Washington developed some serious ideas that he passed on to his step-grandson.

Washington prided himself in his financial success, which was almost entirely caused by his enterprise. This included cold bloodedly buying, working and selling slaves as needed. But something changed in him as he led the new nation. He began to question the legitimacy of slavery. The institution didn't square up with the republic's ideals.

Many Revolutionary leaders, such as Jefferson, had moral concerns about slavery but weren't willing to do anything about it. Too many pro-slavery patriots threatened destruction of the fragile union if the problem of slavery was addressed. None of those leaders, though, had the stature of Washington. Washington knew his moral leadership was just as important, if not more so, as his practical leadership. He did not go so far as to advocate for abolition or even widescale emancipation, but he put his heart over the financial welfare of his family and willed that every person he owned would be freed after his death. That was meaningful action to him and to his step-grandson.

Custis witnessed Washington's behavior and learned many important, if confusing, supposed truths. Chiefly, he believed, there existed a line that well-intentioned slave owners could approach but not cross. That line was mortality. You could own slaves for your lifetime as long as you freed them when you died. So he did.

Custis was the type to see himself as building on the lessons of the Revolution. He wasn't the type to see the Revolution as a static event. To him, it was an ongoing event to be kept going in the proper direction. It was about progress—what could improve the country. That included conditional, gradual emancipation but not abolition. Like Washington, Custis drew a line at that. This confused some abolitionists who knew of Custis's plans for his enslaved and expected him to be sympathetic to their cause. When approached for his support in abolishing slavery in the District of Columbia, he flatly refused.

Abolition was a destabilizing force to him. It was the gravest existential threat to the country at that time, he believed, and he publicly denounced it. It may have been well intentioned but it threatened the country's survival. And for those desperate to save the Union it was dangerous. The South wouldn't tolerate abolition. Its leaders would secede and plunge the nation into a war that could destroy everything Washington had created. Custis worried greatly about disunion. At every opportunity he lectured the nation's leaders about what their priorities should be. For a time, one of those priorities was to fully fund colonization of slaves in Africa.

It was the only hope of solving the problem, he believed, and it fit best his vision for America.

That was: America belonged to white people. Black people did not belong here. Slavery had so debased them, he felt, that they could never be the equal to the white man in America. They could never fully be a part of a free society. He believed this, he said, not because of ill will toward Blacks but rather the opposite. It was through no fault of their own that they had been so debased. Their homeland was Africa and they were violently forced over the Atlantic and subjected to the evil brutality of the shackles and the lash. They never should have been brought here. America belonged to those who came here willingly, seeking to create something new. The evils of white forefathers had cursed this land with slavery. He openly expressed sympathy for the Africans and wanted to help them. To benefit both races, he believed, Blacks must be returned to Africa. Custis claimed that he didn't want to be a master—that he didn't want there to be masters in America. He wanted Africans to be free and happy and successful, just not in America. Those who opposed colonization, in his mind, wanted only to maintain an immoral status quo. Ultimately, when it became obvious that colonization wasn't solving anything, he abandoned that thinking and accepted the reality that confronted all white Americans: the future included Black Americans. The question was: would they be free or enslaved?

Custis stuck to his plan of eventual emancipation. It was the role he could best play in this national pageant. It was a role he took seriously. He knew the world was watching, and that was no exaggeration. In his way, Custis was attempting to show other slave owners a practical way of doing the right thing—the patriotic thing. He believed it would further the cause of the Revolution. To him, it wasn't about how long it would take, it was about doing it correctly and that meant doing it as Washington had done. End the generational aspect of it. Don't burden his child and her children with the abomination.

If every slave owner followed his and Washington's example, slavery would be gone peacefully within a couple generations, he surmised.

To his credit, Custis accomplished a great deal in his lifetime. In his mind, his accomplishments had little or nothing to do with owning slaves. If anything, he believed he accomplished them in spite of it. Of course, that isn't true. Having a labor force to hold him up at a certain status provided him the opportunities for his achievements. Nonetheless, he saw slave ownership as a burden, a distraction.

Truth is, Custis just didn't want to be bothered by slavery except how much he could use his public antipathy of it to further public debate on the meaning of race in America. He demanded that his countrymen examine it, not hide from it. Often, it blew back hard on him as with allegations of his fathering dozens of children by rape of enslaved women. But it won him the posthumous praise of many abolitionists who promoted his example of manumission as a lesson to all slave owners.

During my years at Arlington House another theme grew in importance in my mind. I had begun there thinking of Custis as a son of Washington and I minimized his role as a father of Robert E. Lee. That changed for me with the birth of my own son. My perception of myself changed from son to father over night and it opened my eyes to a whole different way in which Custis has been forgotten.

Fatherhood was a complicated and painful subject for Custis. Not only was there the shame and immorality of fathering an enslaved child or children there was the agony of losing three children in his marriage, including his only son, during the early years at Arlington. Only his daughter Mary survived childhood. Naturally, he doted on her. Her love and reverence for Washington must rival his. One day she would marry and bring a son-in-law into his life and that son-in-law would have to take his role seriously too.

The relationship between Custis and Lee was a curious one. Each man filled a role that the other needed desperately: Custis the father, Lee the son. Custis perhaps reflected on the idea that he now played the part Washington had played in his life. Lee perhaps reflected on the idea that he now played the part Custis had played in Washington's life. Lee certainly pondered his place in the first First Family. Technically, he was the step-great-grandson-in-law to the first president, but that hardly seemed like a relationship at all. It seemed too distant to carry any weight. But if you think of Custis as the only son of the Father of the Country and Lee as Custis's only son of any kind, the relationship becomes more immediate and intimate. As Custis's son-in-law, Lee stood to inherit the mantle of head of the family once Custis died. Mary would inherit the house but Lee would inherit the station: the head of the first First Family. There's every evidence that Lee took it seriously, especially after Custis died and Civil War drew near.

It's not known what Custis might have said to Lee during those last months of his life. Southern secession was an almost daily threat, but it had been for years. The slavery question was intensifying, but Custis had already made provisions to free all of his slaves. Besides, Lee was in Texas commanding U.S. cavalry.

Custis was proud of his Mexican War hero son-in-law. He was glad that Lee had resisted his desire for him to resign before marrying his daughter. No doubt he expected Robert to stay steadfast and true to the Union—to be Washington-like in saving it no matter what. Perhaps they never discussed it. Perhaps they both thought it was a given.

Certainly, Lee knew well Custis's view on secession. Custis had publicly hailed Andrew Jackson for threatening to use military force on South Carolina when it threatened to secede during the Nullification Crisis. Custis spoke with gusto at every turn regarding the preservation of the Union. Lee knew and it made him wary of disunionist talk. He stated clearly that he did not believe in the right of secession except in the most extreme circumstances. Nothing he imagined came close to meeting that threshold, he thought. He would cling to the Union for as long as he could, as long as Virginia would adhere as well. When he made the decision to fight for Virginia and against the U.S. Government it was with a heavy heart and great reluctance. Much of Lee's concern had to do with the future of Arlington. Its proximity to Washington, D.C., made it of the utmost strategic value to the federal government. Union troops would occupy it and, during the war, make it into a national cemetery to punish Lee and forever remind Americans of the price of his decision. It's interesting to consider what decision Lee might have made if Custis was still alive in 1861. As a son, would he have been able to defy his father-in-law's beliefs? Would pressure from Custis have made Lee the savior of the Union rather than its near-destroyer?

During the war, Custis's influence on Lee never waned, though it did change. At first, Lee was convinced that secession went against Washington's legacy but he came to see himself as others saw him—as a second coming of Washington, leading a revolutionary cause. It could be no coincidence that he was head of the first First Family. He even owned one of Washington's swords, gifted him by Custis. The governor of Virginia saw Lee's attitude and ribbed his commanding general: "You try awfully hard to BE Washington."

"To BE Washington," not be *like* him.

When that failed and he found himself a disgraced surrendered general, Lee dug deep inside himself to face the humiliation and disappointment and create something positive for himself, his family and the country.

The last portrait of George Washington Parke Custis, an 1856 photograph by an unknown portraitist (National Portrait Gallery, Smithsonian Institution).

He became an educator and spoke and acted as someone who truly wanted to see the nation heal, setting an example for other former Confederates. How much of this was Custis' conscience acting on him? For Custis was his father and Lee was Custis's son—the last son of the first First Family and of the old republic.

Lee would be hailed for his magnanimity of spirit. Presidents Theodore Roosevelt and Dwight Eisenhower celebrated Lee as one of the greatest of all Americans because of his effort to promote peace and reunion and to bury the animosity that had nearly destroyed the nation. Eisenhower framed Lee's effort in the context of the Cold War. He believed Lee's example was critical in galvanizing Americans in the battle against international Communism. In 1960, Dwight D. Eisenhower wrote:

> A nation of men of Lee's calibre would be unconquerable in spirit and soul. Indeed, to the degree that present-day American youth will strive to emulate his rare qualities, including his devotion to this land as revealed in his painstaking efforts to help heal the Nation's wounds once the bitter struggle was over, we, in our own time of danger in a divided world, will be strengthened and our love of freedom sustained.

History is an organism. It grows as a living entity. All things are connected. A direct line can be drawn between Washington, Custis, Lee, and Eisenhower. They are joined by common purpose and an understanding of certain truths about what it means to unite a people for the sake of their nation. Custis built his Arlington House to honor Washington. Lee's choice to fight against the U.S. Government cost his family their beloved home, but his work to promote reconciliation would turn Arlington House into a shrine to him. And in 1955, President Eisenhower signed legislation making Arlington House a permanent national memorial to Lee, elevating him to the stature of Washington in the public memory.

So, Custis became the man in the middle, the hyphen between Washington and Lee. Perhaps there is no other reason as to why he has been so overlooked by history. He has been simply overshadowed.

Now, our country is changing again. Previously, where Lee was rescued from the trash heap of history and elevated from traitor to national hero his legacy is once again being reexamined. He is being torn down from his pedestal, a pedestal he never wanted, and placed back in that heap of maligned persons. Across the south, his name has been removed from streets and schools. Monuments to him have been seized by the public and remade into symbols of defiance against white supremacy and our flawed memory of the past. What does that mean to our study of Custis?

The mission at Arlington House has evolved since the beginning of the new millennium to more completely represent the entire two-century story of one of the National Park Service's most visited and visible sites. Gone is the focus on the white man in the center. Advanced is the study of the plantation as a dynamic whole, emphasizing more the lives of the enslaved and those enslaved who seized the opportunity of war to gain their freedom and lived at Freedman's Village. Both Custis and Lee have been placed in a different context—as part of the story, not the entirety of it. Will this become just another way of not remembering?

During my last years as a park ranger I worked hard to lead an examination into the modern meaning of Arlington House and the life of Custis. Through it, I discovered that memory is more durable than we might think. Perspective may be constantly shifting. The beliefs on how to frame memory don't remain static and they don't always respect historical record. We choose how we remember; we are never objective. But that's because we care, not because we don't. The Revolution has never ended. We are always remaking ourselves. There is no reason to be fearful. We remember what we need to remember—if we are reminded.

So, this book was written. Custis has been too long forgotten, as has been his uniquely significant contribution to the creation of the American identity. As Custis believed, we have an obligation to remember the history in its pages—to remember who we were. It is in the study of our past that we learn what it is to be American today.

Afterword author and overall consultant Matt Penrod is a retired National Park Service ranger interpreter/historian and education program manager at Arlington House, the Robert E. Lee Memorial, where he spent 28 years. An award-winner, he was responsible for developing and managing new exhibits, education programs, special events, and social media as well as training new employees and volunteers. He has published magazine articles on the site's history and has lectured on Custis.

Key Dates
in the Life of Custis

April 30, 1781: George Washington Parke Custis born, Mount Airy, Maryland.

November 5, 1781: Father Jacky Custis dies of camp fever, George and Martha Washington adopt the boy and sister Nelly.

November 20, 1783: Widowed mother Eleanor Calvert Custis remarries, to David Stuart.

1784: Young Custis meets Marquis de Lafayette among many other dignitaries at Mount Vernon.

1789: Travels to New York City to live with first presidential family.

1791: Moves with first family to Philadelphia, later enrolls at University of Pennsylvania academy.

1796: Enrolls at College of New Jersey (Princeton), is expelled.

1798: Enrolls at St. John's College Annapolis, Maryland.

1799: Returns without degree to Mount Vernon, named by Washington as cornet in temporary new army.

December 14, 1799: Washington dies, naming him an executor and heir to Custis fortune (including slaves) when he comes of age.

May 22, 1802: Grandmother Martha Washington dies, leaving Custis large estate, including relics of George Washington.

1802: Begins sixteen-year construction of Potomac-side Arlington House as tribute to Washington.

1804: Marries Mary Lee Fitzhugh, who soon inherits part of Fitzhugh estate.

1805: Begins sheep shearings at Arlington House.

1808: Daughter Mary Anna Randolph Custis born, only one of four children to survive infancy.

September 1, 1812: As war with England starts, Custis gives major speech, eulogy for slain Gen. James Lingan.

August 1814: Sees action against British troops at Bladensburg.

1820s: Becomes active in American Colonization Society.

October 1824: Hosts Lafayette at Arlington House and Mount Vernon during Frenchman's triumphal tour.

1825: Begins publishing what will become memoirs of life with George Washington.

1827: Begins 10-year career as patriotic playwright.

June 30, 1831: Daughter Mary marries Robert E. Lee.

1845: Takes triumphal tour of New York and New England to see historic sites from 50 years ago and supports preservation.

1830s–50s: Career as painter of historic battles scenes.

July 15, 1852: Sister Nelly dies at Audley.

April 23, 1853: wife Molly dies at Arlington House.

October 10, 1857: Custis dies at Arlington House.

1860: Publication of memoirs edited by daughter Mary and author-archivist Benson Lossing.

In the Footsteps of Custis

Here are some mid–Atlantic regional sites readers may like to visit:

Arlington House—The Robert E. Lee Memorial (www.nps.gov/arho/index. htm): Run by the National Park Service, this home outside Washington, D.C., planned by George Washington Parke Custis and occupied by him for 55 years, is easily paired with a visit to Arlington National Cemetery. It was closed from 2018 to 2021 for extensive renovations to strengthen the presentation of slavery.

George Washington's Mount Vernon (www.mountvernon.org/): Privately owned and one of the nation's top tourist destinations, this Fairfax, Virginia, home of the first president was young Custis's main residence for two decades, and contains many original furnishings. Be greeted by the modern statue of Custis as a boy with the Washington family. See the North Garden House, where Custis was tutored by Tobias Lear.

Mount Airy (www.mountairymansion.org): The birthplace of Custis in Upper Marlboro, Maryland, is marked as such with a historical sign; the mansion is open for rentals.

Bladensburg Waterfront Park in Prince George's County, Maryland, is the site of the War of 1812 battlefield, where Custis fought the British invaders in 1814.

Abingdon Plantation ruins, where Custis's father and mother lived and where he spent many hours as a child, have been reconstructed on the site accessible from a parking garage at Reagan National Airport.

Ravensworth, the Fairfax County mansion built by Custis's father-in-law William Fitzhugh and later enjoyed by the Lees, burned in 1926; it is marked by a historical sign near Braddock Road and the Capital Beltway in North Springfield, Virginia.

Hope Park, where Custis frequently visited the Stuarts (his mother and stepfather), still stands as a private home on Pope's Head Rd. in Fairfax, Virginia, along with a nearby nineteenth century grist mill; the Stuarts also lived in nearby home called Ossian Hall, near the current site of Annandale High School.

Woodlawn Mansion (www.woodlawnpopeleighey.org/), in Fairfax, Virginia, was built by Custis's sister Nelly and husband Lawrence Lewis on land given as a

The North Garden House at Mount Vernon, where the young Custis was tutored. Courtesy Mount Vernon Ladies' Association.

wedding gift from George Washington. The Mount Vernon cupola is visible from the second floor, and a Custis painting decorates a wall.

Tudor Place (www.tudorplace.org/), the luxury home built on a historic hill in the Georgetown section of Washington, D.C., by Custis's sister Martha and husband Thomas Peter, is open for tours and lectures about the family. A Custis painting of the façade is on display.

Law House on Southeast 6th Street in Washington, D.C., known as "the Honeymoon House," was built in the 1790s for Custis's sister Eliza Parke Custis and her husband Thomas Law. Now a private residence, with historical marker.

Old Town Alexandria, Virginia, offers numerous Custis sites and streets on which Custis trod as a boy living at Mount Vernon and an adult living at Arlington House; the **Lee Boyhood Home**, as it is designated on the historical marker, was owned by Custis's father-in-law William Fitzhugh, is where the Custises were married in 1804, and was rented to the Lee family so that Robert E. Lee lived his teen years there; **Christ Church**, in which the Washingtons, Custises and Lee in-laws were parishioners, remains an active Episcopalian Church (the Custis-gifted George Washington Bible is displayed on special occasions**; the Lyceum**, where Custis often spoke, is today a museum and the Office of Historic Alexandria (www.alexandriava.gov/Historic), **Carlyle House**, where he was feted, **Market Square**, where he spoke often and near where the Mason-run Alexandria Museum was located, remains a central square; and **Gadsby's Tavern Museum**, where Custis spoke and often dined, is an active restaurant. The **George Washington Masonic National Memorial** (www. gwmemorial.org/) displays Custis's painting "Washington at Yorktown." There's also an East Custis Avenue.

Black Heritage Museum of Arlington, VA (www. arlingtonblackheritage.org/) on Columbia Pike was organized by descendants of the Syphax family of enslaved persons from Arlington House; it contains exhibits on Custis, the Washingtons and the enslaved individuals. Arlington County has a Nelly Custis Drive, and its portion of Interstate-66 is officially the Custis Memorial Parkway (next to a bike trail, both named for Nelly).

Audley, the rural home of Custis's sister Nelly and Lawrence Lewis after they left Woodlawn, is today a prosperous farm with an historical marker outside Berryville, Virginia.

Chatham, the plantation of Custis's father-in-law William Fitzhugh overlooking downtown Fredericksburg, Virginia, is maintained by the National Park Service and is open to visitors.

Arlington Plantation, the seventeenth-century home of ancestor John Custis IV near Cape Charles on Virginia's Eastern Shore (for which Arlington House on the Potomac is named) exists as ruins marked by historical signage.

Romancock, the Custis plantation on the Pamunkey in King William County near West Point, Virginia, exists today only as a rural road of that name (a related road nearby is Custis Millpond Road).

White House, on the opposite side of the Pamunkey in New Kent County, is now a residential neighborhood. The area is marked by an historical sign noting that George and Martha Washington were married there and that at the end of the American Revolution, Washington passed by there with the Count de Rochambeau. Both plantations were the site of archaeological digs in the 1930s. Visitors to the area may also wish to see site of Chestnut Grove, where Martha Washington was born, and Eltham, where Custis's father Jacky died, as well as the still-active **St. Peters Episcopal Church**, were many of the family worshiped.

In Philadelphia, **the Museum of the American Revolution** (www.amrevmuseum. org/) proudly displays the battlefield tent used by Washington during the Revolution, which for decades belonged to Custis. Other parts of the tents are on display by the National Park Service at the Yorktown battlefield in Virginia. One can also view the reconstructed home of the First Family and the still-active **Walnut Street Theater**, where Custis's plays were performed.

Chapter Notes

Abbreviations: GW George Washington; **GWPC** George Washington Parke Custis; **GWD** *Diaries of George Washington* 6 vols. (Charlottesville: University Press of Virginia, 1976–79); **GWP Col. Series** *Papers of George Washington, Colonial Series;* **GWP Con. Series** *Papers of George Washington, Confederation Series;* **GWP Pres. Series** *Papers of George Washington, Presidential Series;* **GWP Ret. Series** *Papers of George Washington, Retirement Series;* **GWP Rev. Series** *Papers of George Washington, Revolutionary War Series;* **GWW** John C. Fitzpatrick, ed., *The Writings of Washington*, 39 vols. (Washington: Government Printing Office, 1931–1944); **MW** Martha Washington; **MWP** Joseph E. Fields, ed., *Worthy Partner: The Papers of Martha Washington* (Westport, Connecticut: Greenwood Press, 1994)

Chapter 1

1. Constance Cary Harrison, "Washington at Mount Vernon After the Revolution," *Century Illustrated Magazine* (1881–1906); XXXVII, April 6, 1889; ProQuest, 834.

2. August Levasseur, *Lafayette in America in 1824 and 1825: Journal of a Voyage to the United States (Private Secretary to General Lafayette during his Trip)*, 1829, translated by Alan R. Hoffman (Manchester, N.H: Lafayette Press, 2006), 264.

3. Unsigned letter, Tudor Place Archives.

4. Murray H. Nelligan, *Arlington House: The Story of the Lee Mansion Historical Monument* (Burke, Virginia: Chateleine Press, 2001, 2005, revised version of 1953 edition), 143; *New York Herald,* September 24, 1845.

5. Levasseur, *Lafayette in America*, 264.

6. George Washington Lafayette to Eliza Parke Custis, April 7, 1825, Maryland Historical Society.

7. Cassandra A. Good, *Founding Friendships: Friendships between Men and Women in the Early American Republic* (New York: Oxford University Press, 2015), 147.

8. John Foster, *A Sketch of the Tour of General Lafayette on His Late Visit to the United States, 1824* (Portland, Maine: A.W. Thayer in Statesman Office), 195.

9. Jane Bacon MacIntire, *Lafayette: The Guest of the Nation: The Tracing of the Route of Lafayette's Tour of the United States in 1824–25* (Newton, Massachusetts: Anthony J. Simone Press, 1967), 114–116.

10. George Washington Lafayette to Custis, December 8, 1824, Tudor Place Archives.

11. George Washington Parke Custis, *Recollections and Private Memoirs of Washington, by his Adopted Son, George Washington Parke Custis, with a Memoir of the Author, by his Daughter; and Illustrative and Explanatory Notes, by Benson J. Lossing with Illustrations* (Bridgewater, Virginia: American Foundation Publications, first published 1860, reprinted 1999), 67, 591 ff.

12. Nelligan, *Arlington House*, 143.

13. Nelligan, *Arlington House*, 146.

14. *Phenix Gazette* (Alexandria), Vol. 1, No. 113, September 22, 1825.

15. *Phenix Gazette* (Alexandria), October 29, 1825.

16. Custis, *Recollections*, 120.

17. *National Intelligencer*, February 22, 1828.

18. Custis to Samuel Harrison Smith, September 7, 1832, Custis-Lee papers, Library of Congress.

19. Lafayette to Eliza Parke Custis, August 3, 1828, Maryland Historical Society.

Chapter 2

1. See William Meade, *Old Churches, Ministers and Families of Virginia* (Philadelphia: J.B. Lippincott & Co., 1857). Also Milton Rubincam, "The Royal Ancestry of George Washington Parke Custis," *Virginia Magazine of History and Biography* 65, no. 2 (April 1957): 222–228.

2. George Washington Parke Custis, *Recollections and Private Memoirs of Washington* (New York: Derby & Jackson, 1860, 26.

3. See Helen Hill Miller, *Colonel Parke of Virginia: "The Greatest Hector in the Town," A Biography* (Chapel Hill, N.C.: Algonquin Books, 1989).

4. Kathryn Gehred, "The Dunbar Lawsuit: How a Decades-Long Scandalous Court Case Threatened George Washington's Estate," Miller Center, University of Virginia, "The Presidency," 2019. https://millercenter.org/president/washington/washington-papers/dunbar-lawsuit.

5. James Lynch, *The Custis Chronicles: The Virginia Generation* (Camden, Maine: Picton Press, 1997), 102.

6. "A Marriage Contract," *Virginia Magazine of History and Biography* 4, no. 1 (July 1896): 64–66.

7. Custis, *Recollections*, 15.

8. Custis, *Recollections*, 19.

9. Douglas Southall Freeman, *George Washington, Vol. Two: Young Washington* (New York: Charles Scribner's Sons, 1948), 297.

10. *Ibid.*, 299. Custis, *Recollections*, 496.

11. GW to Jonathan Boucher, December 16, 1770. *The Papers of George Washington, Colonial Series, 10 volumes* (Charlottesville: University Press of Virginia, 1983–1995), 8:411–412.

12. GW to Jonathan Boucher, May 30, 1768. *GWP Col. Series*, 8:89–91.

13. Elswyth Thane, *Mount Vernon Family: A Chronicle of the Young People Who Looked to Our First President for Love, Guidance and Support* (New York: Crowell-Collier Press, 1968), 25.

14. Alice Coyle Torbert, *Eleanor Calvert and Her Circle* (New York: William-Frederick Press, 1950), 10.

15. John Perry, *Lady of Arlington: The Life of Mrs. Robert E. Lee* (Sisters, Oregon: Multnomah Publishers, 2001), 24.

16. William D. Hoyt, Jr., "Self-Portrait: Eliza Custis, 1808," *The Virginia Magazine of History and Biography* 53, no. 2 (April 1945), 92.

17. Torbert, *Eleanor Calvert*, 29.

18. GW to John Parke Custis, February 28, 1781. *GWW*, 21:318–321.

19. Perry, *Lady of Arlington*, 26.

20. Charles W. Stetson, *Four Mile Run Land Grants* (Washington, D.C.: Mineoform Press, 1935), 60.

21. Lynch, *Custis Chronicles*, 49.

22. Torbert, *Eleanor Calvert*, 32.

23. Murray H. Nelligan, *Arlington House: The Story of the Lee Mansion Historical Monument*, 1.

24. Stetson, *Four Mile Run*, 30.

25. Lynch, *Custis Chronicles*, 222, Jacky Custis to GW, July 11, 1781, privately owned letter on Founders.archives.gov. https://founders.archives.gov/?q=kind%20of%20a%20bloody%20flux&s=1111311111&sa=&r=5&sr=.

26. Thane, *Mount Vernon Family*, 42.

27. Freeman, *George Washington, Vol. Five: Victory with the Help of France*, 401.

28. Custis, *Recollections*, 255, 38. Lynch, p. 242, points out that at the time there was no legal process for adoption, so Washington, to the extent he focused on legality, was relying on English law.

29. Louis Gottschalk, ed., *Letters of Lafayette to Washington 1777–1799* (New York: Helen Fahnestock Hubbard, 1944), 303.

30. Custis, *Recollections*, 38.

31. MW to Fanny Bassett Washington, February 25, 1788. *MWP*, 205–206.

32. Martha Washington to Fanny Bassett, August 7, 1784. *MWP*, 195.

33. Ron Chernow, *Washington: A Life* (New York: Penguin Press, 2010), 513.

34. Stephen Decatur, Jr., *Private Affairs of George Washington, from the Records and Accounts of Tobias Lear, Esquire, His Secretary* (New York: Houghton Mifflin, 1933), 29.

35. Chernow, *Washington*, 470.

36. *GWD*, 4:158.

37. Custis to Snow, April 12, 1787, Torbert, *Eleanor Calvert*, 52.

38. Custis, *Recollections*, 39.

39. GWPC to Elizabeth Willing Powel, January 17, 1783, original in collection of the Mount Vernon Ladies' Association, Fred W. Smith National Library for the Study of George Washington. Powel and

Martha Washington letters from *MWP*, 199–201.

40. GW to Rev. William Gordon, March 8, 1785. *GWP Col. Series* 2:411–413. GW to George William Fairfax, November 10, 1785. *GWP Col. Series*, 3:348–350.

41. Chernow, *Washington*, 409.

42. Mount Vernon Ladies' Association, digital encyclopedia. https://www.mountvernon.org/library/digitalhistory/digital-encyclopedia/article/edward-savage/.

43. Custis comments made to Augusta Blanche Berard, reported in Clayton Torrence, "Arlington and Mount Vernon 1856," *Virginia Magazine of History and Biography* 57, no. 2 (April 1949): 140–175.

44. James Thomas Flexner, *George Washington: Anguish and Farewell (1793–1799)* (Boston: Little, Brown, 1970), 348.

45. Patricia Brady, ed., *George Washington's Beautiful Nelly: The Letters of Eleanor Parke Custis Lewis to Elizabeth Bordley Gibson, 1794–1851* (Columbia: University of South Carolina Press, 1991), 22.

46. GW to Robert Morris, May 5, 1787. *GWP Col. Series*, 5:171.

47. Patricia Brady, *Martha Washington: An American Life* (New York: Viking, 2005), 4–5. See also William D. Hoyt, Jr., "Self-Portrait: Eliza Custis, 1808," *The Virginia Magazine of History and Biography* 53, no. 2 (April 1945), 97.

48. Nelligan, *Arlington House*, 30.

49. Custis, *Recollections*, 394.

50. Richard Norton Smith, *Patriarch: George Washington and the New American Nation* (Boston: Houghton Mifflin, 1993), xiv.

51. *Ibid.*, 196.

52. Brady, *Martha Washington*, 189.

53. Flexner, *George Washington: Anguish and Farewell*, 29.

54. Chernow, *Washington*, 615.

55. Decatur, *Private Affairs of George Washington*, 67, 102.

56. Decatur, 255.

57. Lynch, *Custis Chronicles*, 225, and Brady, *Martha Washington*, 188.

58. Perry, *Lady of Arlington*, 29.

59. Custis, *Recollections*, 420.

60. Mount Vernon Ladies' Association digital library. https://www.mountvernon.org/library/digitalhistory/digital-encyclopedia/article/arthur-st-clair/.

61. Martha Washington to Mary Stillson Lear, August 24, 1794, 273.

62. Founders Online at National Archives. https://founders.archives.gov/documents/Washington/01-06-02-0005-0001.

63. Eleanor Custis Stuart, to Tobias Lear, February 7, 1790. Fred W. Smith National Library for the Study of George Washington, Mount Vernon.

64. Miriam Anne Bourne, *First Family: George Washington and His Intimate Relations* (New York: W.W. Norton, 1982), 135.

65. GW to GWPC, November 28, 1796, *GWW*, 35:294–296.

66. Chernow, *Washington,* 617. See also Bourne, 135, and Ray Brighton, *The Checkered Career of Tobias Lear* (Portsmouth, N.H.: Portsmouth Marine Society, 1985), 99. In Custis's defense, one might note that as young as age nine, he was expected to study a two-volume work on Telemachus, the mythical Greek character in Homer's *Odyssey.* See Decatur, *Private Affairs of George Washington*, 242.

67. MW to Frances Bassett Washington, September 29, 1794. *MWP*, 276–277.

68. Brady, *Martha Washington*, 203.

69. Paul K. Longmore, *The Invention of George Washington* (Berkeley: University of California Press, 1988), 215–216.

70. Custis, *Recollections*, 114–116.

71. Lynch, *Custis Chronicles*, 227.

72. GWPC to GW, March 25, 1797. *GWP Ret. Series*, 1:48–49. See 1:175–176; 1:168–169.

73. GW to Samuel Stanhope Smith, May 24, 1797. *GWP Ret. Series*, 1:153–154.

74. GWPC to GW, May 29, 1797. *GWP Ret. Series*, 1:158–159.

75. GWPC to GW, June 8, 1797, "Letters from Custis to Washington," *The Virginia Magazine of History and Biography* 20, no. 3 (July 1912): 299.

76. Custis, *Recollections*, 87.

77. Charles Moore, *The Family Life of Washington* (Boston: Houghton Mifflin, 1926), 154.

78. GWPC to Thomas Law, June 5, 1796. Fred W. Smith National Library for the Study of George Washington, Mount Vernon.

79. GW to Zechariah Lewis, August 14, 1797, *GWP Ret. Series*, 1:298–299.

80. GWPC to GW, "Letters from Custis to Washington," *The Virginia Magazine of History and Biography* 20, no. 3 (July 1912): 303.

81. Custis, *Recollections*, 95.

82. Custis, *Recollections*, 98.

83. Lynch, *Custis Chronicles*, 229, citing Donald D. Egbert, *Princeton Portraits* (Princeton, 1947), 325.

84. Matthew R. Costello, *The Property of the Nation: George Washington's Tomb, Mount Vernon, and the Memory of the First President* (Lawrence: University of Kansas Press, 2019), 128.

85. GW to Jean Pierre le Mayeur, August 30, 1784, Fitzpatrick, 27: 465.

86. Patricia Brady, ed., *George Washington's Beautiful Nelly*, 41.

87. Custis, *Recollections*, 459.

88. Lynch, *Custis Chronicles*, 232.

89. GW to David Stuart, February 26, 1798. *GWP Ret. Series*, 2:104–106.

90. David Stuart to GW, January 26, 1798, Founders Online. https://founders.archives.gov/documents/Washington/06–02–02–0045.

91. Custis, *Recollections*, 99.

92. GW to John McDowell, March 5, 1798. *GWP Ret. Series*, 2:118–119.

93. John McDowell to GW, March 8, 1798, *GWP Ret. Series*, 2:123.

94. Custis, *Recollections*, 100.

95. Custis, *Recollections*, 101.

96. Custis, *Recollections*, 105.

97. Custis to Lawrence Lewis, May 21, 1798, New York Public Library, Digital Custis Lenox Collection, Digital Custis Lenox Collection, I.D. 5681532.

98. David Ribblett, *Nelly Custis: Child of Mount Vernon* (Mount Vernon, Virginia: Mount Vernon Ladies' Association, 1993), 41.

99. Thane, *Mount Vernon Family*, 84.

100. GW to GWPC, April 15, 1798. *GWD*, 2:288. Editors of *The Papers of George Washington* say the female is probably Elizabeth Jennings, daughter of Thomas Jennings (see *GWP Ret. Series*, 2:336n1).

101. Custis, *Recollections*, 106.

102. Custis, *Recollections*, 107.

103. Custis, *Recollections*, 109.

104. Custis, *Recollections*, 110.

105. GW to David Stuart, August 13, 1798. *GWP Ret. Series*, 2:525–526.

106. John McDowell to GW, August 13, 1798, *GWP Ret. Series*, 2:519–120.

107. GW to John McDowell, September 2, 1798. *GWP Ret. Series*, 2:578–579.

108. Brady, *Beautiful Nelly*, 54.

109. MW to Sally Cary Fairfax, May 17, 1798, *MWP*, 314–315.

110. GW to Bartholomew Dandridge, January 25, 1799. *GWP Ret. Series*, 3:338–339.

111. Custis, *Recollections*, 38.

112. Thane, *Mount Vernon Family*, 47.

113. Woody Holton, ed., *My Dearest Friend: Letters of Abigail and John* Adams (Cambridge: Harvard University Press, 2007), 290.

114. Custis, *Recollections*, 450.

115. T. Michael Miller, *Murder & Mayhem: Criminal Conduct in Old Alexandria, Virginia, 1749–1900* (Bowie, Maryland: Heritage Books, 1988), 183.

116. William H. Gaines, Jr., "The Forgotten Army: Recruiting for a National Emergency (1799–1800)," *The Virginia Magazine of History and Biography* 56, no. 3 (July 1948): 267–279.

117. GW to David Stuart. *GWP Ret. Series*, 3:299–299.

118. James McHenry to Custis, December 14, 1798, Virginia Historical Society.

119. Custis, *Recollections*, 51.

120. GW to James McHenry, March 25, 1799. *GWP Ret. Series*, 3:438–443.

121. GW to Clement Biddle, June 7, 1799. *GWP Ret. Series*, 4:111n1. This letter, known from a letterpress copy in the Washington Papers at the Library of Congress, was probably never sent to Biddle. On the same day, Washington also wrote to James McHenry: "When I began the enclosed letter … I intended to address it to Colo. Biddle, who transacts all matters of the sort for me in Philadelphia, but as I wrote on, it occurred to me that possibly the Quarter Master might be a more appropriate choice to accomplish my order…" McHenry subsequently engaged Tench Francis, the purveyor of public supplies, to secure the articles for GWPC.

122. Nelligan, *Arlington House*, 39.

Chapter 3

1. Frank E. Grizzard, Jr., *George Washington: A Biographical Companion* (Santa Barbara, California: ABC-CLIO, 2002), 67.

2. Copy of letter, owned by Joseph Fields, courtesy Mount Vernon Ladies' Association.

3. John C. Fitzpatrick, ed., *The Last Will and Testament of George Washington, Introduction by the Honorable Lewis F. Powell Jr.,*

Including Martha Washington's Will, Genealogy, Family Trees and a Complete Index of Beneficiaries (Fairfax, Virginia: Foley and Lardner for Mount Vernon Ladies' Association, 1939), 23. Lot 21 was between Georgetown and Rock Creek, in the modern neighborhood of Foggy Bottom.

4. Eugene E. Prussing, *The Estate of George Washington, Deceased* (Boston: Little, Brown, 1927), 68.

5. Estimates vary because Jacky Custis died intestate. These numbers came from Henry Wiencek, *An Imperfect God: George Washington, His Slaves, and the Creation of America* (New York: Farrar, Straus, Giroux, 2003), 81. For a thorough discussion of the estimates, see James Lynch, *The Custis Chronicles: The Virginia Generation* (Camden, Maine: Picton Press, 1997), 156.

6. Murray Nelligan, *Arlington House*, 41.

7. Joseph Fields, ed., *"Worthy Partner": The Papers of Martha Washington* (Westport, Connecticut: Greenwood Press, 1994), 396, MWP.

8. George Washington Parke Custis, *Recollections*, 57.

9. John Quincy Adams diary 24, 1 March 1795–31 December 1802, page 343, copyright 2020, Massachusetts Historical Society. http://www.masshist.org/jqadiaries, accessed January 15, 2020.

10. Fitzpatrick, *The Last Will*, 57.

11. Cassandra Good, "Washington Family Fortune: Lineage and Capital in Nineteenth-Century America," *Early American Studies*, Winter 2020, 90–133.

12. Jennifer Hanna, "Arlington House: The Robert E. Lee Memorial: Cultural Landscape Report, History," 1, Interior Department, National Park Service, October 2001, 28.

13. Mary Thompson, *"The Only Unavoidable Subject of Regret": George Washington, Slavery, and the Enslaved Community at Mount Vernon* (Charlottesville: University of Virginia Press, 2019), 340.

14. Murray H. Nelligan, *Arlington House: The Story of the Lee Mansion Historical Monument* (Burke, Virginia: Chateleine Press, 2001, revised version of 1953 edition), 49.

15. C.B. Rose, *Arlington County, Virginia: A History* (Arlington, Virginia: Arlington Historical Society, 1976), 72.

16. Woody Holton, ed., *My Dearest Friend: Letters of Abigail and John* Adams (Cambridge: Harvard University Press, 2007), 290.

17. Charles W. Stetson, *Four Mile Run Land Grants* (Washington, D.C.: Mimeoform Press, 1935), 39.

18. Karl Decker and Angus McSween, *Historic Arlington* (Washington, D.C.: Decker and McSween Publishing Co., 1892), 14.

19. Hanna, "Cultural Landscape Report," 28.

20. Murray H. Nelligan, "The Building of Arlington House," *Journal of the Society of Architectural Historians* 10, No. 2 (May 1951), 11–15. The lack of documentation on Custis's contract with Hadfield prompted some modern historians to doubt the architect's role. National Park Service historian Nelligan cites the reference in Hadfield's 1826 obituary.

21. Jennifer Hanna, *Arlington House*, 6.

22. Murray H. Nelligan, *Arlington House*, 50.

23. Jennifer Hanna, *Arlington House*, 29.

24. Rosalie Stier Calvert to Mary Louise Peeters Stier, December 29, 1803. See Margaret Law Callcott, ed., *Mistress of Riversdale: The Plantation Letters of Rosalie Stier Calvert 1795–1821* (Baltimore: The Johns Hopkins University Press, 1991), 70.

25. Rosalie Stier Calvert to Mary Louise Peeters Stier, May 12, 1804. *Mistress of Riversdale*, 82.

26. Rosalie Stier Calvert to Isabelle van Havre, May 5, 1808, *Mistress of Riverdale*, 188.

27. Custis to James Anderson, June 3, 1804, cited in Douglas Eugene Pielmeier, *Arlington House: The Evolution of a Nineteenth-Century Virginia Plantation*, 1996, unpublished doctoral dissertation at Arlington House Archives, 99.

28. Nelligan, *Arlington House*, 64.

29. Alice Coyle Tobert, *Eleanor Calvert and Her Circle* (New York: The Williams-Frederick Press), 112. For more on the Lee family, see https://www.stratfordhall.org/collections-research/staff-research/thomas-lee-of-stratford-1690–1750/

30. Lynch, *The Custis Chronicles*, 45.

31. Rosalie Stier Calvert to Isabelle van Havre, May 6, 1807, *Mistress of Riversdale*, 168.

32. Rose, *Arlington County*, 4.

33. Lynch, *Custis Chronicles*, 244.

34. Douglas Eugene Pielmeier, 96.

35. Library of Congress Custis-Lee papers, Arlington House Archives.

36. Invoices in the Stabler-Leadbeater Apothecary Museum, City of Alexandria, Virginia. https://www.alexandriava.gov/Apothecary.

37. Custis to Molly Custis, no date, 1810, Virginia Historical Society.

38. Jennifer Hanna, *Arlington House*, 46. Original at Virginia Historical Society.

39. "Arlington House—The Robert E. Lee Memorial," National Park Service brochure. Also Jennifer Hanna, *Arlington House*, 48.

40. Robert Cohen, "History of the Long Railroad Bridge Crossing Across the Potomac River," National Railway Historical Society, D.C. Chapter, 2003. http://www.dcnrhs.org/learn/washington-d-c-railroad-history/history-of-the-long-bridge.

41. Jennifer Hanna, *Arlington House*, 38.

42. Quoted in the *National Intelligencer*, May 7, 1811.

43. Custis to J. Littlejohn, June 23, 1817, Washington and Lee University.

44. *City of Washington Gazette*, May 7, 1818.

45. *National Intelligencer*, May 7, 1811.

46. Custis, *Recollections*, 52.

Chapter 4

1. George Washington Parke Custis, *An Address to the People of the United States on the Importance of Encouraging Agriculture and Domestic Manufacture: Together with An Account of the Improvements of Sheep at Arlington* (Alexandria, Virginia: S. Snowden, 1808), quotes from pages 7, 11, 12, Library of Congress. Jefferson had the pamphlet custom-bound with other works.

2. Custis, *Recollections*, 595.

3. John Naismith, *General View of the Agriculture of the County of Clydesdale, with Observations on the Means of Its Improvement, Drawn Up for Consideration of the Board of Agriculture and Internal Improvement* (Glasgow: Printed by J. Mundell, 1798), Library Company of Philadelphia. This copy, sent to George Washington, arrived after his death. It bears the signature of his widow Martha as well as that of Custis.

4. Jennifer Hanna, "Arlington House, The Robert E. Lee Memorial: Cultural Landscape Report, Volume 1, History," 1,

Interior Department, National Park Service, October 2001, 16. See inventories by George Washington and Lund Washington cited in *The Papers of George Washington*, Colonial Series, 6: 283–301.

5. Hanna, *Arlington House*, National Park Service, 29.

6. Nelligan, *Arlington House*, 53, 55, 51.

7. Jonathan Horn, *Washington's End: The Final and Forgotten Struggle* (New York: Scribner, 2020), 101.

8. Custis to James Anderson, November 28, 1804. Library of Virginia.

9. Custis to James Anderson, February 16, 1806, Lee family letters, copies at Virginia Historical Society.

10. Lee family letters, copies at Virginia Historical Society.

11. James Anderson to Custis, March 1806, Virginia Historical Society.

12. Richard Young to Custis, April 22, 1808, Virginia Historical Society.

13. Lee family letters, copies at Virginia Historical Society.

14. Letters to Custis from a Mr. Coftin of Northampton County, Virginia Historical Society.

15. Benson J. Lossing, "The Historic Buildings of America"; "The Arlington House," 1876, *Potter's American Monthly* VI, no. 50 (Philadelphia: John E. Potter & Co., 1879): 81–88.

16. Nelligan, *Arlington House*, 52, taken from *The Federalist*, March 7, 1803, and *Alexandria Gazette*, November 15, 1803.

17. Sara Bearss, "The Farmer of Arlington: George W. P. Custis and the Arlington Sheep Shearings," *Virginia Cavalcade* 38, no. 3 (Winter 1989).

18. U.S. Agriculture Department website, "A Condensed History of American Agriculture 1776–1999," AppData/Local/Microsoft/Windows/INetCache/IE/CXXKU1H7/history-american-agriculture.pdf.

19. Nelligan, *Arlington House*, 101.

20. *National Intelligencer and Washington Advertiser*, April 30, 1808.

21. Charles Cotesworth Pinckney to Custis, September 17 and 24, 1807, Tudor Place Archives.

22. John Perry, *Lady of Arlington: The Life of Mrs. Robert E. Lee* (Sisters, Oregon: Multnomah Publishers, 2001), 46.

23. *Alexandria Gazette*, November. 4, 1850.

24. James Madison to Custis, June 3, 1810, Tudor Place Archives.

25. Advertisement in the *Star* (Raleigh, N.C.), February 9, 1809.

26. Custis to James Hooe, October 30, 1810, New York Public Library.

27. Nathaniel Atkinson to Custis, July 10, 1815, Virginia Historical Society.

28. George Logan to Custis, February 17, 1810, Tudor Place Archives.

29. D.B. Warden to Custis, May 23, 1811, Virginia Historical Society.

30. Robert Livingston to Custis, June 29, 1810, Virginia Historical Society. For details see also Richmond (Virginia) *Enquirer,* September 21, 1810.

31. Bearrs, "The Farmer of Arlington."

32. *Spirit of Seventy-Six* (Richmond, Virginia), July 6, 1810. "Cornplanter" in the 20th century would be unmasked as Virginia Congressman James Mercer Garnett. See James Mercer Garnett, *Genealogy of the Mercer-Garnett Family of Essex, Virginia* (Richmond: Whittet & Shepperson Printers, 1910), 8.

33. Bearss, "The Farmer of Arlington."

34. *Spirit of Seventy-Six,* July 17, 1810.

35. *The Monitor,* May 2, 1809.

36. Nelligan, *Arlington House,* 86, 91.

37. *Federal Republican,* September 8, 1813.

38. C.B. Rose, Jr., *Arlington County, Virginia: A History* (Arlington Historical Society, 1976), 69.

39. Virginia Congressman Thomas M. Bayly to Custis, January 14, 1816, Virginia Historical Society.

40. George Washington Parke Custis to Molly Custis, 1810, Virginia Historical Society.

41. Will Costin to Custis, April 9, 1814, Virginia Historical Society. Custis later declined an offer from the British to reimburse him for their takings from Smith's Island. See James Lynch, *The Custis Chronicles: The Virginia Generation* (Camden, Maine: Picton Press, 1997), 249.

42. Thomas Stuart to Custis from White House, November 5, 1814, Virginia Historical Society.

43. Letter to Custis from William Sherrill near Point Pleasant (modern-day West Virginia), July 11, 1809, Virginia Historical Society.

44. Letters from Custis to James Hooe, June 14, 1813, and October 15, 1813, New York Historical Society.

45. Plat from Virginia Historical Society. See also Ralph T. Whitelaw, *Virginia's Eastern Shore: A History of Northampton and Accomack Counties* (Camden, Maine: Picton Press, 1989).

46. Jennifer Hanna, *Arlington House, 39.*

47. Christopher Johnson to Custis, July 1, 1818, Virginia Historical Society.

48. Custis April 24, 1825 letter to *American Farmer,* "Banking with the Spade," May 6, 1825, 7, no. 7, 51.

49. *Ibid.*

50. Brumley to Custis from White House, August 1, 1824, Virginia Historical Society.

51. Lynch, *The Custis Chronicles,* 245–46, citing letters from New York Historical Society. June 3, 1804, and affidavit from Walden. February 9, 1824, Virginia Historical Society.

52. William Bromley at New Kent Courthouse letter to Custis at Arlington House, October 9, 1832, Virginia Historical Society.

53. *Alexandria Gazette,* November 4, 1850.

54. Custis, *An Address to the People of the United States on the Importance of Encouraging Agriculture,* 28–29.

Chapter 5

1. *Encyclopedia of Virginia.* https://www.encyclopediavirginia.org/Custis_George_Washington_Parke_1781–1857#start_entry.

2. Custis letter to editor Samuel Snowdon, *Alexandria Gazette,* May 3, 1802.

3. Sara B. Bearss, "The Federalist Career of George Washington Parke Custis," *Northern Virginia Heritage* (February 1996), 15–20.

4. *Cleveland Herald,* April 20, 1853. Easton (Maryland) *Star,* August 27, 1850.

5. *Richmond Whig,* November 3, 1848.

6. Custis, *Recollections,* 340.

7. Recollections, 360.

8. Nelligan, *Arlington House,* 98,

9. *Dartmouth Gazette,* January 11, 1805.

10. Custis (unsigned) in *National Intelligencer,* February 23, 1857.

11. *Alexandria Gazette,* May 3, 1810; Nelligan, *Arlington House,* 110.

12. Sara B. Bearss, "The Disgrace and

Ruin of the Country: George Washington Parke Custis and the War of 1812," *An Occasional Bulletin* 50 (June 1985): 15.

13. Ella Loraine Dorsey, "A Biographical Sketch of James Maccubbin Lingan, One of the Original Proprietors," Historical Society of Washington D.C: *Records of the Columbia Historical Society,* 13(1910):1–48. https://www.jstor.org/stable/40067009?seq=1#metadata_info_tab_contents.

14. Anthony S. Pitch, *The Burning of Washington: The British Invasion of 1814* (Annapolis, Maryland: Naval Institute Press, 1998). 10.

15. Sara B. Bearss, "The Federalist Career of George Washington Parke Custis."

16. Custis, *Recollections,* 571.

17. *Federal Republican,* September 4, 1812.

18. *Ibid.*

19. *American Watchman* (Wilmington, Delaware), September 19, 1812.

20. Custis, *Recollections,* 585.

21. Nelligan, *Arlington House: The Story of the Lee Mansion Historical Monument* (Burke, Virginia: Chateleine Press, 2001), 115, citing *Alexandria Gazette,* July 6 and September 24, 1810.

22. Nelligan, *Arlington House,* 112.

23. *Federal Republican,* September 1, 1814.

24. Diaries of Mrs. William (Anna) Thornton, September 24, 1814, Papers of William Thornton, Library of Congress.

25. See the account "Dolley Madison Rescues George Washington" from the Mount Vernon Ladies' Association at https://www.mountvernon.org/george-washington/artwork/dolley-madison-comes-to-the-rescue/.

26. Nelligan, *Arlington House,* 120. John S. Bassett, ed., *Correspondence of Andrew Jackson* (Washington D.C.: Carnegie Institute of Washington, 1935), II, 119f.

27. *National Intelligencer,* January 6, 1824. Benson J. Lossing, *The Home of Washington: Or Mount Vernon and Its Associations, Historical, Biographical, Pictorial* (Washington, D.C.: Virtue & Yorkston, 1871), 239.

28. Merrill D. Peterson, *The Jefferson Image in the American Mind* (Charlottesville: Thomas Jefferson Memorial Foundation and University of Virginia Press, 1998), 223.

29. Nelligan, *Arlington House,* 157.

30. *Alexandria Gazette,* September 16, 1840.

31. *Newark Daily Advertiser,* November 14, 1840.

32. T. Michael Miller, "If Elected…: An Overview of How Alexandrians Voted in Presidential Elections from 1789–1984," *Fireside Sentinel* II, no. 10 (October 1988): 1.

33. *Richmond Whig,* November 3, 1848.

34. *Port Gibson Herald* (Mississippi) September 29, 1848.

35. *Alexandria Gazette,* September 25, 1848.

36. *New Orleans Weekly Delta,* February 11, 1850.

37. *American Commercial and Daily Advertiser,* February 23, 1850.

38. Henry S. Foote, *Oration Delivered by the Hon. Henry S. Foote, on the Fourth of July, 1850, at Monument Place* (Washington: National Monument Society, Printed by H. Polkinhorn, 1850), 20.

39. Bob and Jan Young, *Old Rough and Ready: Zachary Taylor* (New York: Juliann Messner, a division of Simon & Schuster, 1970), 178.

40. Custis speech to Washington Society of Alexandria, February 1820. Printed by S.H. Davis, electronic resource, New York Public Library, original at Albert and Shirley Small Special Collections Library, University of Virginia.

41. Nelligan, *Arlington House,* 181.

42. Congressional proceedings quoted in the Philadelphia *Inquirer,* March 29, 1848.

43. *Daily Crescent* (New Orleans), April 7, 1848.

44. Nelligan, *Arlington House,* 156. *Daily National Intelligencer,* January 27, 1829.

45. *Alexandria Gazette,* June 23, 1826.

46. "Proceedings of a Meeting of the Friends of Civil & Religious Liberty, Residing in the District of Columbia, assembled at the City Hall," arranged and published by John Boyle, in larger volume: T. Forster, *England's Liberty and Prosperity Under the Administration of the Duke of Wellington, Based on Independence of Election,"* second edition (London: Printed by P. Force, 1830), 16–17, 24.

47. James A. Barry to Custis, March 18, 1829, Virginia Historical Society.

48. *Daily National Intelligencer,* February 3, 1833.

49. *The Truth Teller* (New York City), April 13, 1836, and *Phenix Gazette* (Alexandria, Virginia), May 8, 1833.

50. *Metropolia,* Washington, reprinted in *Truth Teller* (New York City), April 13, 1836.

51. *Native American,* March 31, 1838.

52. *Truth Teller* (New York City), March 18, 1839.

53. Speech delivered March 18, 1844, reported by the *National Intelligencer,* reprinted in the *New York Freeman's Journal and Catholic Register,* April 6, 1844.

54. *Baltimore Sun,* September 21, 1852, William Higginbotham from Baltimore to Custis, September 22, 1852, Virginia Historical Society.

55. For a discussion of the District of Columbia boundaries, see http://www.virginiaplaces.org/boundaries/retrocession.html.

56. No. 18 Letter from George W.P. Custis (Chairman) addressed to the Speaker, from Arlington House, District of Columbia, December 11, 1804. District of Columbia History Center.

57. Virginia Places, "Cession and Retrocession of the District of Columbia," http://www.virginiaplaces.org/boundaries/retrocession.html, accessed March 25, 2020.

58. C.B. Rose, *Arlington County, Virginia: A History* (Arlington, Virginia: Arlington Historical Society, 1976), 82.

59. *Alexandria Gazette and Virginia Advertiser,* February 5, 1846. Discussed in Carole L. Herrick, *Ambitious Failure: Chain Bridge: The First Bridge Across the Potomac River* (Reston, Virginia: Higher Education Publications, 2012), 141.

60. Dean C. Allard, "When Arlington Was Part of the District of Columbia," *Arlington Historical Magazine* 6, no. 2 (1978): 36.

61. *Alexandria Gazette,* September 3, 4, 1846. Cited in Mark David Richards, "The Debates Over the Retrocession of the District of Columbia, 1801–2004," *Washington History,* Spring/Summer, 2004, 1–29.

62. *Alexandria Gazette,* March 23, 1846.

63. Custis to Francis Nelson, January 6, 1847, Library of Congress Custis-Lee Papers.

64. *Richmond Whig,* November 3, 1848.

65. Nelligan, Arlington House, 159, *Daily National Intelligencer,* October 16, 1829.

66. Custis speech, undated, Tudor Place Archives.

67. T. Michael Miller, *Fireside Sentinel,* Alexandria, Virginia: The Alexandria Library, Lloyd House, 1, No. 7 (September 1987).

68. *Alexandria Gazette,* September 8, 1847.

69. Coverage in the *Albany Evening Journal,* January 9, 1855, *Plattsburgh Republican,* January 20, 1855.

70. *Charleston Courier,* January 11, 1856.

71. *Baltimore Sun* coverage taken from the *Washington Sentinel,* December 20, 1855.

72. *Daily National Intelligencer,* August 27, 1850.

73. Frances Scott and Anne Cipriani Webb, *Who Is Markie? The Life of Martha Custis Williams Carter, Cousin and Confidante of Robert E. Lee* (Westminster, Maryland: Heritage Books, 2007), 113.

74. Custis himself raised a toast to Fillmore in March 1856 ("we bow to him whose race is run") at a dinner in Georgetown, as reported in the *Daily Evansville Journal* (Indiana), March 14, 1856.

75. Republished in the *True Democrat* (Little Rock, Arkansas), April 29, 1856.

Chapter 6

1. Benson J. Lossing, *The Historic Buildings of America;* "The Arlington House," 1876 (Philadelphia: Potter's American Monthly, John E. Potter & Co., VI, No. 50), 81–88; Stephen Decatur, Jr., *Private Affairs of George Washington, from the Records and Accounts of Tobias Lear, Esquire, His Secretary* (New York: Houghton Mifflin, 1933, New York: De Capo Press, 1969). See also Custis, *Recollections,* 119–120, introduction by daughter Mary.

2. Custis to John Varden, March 10, 1856, Fred W. Smith National Library for the Study of George Washington, Mount Vernon.

3. *New York Herald,* September 24, 1845, "Jaunt to Arlington House." The four, by the ladies' inventory, are Houdon (for a bas relief), Trumbull, Sharples and Peale.

4. *Wisconsin Daily Patriot* (Madison), June 10, 1861 (dispatch by *Herald* correspondent).

5. Nelligan, *Arlington House,* 191, and *Alexandria Gazette,* January 4, 1833.

6. Isiah Thomas, *An Account of the American Antiquarian Society* (Boston, 1813).

7. Custis to Nicholas Lloyd Rogers, November 22, 1826. See also Custis to Col. J.E. Howard, August 26, 1824, both at Society of the Cincinnati.

8. Josephine Seaton, *William Seaton: A Biographical Sketch: With Passing Notices of His Associates and Friends* (Boston: James Osgood and Co., 1871).

9. William E. Ames, "The National Intelligencer: Washington's Leading Political Newspaper," *Records of the Columbia Historical Society* 66/68 (1966), 71–83.

10. Josephine Seaton, 178.

11. In his final volume, Custis's editors credit John Watson, a "venerable annalist of Philadelphia and New York," with encouraging the effort. *Recollections*, 120.

12. Nelligan, *Arlington House,* 102.

13. *National Intelligencer*, February 22, 1828.

14. *National Intelligencer*, August 25, 1828.

15. Custis, *Recollections*, 354–363.

16. Tribute delivered at American Colonization Society meeting, *Daily National Intelligencer*, May 9, 1835.

17. Original manuscript, Library of Virginia.

18. Custis, *Recollections*, 384–392.

19. James Longacre and James Herring, *The National Portrait Gallery of Distinguished Americans*, Vol. 1 (Philadelphia: Henry Perkins for American Academy of the Fine Arts, 1834), 10. See also Custis, *Recollections*, 495.

20. Custis from Arlington House to Molly and Mary Custis, at Point Comfort July 19, 1833, New York Public Library. See also *Recollections*, 60.

21. *Alexandria Gazette,* July 11, 1839.

22. Mount Vernon Place (Baltimore) website. http://mvpconservancy.org/history/.

23. William Meade, "Old Church, Ministers and Families of Virginia," published 1857 in Philadelphia, Vol. 1 and 2. Reprinted by Genealogical Co. Inc., in Baltimore, 1966, 1978, 2:169.

24. Seth C. Bruggeman, *Here, George Washington Was Born: Memory, Material Culture, and the Public History of a National Monument* (Athens: University of Georgia Press, 2008), 24–26.

25. *Alexandria Gazette*, March 6, 1832. In the 20th century, the National Park Service revitalized the site.

26. Matthew R. Costello, *The Property of the Nation: George Washington's Tomb, Mount Vernon, and the Memory of the First President* (Lawrence: University of Kansas Press, 2019), 40.

27. *Gales and Seaton's Register of Debates in Congress, Comprising Debates and Incidents of the First Session of the Twenty-Second Congress* (Washington, D.C., 1833), February 13, 1832, 1782 ff.

28. Custis, *Recollections*, 440.

29. Nelligan, *Arlington House*, 172. Mount Vernon digital library. https://www.mountvernon.org/library/digitalhistory/digital-encyclopedia/article/lawrence-lewis/.

30. Custis, *Recollections,* 439.

31. Gales and Seaton, *Register of Debates in Congress, Comprising Debates and Incidents of the First Session of the Twenty-Second Congress* (Washington, D.C., 1833), Part 1 of VIII, 414.

32. *Ibid.*, 441.

33. Custis, *Recollections,* 129; original essay published May 13, 1826, in the *National Gazette.*

34. Craig Shirley, *Mary Washington: The Untold Story of George Washington's Mother* (New York: Harper, 2020), 283.

35. Custis, *Recollections*, 148.

36. Gary Kelly, ed., *Lydia Sigourney: Selected Poetry and Prose* (Peterborough, Ontario, Canada: Broadview Editions), 2007, 97.

37. Martha Saxton, *The Widow Washington: The Life of Mary Washington* (New York: Farrar, Straus, Giroux, 2019), 292.

38. Custis to George Bassett, May 4, 1833, Virginia Historical Society.

39. *Ibid.*

40. National Park Service, Arlington House. https://www.nps.gov/museum/exhibits/arho/exb/Military/medium/ARHO-2552-Page-1-of-Letter-.html.

41. Custis to George D. Meade, June 4, 1812, Library of Congress. Nelligan, *Arlington House,* 105.

42. *The Spectator* (New York) February 32, 1832.

43. The cornerstone marked by Jackson lay in pieces for 60 years, until a new monument was built nearby in 1893, dedicated the next year by President Grover

Cleveland. http://kenmore.org/genealogy/washington/monument.html.

44. Nelligan, *Arlington House,* 287; *Alexandria Gazette,* April 5, 16, 1851.

45. *Boston Evening Transcript* (from *New York Express*), August 2, 1845.

46. Reported, with some variations in details in the *New York Express* and *Journal of Commerce,* August 14, 1845.

47. *Evening Journal* (Boston), reprinted in *Daily National Intelligencer,* August 22, 1845.

48. National Park Service, Bunker Hill website. https://www.nps.gov/bost/learn/historyculture/bhm.htm.

49. Nelligan, *Arlington House,* 249–50; *Daily National Intelligencer,* February 23, 1846.

50. *Ibid.,* 251.

51. *Daily National Intelligencer,* May 1, 6, 1847.

52. Frederick L. Harvey, *History of the Washington National Monument and the Washington National Monument Society* (Washington, D.C.: Press of Norman T. Elliott Printing Co., 1902).

53. Nelligan, *Arlington House,* 269; letters of May 16, 1848, in National Archives Washington Monument papers.

54. *National Intelligencer,* June 10, 1848.

55. National Park Service Washington National Monument website. https://www.nps.gov/wamo/learn/historyculture/index.htm.

56. Judith M. Jacob, "The Washington Monument: A Technical History and Catalog of the Commemorative Stones," National Park Service, Interior Department, Northeast Region, Design, Construction, and Facility Management Directorate, Architectural Preservation Division (2005), 54.

57. New York tour site, August 31, 2016, article by Dana Schulz. https://www.6sqft.com/the-upper-east-sides-never-built-washington-monument-would-have-been-the-citys-tallest-structure/.

58. Custis to Frances Nelson, October 26, 1847, College of William and Mary, Swem Library.

59. *The Republic* (Washington, D.C.), July 7, 1851.

60. President Pierce to Custis, April 5, 1854, Tudor Place Archives, *Alexandria Gazette,* April 6, 1854.

61. Custis to Washington Lewis, February 6, 1857, Virginia Historical Society.

62. *Manchester Daily Mirror,* November 9, 1863.

63. Jared Sparks to Custis, January 11, 1855, Tudor Place Archives.

64. Rembrandt Peale to Custis, August 20, 1857, Tudor Place Archives.

65. Nelligan, *Arlington House,* 206, citing Custis and Jared Sparks letters at Harvard University.

66. Joel Tyler Headley to Custis (no date for letter, but book published in 1859), Tudor Place Archives.

67. Leutze to Custis, November 10, 1850, printed in *National Intelligencer,* December 5, 1850.

68. Custis, George Washington Parke, and M. Russell Thayer, "George Washington Parke Custis' Opinion of Portraits of Washington," *The Pennsylvania Magazine of History and Biography* 18, no. 1 (1894), 81–84. *JSTOR,* www.jstor.org/stable/20083580. Custis got that fact wrong; Wertmuller is now credited with the painting done in 1795. https://www.mountvernon.org/george-washington/artwork/george-washington-portrait-by-adolf-ulrik-wertmuller/.

69. Montgomery Meigs to Custis, January 19, 1856, Tudor Place Archives.

70. Custis letter to D. Tefflt, December 11, 1834, New York Public Library.

71. Both letters from Arlington House archives. Custis to L.G. Lyon, 595 Broadway, New York City, January 5, 1848, and to Daniel Bryan April 26, 1849.

72. Robert Bolton to Custis, October 30, 1848, Tudor Place Archives.

73. Custis to J. Pickett, April 17, 1857, Fred W. Smith National Library for the Study of George Washington, Mount Vernon.

74. The *American Antiquarian,* August 1870, 1, No. 1, "Washingtonia" catalog of Charles de F. Burns of 127 Mercer Street, New York, N.Y.

75. Custis to Washington Lewis, February 6, 1857, Virginia Historical Society.

76. Custis to N.H. Washington in Baltimore, June 1857, Fred W. Smith National Library for the Study of George Washington, Mount Vernon.

77. Lyman C. Draper to Custis, May 6, 185?, Tudor Place Archives.

78. Joseph Henry to Custis, November 21, 1854, Tudor Place Archives.

Chapter 7

1. Paul C. Nagy, *The Lees of Virginia: Seven Generations of an American Family* (Oxford: Oxford University Press, 1990), 235.

2. Elizabeth Brown Pryor, *Reading the Man: A Portrait of Robert E. Lee Through His Private Letters* (New York: Penguin Books, 2007), 49.

3. Eliza Lewis Carter Tucker to Mary Custis, December 18, 1828. University of Virginia, Albert and Shirley Small Special Collections Library.

4. Eleanor Parke Custis Lewis to Elizabeth Bordley Gibson, June 24, 1827, Patricia Brady, ed., *George Washington's Beautiful Nelly: The Letters of Eleanor Parke Custis Lewis to Elizabeth Bordley Gibson, 1794–1851* (Columbia: University of South Carolina Press, 1991), 191.

5. Michael Korda, *Clouds of Glory: The Life and Legend of Robert E. Lee* (New York: HarperCollins, 2014), 48.

6. Mary Custis Lee to Hortensia Monroe Hay, October 14, 1830, Arlington House Archives.

7. John Perry, *Lady of Arlington: The Life of Mrs. Robert E. Lee* (Sisters, Oregon: Multnomah Publishers, 2001), 82.

8. Custis to F. Dodge, July 20, 1831. Library of Congress, Custis-Lee Papers, Murray H. Nelligan, "American Nationalism and the Stage: The Plays of George Washington Parke Custis (1781–1857)," *The Virginia Magazine of History and Biography* 58, no. 3, July 1950, 316.

9. Emory M. Thomas, *Robert E. Lee: A Biography* (New York: W.W. Norton & Co., 1995), 62.

10. *Cincinnati Gazette*, reprinted in *Columbian Register* (New Haven, Connecticut), April 29, 1865.

11. Douglas Southall Freeman, *R. E. Lee: A Biography* (New York: Scribner's Sons, 1934–1935), I, 92–93, 105–106.

12. National Park Service, *A Guide to Arlington House, the Robert E. Lee Memorial* (Washington, D.C.: Department of the Interior, 1985), 19. Letter at Arlington House archives.

13. Perry, *Lady of Arlington*, 84.

14. Lee to Andrew Talcott, July 13, 1831, Elizabeth Brown Pryor, *Reading the Man: A Portrait of Robert E. Lee Through His Private Letters* (New York: Penguin Books, 2007), 70–71, original at Stratford Hall Lee Family

Archive. https://leefamilyarchive.org/9-family-papers/747-robert-e-lee-to-andrew-talcott-1831-july-13.

15. Custis to Ann Bronaugh, June 28, 1811, Arlington House Archives.

16. Rosalie Stier Calvert to Mary Louise Peeters Stier, December 29, 1803. See Margaret Law Callcott, ed., *Mistress of Riversdale: The Plantation Letters of Rosalie Stier Calvert 1795–1821* (Baltimore: The Johns Hopkins University Press, 1991), 72.

17. William D. Hoyt, Jr., "Self-Portrait: Eliza Custis, 1808." *The Virginia Magazine of History and Biography* 53, no. 2 (April 1945): 95.

18. Rosalie Stier Calvert to sister Isabelle van Havre, May 5, 1808, Margaret Law Callcott, ed., *Mistress of Riversdale*, 188.

19. *Ibid.*, 92.

20. Josephine Seaton, *William Winston Seaton of the National Intelligencer* (Boston: James R. Osgood & Co., 1871), 119.

21. Wendy Kail, "The Court Will Come to Order: Dandridge vs. Executors of Martha Washington's Will," (Washington, D.C.: Tudor Place Foundation, 2015). https://www.tudorplace.org/wp-content/uploads/2015/02/The-Court-Will-Come-to-Order-Dandridge-v-Executors_.pdf.

22. Eleanor Parke Custis Lewis to Elizabeth Bordley Gibson, December 4, 1804. Brady, ed., *George Washington's Beautiful Nelly*, 65–66.

23. Eleanor Parke Custis Lewis to Mary Custis, April 3, 1823, Library of Virginia.

24. Eleanor Parke Custis Lewis to Elizabeth Bordley Gibson, Brady, *George Washington's Beautiful Nelly*, 138.

25. Custis to Nelly Lewis, October 4, 1845, Fred W. Smith National Library for the Study of George Washington, Mount Vernon.

26. Mary Custis to George Washington Parke Custis, undated letter, while Mary was at Port Comfort and he at Arlington House, Library of Virginia.

27. Louis R. Wilson, "The First Book in the Library of The First State University," *College and Research Libraries*, January 1961, 35–39. file:///C:/Users/Charles/Downloads/11389–14590–1-PB.pdf.

28. Philip Slaughter, *Memoir of the Life of the Rt. Rev. William Meade, D.D., Bishop of the Protestant Episcopal Church of the Diocese of Virginia* (Cambridge: J. Wilson & Son, 1885), 11.

29. The Rev. Edward L. Goodwin

(Historiographer of the Diocese of Virginia), "Bishop William Meade of Clarke Co.," *Virginia Churchman* 39, no. 1 (January 1923), 4.

30. John J. Johns, *Memoir of the Life of the Right Rev. William Meade, D.D., Bishop of the Protestant Episcopal Church in the Diocese of Virginia* (Baltimore: Innes & Co., 1867), 28.

31. Perry, *Lady of Arlington*, 77.

32. Nagy, *The Lees of Virginia*, 161. Custis, *Recollections*, 173.

33. Custis to J.S. Smith, October 13, 24, 1848, Maryland Historical Society. Printed in *Military Art & Historian* III, 3 (March 1951): 21ff.

34. Custis to James Scott, August 3, 1841, Fred W. Smith National Library for the Study of George Washington, Mount Vernon.

35. John Moncure Conway at Stafford Courthouse, Virginia, to Custis at Arlington House, January 18, 1826, Virginia Historical Society.

36. Perry, *Lady of Arlington*, 89.

37. James G. Berret to Custis, September 3, 1855, Tudor Place Archives.

38. Custis, *Recollections*, 57.

39. Frances Scott and Anne Cipriani Webb, *Who Is Markie? The Life of Martha Custis Williams Carter, Cousin and Confidante of Robert E. Lee* (Westminster, Maryland: Heritage Books, 2007), 100.

40. Custis, *Recollections*, 54.

41. Nelligan, *Arlington House*, 168.

42. Mary Fitzhugh Custis to Custis, ND, Arlington House Archives.

43. Custis to Mary Custis, Robert E. Lee and Mary Custis, July 26, 1831. Nelligan, *Arlington House*, 175, Historical Society of Pennsylvania.

44. Frances Scott and Anne Cipriani Webb, *Who Is Markie*, 98.

45. "A Jaunt to Arlington House," *New York Herald*, September 24, 1845.

46. Nelligan, *Arlington House*, 278. From Mary Elizabeth Wilson Sherwood, "Washington Before the War," *Lippincott's Monthly Magazine* 54 (August 1894), 261.

47. Constance Cary Harrison, "Washington at Mount Vernon After the Revolution," *Century Illustrated Magazine* 37, no. 6 (1881–1906); ProQuest, 834.

48. Elizabeth Randolph Calvert, "Childhood Days at Arlington: Mixed with after memories," 1845, Arlington House Archives.

49. Robert E. Lee to Molly Custis from Old Point Comfort, May 1833, Duke University, David M. Rubenstein Rare Book and Manuscript Library.

50. Lee to daughter Annie from Mexico City, February 29, 1848. Lee papers, Washington and Lee University Special Collections Library.

51. Custis to Anna Maria Sarah Goldsborough, October 4, 1853, Virginia Historical Society.

52. *Alexandria Gazette*, November 4, 1802; Nelligan, *Arlington House*, 62.

53. Agnes Lee, "Growing Up in the 1850s," *The Journal of Agnes Lee*, edited by Mary Custis Lee DeButts (Chapel Hill: University of North Carolina Press for the Robert E. Lee Memorial Association, 1984), 118.

54. Elizabeth Randolph Calvert memories.

55. Clayton Torrence, ed., "Arlington and Mount Vernon 1856. As Described in a Letter of Augusta Blanche Berard," *Virginia Magazine of History & Biography* 57, no. 2 (1949), 151. See also Cassandra Good, "Washington Family Fortune: Lineage and Capital in Nineteenth-Century America," *Early American Studies* (Winter 2020). The McNeil Center for Early American Studies, 108.

56. El Marques de Monserrate from Washington City, to Custis at Arlington House, August 8, 1813, Tudor Place Archives.

57. Seaton, 179.

58. Custis, *Recollections*, 70.

59. Nelligan, *Arlington House*, 260.

60. Daily *National Intelligencer*, July 5, 1852.

61. *Alexandria Gazette*, June 7, 1852, via *Baltimore Sun*.

62. Sarah E. Vedder, *Reminiscences of the District of Columbia: Or Washington City Seventy-Nine Years Ago* (St. Louis: A.R. Fleming, 1909), 68.

63. Karl Decker and Angus McSween, "Historic Arlington: The Story of the National Cemetery," (Washington, D.C., 1892), 35.

64. Cassandra Good, "Washington Family Fortune," from Benson John Lossing, "Arlington House: The Seat of G. W. P. Custis, Esq.," *Harper's New Monthly Magazine*, 1853, 440–41.

65. Elizabeth Randolph Calvert, "Childhood Days at Arlington."

66. *Evening Star,* May 26, 1856.
67. *Cincinnati Gazette,* reprinted in *Columbian Register* (New Haven, Connecticut), April 29, 1865.
68. Custis to Frank Taylor, December 27, 1842, Library of Congress, Lee-Custis papers.
69. National Park Service, A Guide to Arlington House, the Robert E. Lee Memorial, 1985.
70. Custis to Richard Smith, April 30, 1830, Arlington House Archives.
71. T. Michael Miller, "Early 19th-Century Artists Who Worked in Alexandria, Va.," *Fireside Sentinel* 3, no. 7 (July 1989).
72. *Alexandria Gazette,* July 4, 1860, and July 9, 1855.
73. Custis to Benjamin Hallowell, April 10, 1847, Tudor Place Archives. See also Eleanor Lee Templeman, "Benjamin Hallowell, Dedicated Educator," *Arlington Historical Magazine* 2, No. 3, 24–33. http://arlingtonhistoricalsociety.org/wp-content/uploads/2017/02/1963-6-Benjamin.pdf.
74. Nineteenth-century orders provided courtesy of Callie Stapp, City of Alexandria Gadsby's Tavern Museum & Stabler-Leadbeater Apothecary Museum Curator. https://www.alexandriava.gov/historic/apothecary/default.aspx?id=36978.
75. Custis to Robert Ball, August 27, 1854. Arlington House Archives.
76. Mary Custis to daughter Mary Lee, August 11, 1837, Library of Virginia.
77. Charles S. Clark, "Finding the Febrey Household," *Arlington Historical Magazine* 15, no. 3 (2015). Documents recording other sales from Custis were likely lost in a fire at the Alexandria Courthouse in 1871. See Charles Stetson, *Four Mile Run Land Grants* (1935), 62.
78. "Alexandria Canal," City of Alexandria Department of Planning and Community Development, with Alexandria Archaeology, Office of Historic Alexandria brochure, accessed May 2020. https://www.alexandriava.gov/uploadedFiles/historic/info/history/HistoryOfTheAlexandriaCanalBrochure.pdf.
79. Carole L. Herrick, *Ambitious Failure: Chain Bridge: The First Bridge Across the Potomac River* (Reston, Virginia: Higher Education Publications, 2012), 121.
80. *Alexandria Gazette,* January 27, 1836.
81. Custis at Arlington House to wife at Audley in Berryville, Virginia; daughter in St. Louis, September 10, 1839, Tudor Place Archives.
82. "Jackson City," *The North Carolina Standard* (Raleigh), January 14, 1836, Library of Congress: *Chronicling America.*
83. *Daily National Intelligencer,* January 8, 29, 1836.
84. Nelligan, *Arlington House,* 207, 211.
85. John M. Belohlavek, "Assault on the President: The Jackson-Randolph Affair of 1833," *Presidential Studies Quarterly* 12, no. 3, Presidents, Vice Presidents and Political Parties: Performance and Prospects (Summer 1982), 361–368. https://www.jstor.org/stable/27547834?read-now=1&seq=1#page_scan_tab_contents.
86. Robert E. Lee at Fort Monroe to Custis at Arlington House, May 26, 1833, Virginia Historical Society.
87. Nelligan, *Arlington House,* 186.
88. Mary P. Coulling, *The Lee Girls* (Winston Salem, N.C.: John F. Blair, Publisher, 1987), 8.
89. Robert E. Lee at Fort Monroe to Custis at Arlington House, May 26, 1833, Virginia Historical Society.
90. Nelligan, *Arlington House,* 201.
91. Eleanor Lee Templeman, *Arlington Heritage: Vignettes of a Virginia County* (1959), 26.
92. Ruth Preston Rose, "Smith's Island," *Arlington Historical Magazine,* 8, no. 1 (1985), 28–30. Original letter at Duke University, David M. Rubenstein Rare Book and Manuscript Library.
93. Molly Custis to Mary Lee, August 11, 1837, Library of Virginia.
94. Robert E. Lee to Mary Custis and George Washington Parke Custis, August 25, 1837, University of Virginia, Albert and Shirley Small Special Collections Library.
95. John Perry, *Lady of Arlington,* 127.
96. Custis to Mary Lee and Molly Custis in St. Louis, September 10, 1839, Tudor Place Archives.

Chapter 8

1. Custis, *Recollections,* 58.
2. Nelligan, *Arlington House,* 240, quoting letter from Custis to William G. Read, published in *Read's Oration* (Baltimore: J. Murphy, 1842) and *National Intelligencer,* May 10, 25, 1842.

3. Custis quoted in J. Fairfax McClaughlin, "Father George Fenwick, S.J." *United States Catholic* (New York: U.S. Catholic Society, October 1887), 402.

4. National Park Service, Arlington House Archives. Some words in the manuscript are illegible. https://www.nps.gov/arho/learn/historyculture/1914.htm

5. Latin inscription on paper at Tudor Place Archives. Translation by Grant Franks and Claudia Hauer of St. John's College, Santa Fe, N.M.

6. Murray H. Nelligan, "American Nationalism and the Stage: The Plays of George Washington Parke Custis (1781–1857)," *The Virginia Magazine of History and Biography* 58, no. 3 (July 1950), 299–324. The current author is indebted to the late National Park Service historian Nelligan, whose scholarship on Arlington House in the early 1950s expanded to comprise the most comprehensive study of Custis's plays.

7. Custis, *Recollections*, 368.

8. Custis, *Recollections*, 366–368.

9. Charles S. Watson, *The History of Southern Drama* (Louisville: University Press of Kentucky, 1997), 19–24.

10. Mary Custis Lee to Charles Carter Lee, April 14, 1834. Stratford Hall Collection of Lee Family Papers.

11. Murray H. Nelligan, "A Poor Devil of an Author," address given to annual luncheon of Washington chapter of the Association for the Preservation of Virginia Antiquities, Washington, D.C., May 26, 1951, Alexandria Library.

12. Custis, *Recollections*, 300–307.

13. Nelligan, "American Nationalism on the Stage," citing *Democratic Press* of July 5, 1827, 307.

14. *Ibid.*, citing the Washington-based *National Journal*, March 20, 21, 1829.

15. *Ibid.*

16. Custis to John Howard Payne, December 18, 1833, New York Public Library.

17. Custis to F.C. Wemyss, April 24, 1829. Miscellaneous Collection, William L. Clements Library, University of Michigan.

18. Custis to Dr. Carter G. Lee, January 11, 1831. Custis-Lee Papers, Library of Congress.

19. Lafayette to Mrs. Lawrence Lewis, January 11, 1828. Fred W. Smith National Library for the Study of George Washington, Mount Vernon.

20. Nelligan, "American Nationalism on the Stage," 316.

21. Custis to Philip Richard Fendall, March 12, 183?, Washington and Lee University Library Special Collections and Archives.

22. Nelligan, "American Nationalism on the Stage," citing *Daily National Intelligencer*, January 8, 11, 1836.

23. George Washington Parke Custis to Molly Custis, September 12, 1833, *Recollections*, 59.

24. Custis to Molly Custis, September 21, 1833. Virginia Historical Society.

25. Watson, *The History of Southern Drama*, 23.

26. *Metropolitan* (Washington, D.C.), April 13, 1836.

27. *Washington Mirror*, April 16, 1836.

28. *Daily National Intelligencer*, September 2, 1836.

29. Custis to Carter Lee, January 11, 1831. Custis-Lee Papers, Library of Congress.

30. Edmund Law Rogers to Custis, April 7, 1855. Tudor Place Archives.

31. Nelligan, *Arlington House*, 275; *Daily National Intelligencer*, September 18, 1849.

32. Stephen Decatur, Jr., *Private Affairs of George Washington*, 91.

33. James B. Lynch, *The Custis Chronicles: The Virginia Generation* (Camden, Maine: Picton Press, 1997), 257. See Mary Gregory Powell, *The History of Old Alexandria, Virginia: From July 13, 1749 to May 24, 1861* (Richmond: William Byrd Press, 1928), 243. *Alexandria Gazette*, February 21, 1809.

34. Custis to Mary C. Lee, August 14, 1838, Tudor Place Archives.

35. Custis at Arlington House to William G. Williams in Buffalo, New York, October 24, 1838. Tudor Place Archives.

36. Custis to Benson J. Lossing, December 30, 1852, Fred W. Smith National Library for the Study of George Washington, Mount Vernon. Nelligan, *Arlington House*, 301.

37. *New York Herald*, September 24, 1845.

38. Augusta Blanche Berard, "Arlington and Mount Vernon 1856," letter with introduction and notes by Clayton Torrence, *Virginia Historical Magazine* LVII (1949), 140–175.

39. Custis to Benson J. Lossing, December 30, 1852. Fred W. Smith National

Library for the Study of George Washington, Mount Vernon.

40. Custis, *Recollections*, 68.

41. Mary P. Coulling, *The Lee Girls* (Winston Salem, North Carolina: John F. Blair, Publisher, 1987), 56.

42. Custis to Lewis Washington of Beall Air in Jefferson County, Virginia (now West Virginia), February 6, 1857, Virginia Historical Society.

43. Elizabeth Pryor, *Reading the Man: A Portrait of Robert E. Lee through His Private Letters* (New York: Penguin, 2007), 51.

44. Custis to Major William Nowland, April 25, 1836. Quoted in Lynch, *Custis Chronicles,* 255. Lynch and Pryor say the painting in the Capitol was probably "The Battle of Princeton," but Custis's own correspondence suggests "The Surrender of Yorktown." It is likely more than one were displayed at different times.

45. Elizabeth Randolph Calvert, "Childhood Days at Arlington: Mixed with After Memories," 1845, Arlington House archives.

46. John Perry, *Lady of Arlington: The Life of Mrs. Robert E. Lee* (Sisters, Oregon: Multnomah Publishers, 2001), 155.

47. Custis to Callan, August 12, 1854, Fred W. Smith National Library for the Study of George Washington, Mount Vernon. Minutes published in *Daily National Intelligencer*, August 9, 1854.

48. Publisher Robert King advertisement for engravings by John C. McCrae, *Easton Star* (Maryland), February 19, 1861.

49. Robert E. Lee to Carter Lee, May 2, 1836. University of Virginia, Albert and Shirley Small Special Collections Library.

50. *Herald* Correspondent, *Wisconsin Daily Patriot* (Madison), June 10, 1861.

51. *Alexandria Gazette*, 1873 (reprinted August 13, 1940).

52. Custis at Arlington House to Lossing in Poughkeepsie, New York, June 19, 1854, Virginia Historical Society.

Chapter 9

1. *Vermont* (Bennington) *Gazette*, June 29, 1819.

2. John Michael Vlach, "Plantation Landscapes of the Antebellum South," in *Before Freedom Came: African American Life in the Antebellum South*, Edward D.C.

Campbell, Jr., with Kym S. Rice, eds. (Richmond, Virginia: The Museum of the Confederacy, 1991), 21–49.

3. Custis, *Recollections, 157.*

4. Custis *Recollections*, 377–381.

5. Custis, *Recollections*, 501.

6. Custis, *Recollections*, 158.

7. Augusta Blanche Berard, "Arlington and Mount Vernon 1856," letter with introduction and notes by Clayton Torrence, *Virginia Historical Magazine* LVII (1949), 162.

8. John Perry, *Lady of Arlington: The Life of Mrs. Robert E. Lee* (Sisters, Oregon: Multnomah Publishers, 2001), 42.

9. Jennifer Hannah, "Arlington House: The Robert E. Lee Memorial: Cultural Landscape Report, History, Volume 1," Interior Department, National Park Service, October 2001, 48.

10. Sheet of blank passes at Virginia Historical Society.

11. Kark Decker and Angus McSween, "Historic Arlington: The Story of the National Cemetery" (Washington, D.C., 1892 reprinted 1928), 44–45.

12. Mary Thompson, *The Only Unavoidable Subject of Regret* (Charlottesville: University of Virginia Press, 2019), 198.

13. Douglas Eugene Pielmeier, *Arlington House: The Evolution of a Nineteenth-Century Virginia Plantation,* 1996, unpublished thesis at Arlington House Archives, 100. The current author is indebted to this work for in-depth scouring of court and census documents related to slavery at the Custis estate.

14. William Bromley to Custis, October 19, 1832, Virginia Historical Society.

15. Custis Low Country Estates Inventory, Virginia Historical Society.

16. Elizabeth Brown Pryor, *Reading the Man: A Portrait of Robert E. Lee Through His Private Letters* (New York: Penguin, 2007), 128, using Arlington House letters and former slave interviews from 1920. Pryor offers persuasive analysis of the treatment of Custis and Lee's enslaved persons.

17. Pielmeier, *Arlington House*, 120.

18. Custis letter to Silas Burrows, *Alexandria Gazette*, February 27, 1832.

19. Cassandra Good, "Washington Family Fortune Lineage and Capital in Nineteenth-Century America," *Early American Studies*, Winter 2020, 90–133.

20. Mary Custis to George Washington

Parke Custis in Philadelphia, September 20, 1832, Library of Virginia.

21. Edna Greene Medford, "Beyond Mount Vernon: George Washington's Emancipated Laborers and Their Descendants," Philip J. Schwarz, ed., *Slavery at the Home of George Washington,* Mount Vernon, 2001, citing Alexandria deed book, 1803, 153.

22. Custis to James Hooe, January 15, 1812, New York Public Library.

23. Elizabeth Brown Pryor, *Reading the Man,* 267.

24. Augusta Blanche Berard, "Arlington and Mount Vernon 1856," letter with introduction and notes by Clayton Torrence, *Virginia Historical Magazine* LVII (1949), 140–175.

25. *Alexandria Gazette,* January 22, 1858, Annual report of American Colonization Society.

26. Early Lee Fox, *The American Colonization Society, 1817–1840* (Baltimore: The Johns Hopkins University Press, 1919), 23.

27. National Park Service, "Arlington House: The Robert L. Lee Memorial," Guidebook, 24. See also Karen L. Byrne, "The Power of Place: Using Historic Structures to Teach Children About Slavery," National Park Service, *Cultural Resource Management* 23, no. 3.

28. Nelligan, *Arlington House,* 281, Custis letter to R.R. Gurley, Historical Society of Pennsylvania.

29. David M. Streifford, "The American Colonization Society: An Application of Republican Ideology to Early Antebellum Reform," *Journal of Southern History* 45, no. 2 (May 1979): 212, 217.

30. *Annual Reports of the American Society of Colonizing the Free People of Colour of the United States,* Vols. 11–20, 1828–36, 23–24 (Washington, D.C., ACA originals 1818–1910, reprinted New York, Negro Universities Press, Greenwood Publishing Corp., 1969). The title uses the original name of the American Colonization Society.

31. American Colonization Society, 11th Annual Report, 25.

32. American Colonization Society, 13th Annual Report, ix, xvii.

33. William Meade to Molly Custis at Arlington House, May 30, 1825, Albert and Shirley Small Special Collections Library, University of Virginia.

34. *The Emancipator* (New York), April 25, 1839.

35. Custis to R.R. Gurley, circa 1850, Historical Society of Pennsylvania.

36. Ford Risley, *Abolition and the Press* (Evanston, Illinois: Medill School, Northwestern University Press, 2008), 36–37.

37. *"Selections from the Writings of W. L. Garrison:* Extracted from a pamphlet, published in 1832, titled "THOUGHTS ON AFRICAN COLONIZATION: or an Impartial Exhibition of the Doctrines, Principles and Purposes of the American Colonization Society. Together with the Resolutions, Addresses and Remonstrances of the Free People of Color" (Boston: R.F. Wallcut, 1852), re-published 1999 by Stephen Railton and the University of Virginia. http://utc. iath.virginia.edu/abolitn/abeswlgbt.html.

38. Frederick Douglass, *The North Star* (Rochester, New York), January 26, 1849. Republished 2001 by Stephen Railton and the University of Virginia. http://utc.iath. virginia.edu/abolitn/abar03at.html.

39. Douglas Southall Freeman, *R. E. Lee: A Biography,* Four Volumes (New York: Charles Scribners Sons, 1934), 1, 372–373; Letter from Robert E. Lee to Mary Lee, December 27, 1856, Lee Papers, Library of Congress. See also Roy Blount, Jr., "Making Sense of Robert E. Lee," *Smithsonian Magazine,* 2003. See https://www. smithsonianmag.com/history/making-sense-of-robert-e-lee-85017563/.

40. Eleanor Parke Custis Lewis to Harrison Gray Otis, October 17, 1831, copy from Massachusetts Historical Society. http:// www.masshist.org/database/2459.

41. Schomberg Center for Research in Black Culture, "In Motion: The African-American Migration Experience," New York Public Library Digital Library Program. http://www.inmotionaame.org/ migrations/topic.cfm;jsessionid=f8303352 381573098127250?migration=4&topic=4& bhcp=1.

42. Rosabella Burke to Mary Custis Lee, February 20, 1859. Material on Burkes from National Park Service, Arlington House Archives. https://www.nps.gov/arho/learn/ historyculture/burke.htm.

43. Antonio T. Bly, "Slave Literacy and Education in Virginia," *Encyclopedia of Virginia.* https://www.encyclopediavirginia. org/Slave_Literacy_and_Education_in_ Virginia.

44. Frances Scott and Anne Cipriani Webb, *Who Is Markie? The Life of Martha Custis Williams Carter, Cousin and Confidante of Robert E. Lee* (Westminster, Maryland: Heritage Books, 2007), 103.

45. Custis to the Rev. Issac Orr, February 25, 1831, Fred W. Smith National Library for the Study of George Washington, Mount Vernon.

46. *Journal of Martha Custis Williams*, November 2, 1853. See also Karen L. Byrne, "Our Little Sanctuary in the Woods: Spiritual Life at Arlington Chapel," *Arlington Historical Magazine* 12, no. 2 (October 2002), 39.

47. Markie Williams diary entry for November 2, 1853, cited in Holloway.

48. Byrne, "Our Little Sanctuary in the Woods," 40.

49. Augusta Blanche Berard, "Arlington and Mount Vernon 1856," letter with introduction and notes by Clayton Torrence, *Virginia Historical Magazine* LVII (1949), 140–175.

50. Williams diary, cited in Byrne.

51. Scott and Webb, 106.

52. Birth records of Christ Church kept with the Mary Coulling papers of the Lee family, courtesy Special Collections and Archives, Washington and Lee University.

53. Mary Thompson, *"The Only Unavoidable Subject of Regret,"* 210.

54. Custis, *Recollections*, 24.

55. Mary Thompson, *The Only Unavoidable Subject of Regret*, 208.

56. Mary Randolph, *The Virginia Housewife: Or Methodical Cook* (Baltimore: John Plaskitt, 1836), xi.

57. Patricia Brady Schmit, *Nelly Custis Lewis's Housekeeping Book* (New Orleans: The Historic New Orleans Collection, 1982), 20–21.

58. Pielmeier, 139, Arlington House Archives.

59. Elizabeth Brown Pryor, *Reading the Man,* 128, citing letters from Mary Custis Lee.

60. Scott and Webb, *Who Is Markie?,* 105.

61. Agnes Lee, "Growing Up in the 1850s," *The Journal of Agnes Lee*, edited by Mary Custis Lee DeButts (Chapel Hill: The University of North Carolina Press for the Robert E. Lee Memorial Association, 1984), 120.

62. Mary P. Coulling, *The Lee Girls* (Winston Salem, N.C.: John F. Blair, Publisher, 1987), 48.

63. Luthor Morris Leisenring, Interviews with Annie Baker and Ada Thompson, March 3, 1930, summarized by National Park Service at Arlington House.

64. Mary Custis Lee journal, 1890, Virginia Historical Society, cited by Mary P. Coulling, *The Lee Girls,* 33.

65. Unsigned dispatch, *Harper's Weekly*, May 29, 1886, 347.

66. Enoch Aquila Chase, "Ancient Custis Slave Remembers Brilliant Arlington Events," *Sunday Star,* November 4, 1928. Parks, a much-honored maintenance worker at Arlington National Cemetery, gave Arlington House historians crucial first-hand information about the layout of the old plantation. He was about 85 when he gave that interview and died the following year, buried with full military honors. Chase later published a history of the cemetery.

67. Leisenring interviews in 1930.

68. John P. Walden to Custis, November 3, 1823, Virginia Historical Society.

69. Custis to Francis Nelson, June 17, 1849, College of William and Mary, Swem Library.

70. Custis to Francis Nelson, January 28, 1857, Fred W. Smith National Library for the Study of George Washington, Mount Vernon.

71. Court records and *Daily National Intelligencer,* October 29, 1829; cited in National Park Service, National Register of Historic Places Registration Form, 2013, Section 8, p. 71. https://arlingtonva.s3.amazonaws.com/wp-content/uploads/sites/31/2015/04/VA_Arlington_County_Arlington-House_Additional_Doc__Boundary_Increase_FINAL_03–18–2014.pdf.

72. *Daily National Intelligencer,* November 21, 1836.

73. *Weekly Union* (Manchester, New Hampshire), December 29, 1857.

74. Custis at Arlington House to Mary Lee Custis at Audley (Berryville, Virginia), August 31, 1839, Virginia Historical Society.

75. Emory M Thomas, *Robert E. Lee: A Biography* (New York: W.W. Norton & Co., 1995), 110.

76. Mary Custis Lee to Molly Custis, July 4, 1838, Arlington House Archives.

77. Mary Custis Lee to Molly Custis, no date, 1850, cited in Pryor, 127, Virginia Historical Society.

78. Mary Custis Lee to Union General Charles Sanford, May 30, 1861, Virginia Historical Society Enoch Aquila Chase papers, cited in Mary Coulling, *The Lee Girls,* 89.

79. Elizabeth Brown Pryor, *Reading the Man,* 127.

80. John Perry, *First Lady of Arlington,* 137–38.

81. Philip D. Morgan, "'To Get Quit of Negroes': George Washington and Slavery," *Journal of American Studies* 39, no. 3 (2005), 419.

82. See Henry Wiencek, *An Imperfect God: George Washington, His Slaves, and the Creation of America* (New York: Farrar Straus and Giroux, 2003), 285. See also Mary Thompson, "*The Only Unavoidable Subject of Regret,*" 143.

83. Wiencek, *An Imperfect God,* 84–85, 284–290.

84. Mary Thompson, "*The Only Unavoidable Subject of Regret,*" 145.

85. T. Michael Miller, ed., "Scenes of Childhood" by Mary Gregory Powell, *Fireside Sentinel* (Alexandria, Virginia IV, no. 1 (January 1990).

86. The assertion surfaced in the 1930s. See Sterling A. Brown, "The Negro in Washington," *Washington: City and Capital,* Government Printing Office, 1937.

87. *Atchison* (Kansas) *Daily Globe,* Saturday, September 15, 1888, "Lovely Arlington: Graphic Description of a Beautiful Place, Interesting Reminiscences, Its Historic Associations," by a special correspondent, 3.

88. Elizabeth Brown Pryor, *Reading the Man,* 139.

89. Pielmeier, *Arlington House,* 117.

90. Pielmeier, *Arlington House,* 157. See also Delorus Preston, Jr., "William Syphax, A Pioneer in Negro Education in the District of Columbia," *Journal of Negro History* XX, No. 4 (October 1935), 448–476. See also https://www.mountvernon.org/george-washington/slavery/a-community-divided/syphax-family/.

91. Unsigned letter to *Muncie* (Indiana) *Times,* reprinted in *Daily Inter Ocean* (Chicago), September 23, 1865.

92. Arlington House Foundation website, "Women of Arlington House." https://www.arlingtonhouse.org/about/the-stories/women-of-arlington.

93. Allison Keyes, "How the African-American Syphax Family Traces Its Lineage to Martha Washington," Smithsonian Mag.com, March 9, 2018. https://www.smithsonianmag.com/smithsonian-institution/how-african-american-syphax-family-traces-its-lineage-martha-washington-180968439/.

94. Cited in Pielmeier, *Arlington House,* 156; *Congressional Globe, Weekly Alta California,* July 28, 1866.

Chapter 10

1. *Cleveland Herald,* April 20, 1853.

2. *Weekly Union,* Washington, D.C., April 22, 1854.

3. *Alexandria Gazette,* August 14, 1854.

4. Custis to Francis Nelson, January 26, 1855.

5. Custis to Nelson, July 21, 1847, College of William and Mary, Swem Library.

6. Custis to Nelson, December 31, 1847, Schell papers, Library of Congress.

7. Custis to Nelson, February 2, 1847, William and Mary, Swem Library.

8. Custis to Nelson, December 11, 1850, William and Mary, Swem Library

9. Custis to Nelson, November 14, 1846, Schell Papers, Library of Congress.

10. Custis to Nelson, October 23, 1853, William and Mary, Swem Library

11. Custis to Nelson, April 24, 1854, William and Mary, Swem Library.

12. Custis to Nelson, June 30, 1853, William and Mary, Swem Library.

13. Custis to Nelson, June 17, 1854, William and Mary, Swem Library.

14. Custis to Nelson, July 12, 1855, William and Mary, Swem Library.

15. Custis to Nelson, June 29, 1844, Joseph Schell papers, Library of Congress.

16. Custis to Nelson, January 17, 1855, William and Mary, Swem Library.

17. Custis to Nelson, April 9, 1855, William and Mary, Swem Library.

18. Custis to Nelson, February 26, 1856, William and Mary, Swem Library.

19. Custis to Nelson, May 7, 1854, and February 2, 1854, William and Mary, Swem Library.

20. Custis to Nelson, August 18, 1855, William and Mary, Swem Library.

21. Custis to Nelson, May 7, 1854, William and Mary, Swem Library.

22. Custis to Nelson, January 17, 1855, William and Mary, Swem Library.

23. Custis to Nelson, December 5, 1854, William and Mary, Swem Library.

24. Custis to Nelson, June 26, 1856, William and Mary, Swem Library.

25. Lee to Custis, March 2, 1855, Nelligan, Arlington House, 316, from DeButts-Ely papers, Virginia Historical Society.

26. Murray Nelligan, *Arlington House*, 315, from the *Evening Star*, February 23, 1855.

27. *Alexandria Gazette*, February 27, 1854.

28. *Alexandria Gazette*, February 27, 1854.

29. Nelligan, *Arlington House, 305*, U.S. *Agriculture Society Journal* I (July 1853), 19, 148–153.

30. *Port Tobacco Times and Charles County Advertiser*, September 18, 1850.

31. *Alexandria Gazette*, November 4, 1850.

32. Nelligan, *Arlington House*, 313, from *National Intelligencer*, September 7, 1854.

33. *Irish Daily Union* (Washington, D.C.), March 30, 1851.

34. *Alexandria Gazette*, October 8, 1851.

35. Nelligan, *Arlington House*, 295.

36. Nelligan, *Arlington House*, 291, *National Intelligencer*, February 18, 23, 24, 1852.

37. *The Evening Star*, September 13, 1854.

38. *Daily National Intelligencer*, May 19, 1855.

39. *The Evening Star*, February 24, 1855.

40. *Washington Sentinel*, May 23, 1854.

41. Nelligan, *Arlington House*, 306.

42. Mary Custis Lee deButts, ed., *Growing Up in the 1850s: The Journal of Agnes Lee* (Chapel Hill, University of North Carolina Press, 1984), 10.

43. Francis Scott and Anne Cipriani Webb, *Who Is Markie?* (Westminster, Maryland: Heritage Books, 2007), 111.

44. Nelligan, *Arlington House*, 302. See Agnes Lee Journal, July 1853, and Benson Lossing, "Arlington House," *Harper's Magazine*, VII, September 1853, 437.

45. Charles Lanman, "A Day with Washington Irving," *Once a Week*, Series 1, Vol. II (1859–1860).

46. Scott and Webb, *Who Is Markie?*, 102.

47. Josephine Seaton, *William Winston Seaton: A Biographical Sketch: With Passing Notices of His Associates and Friends* (Boston: James Osgood and Co., 1871), 181.

48. Custis to Lewis Washington, August 4, 1852. Fred W. Smith National Library for the Study of George Washington, Mount Vernon.

49. Barre (Massachusetts) *Patriot,* April 1, 1853.

50. *Daily Globe* (Washington, D.C.), September 12, 1854.

51. Custis to John Washington III, September 9, 1852, Letter for sale by Joe Rubenstine in June 2019.

52. *Evening Star*, July 5, 1855.

53. *Evening Post* (New York), August 23, 1855.

54. Custis to Robert Ball, September 2, 1854, Arlington House Archives.

55. Custis to Robert Ball, August 27, 1854, Arlington House Archives.

56. Nelligan, *Arlington House*, 288; Mary Custis to Custis Lee, December 5, 1851. Lee Papers, Library of Congress.

57. Nelligan, *Arlington House*, 289.

58. Nelligan, *Arlington House*, 292. Lee to Mary Custis, March 17, 1852, Lee-Custis Papers, Library of Congress.

59. For Hamilton's role, see the Papers of George Washington project at University of Virginia. https://www.ourdocuments.gov/doc.php?flash=false&doc=15.

60. David L. Ribblett, *Nelly Custis: Child of Mount Vernon* (Mount Vernon, Virginia: Mount Vernon Ladies' Association, 1993), 102.

61. The book published in 1854 was by Rufus Wilmot Griswold. Atlee exchange with Custis in *Daily Globe* (Washington, D.C.), January 4, 1855.

62. Agnes Lee, "Growing Up in the 1850s," *The Journal of Agnes Lee*, edited by Mary Custis Lee deButts (Chapel Hill: University of North Carolina, 1984), 41.

63. Mary Lee to Custis Lee, December 5, 1851, cited in Douglas Eugene Pielmeier, *Arlington House: The Evolution of a Nineteenth-Century Virginia Plantation*, 1996, unpublished thesis at Arlington House Archives, 137.

64. Agnes Lee Journal, entry for May 4, 1853, "Growing Up in the 1850s," 13.

65. *Daily Commercial Register* (Sandusky, Ohio), May 5, 1853.

66. James Lynch, *The Custis Chronicles:*

The Virginia Generation (Camden, Maine: Picton Press, 1997), 246, letter in Virginia Historical Society.

67. William Meade, *Old Churches, Ministers and Families of Virginia* (Philadelphia: J. B. Lippincott & Co., 1857), II, 196.

68. Nelligan, *Arlington House*, 321.

69. National Park Service, Arlington House, Application for Historic Registration, 2013.

70. Nelligan, *Arlington House*, 309, May 10, 18, 1853, Lee-Custis Papers, Library of Congress.

71. Custis, *Recollections*, 53.

72. Custis to Anna Maria Sarah (Goldsborough) Fitzhugh, December 29, 1853, Virginia Historical Society.

73. *Mercury* (N.Y.), March 30, 1854.

74. Custis to Nelson, June 9, 30, 1853, William and Mary, Swem Library.

75. Custis from West Point to Robert Ball at Arlington, September 2, 1854, Arlington House Archives.

76. Scott and Webb, *Who Is Markie?* 95.

77. *Ibid.*

78. Scott and Webb, *Who Is Markie?* 99.

79. Nelligan, Arlington House, 311. Lee to Markie Williams, Entry for January 2, 1854. See Craven Avery, ed., "To Markie": The Letters of Robert E. Lee to Martha Custis Williams, From The Originals in the Huntington Library (Cambridge: Harvard University Press, 1933), 38f.

80. Custis to Lewis Washington, February 6, 1857, Virginia Historical Society.

81. Nelligan, *Arlington House*, 336.

82. Robert E. Lee to Mary Lee, letters April-October, 1856, Custis-Lee Papers, Library of Congress. Nelligan, 330.

83. Jared Sparks to Custis, January 11, 1855, Tudor Place Archives.

84. Custis to John Varden, March 10, 1856, Fred W. Smith National Library for the Study of George Washington, Mount Vernon.

85. Custis to Henry C. Wise, October 15, 1856, William and Mary, Swem Library.

86. Hamilton Fish to Custis, December 27, 1856, Tudor Place Archives.

87. Robert Weir to Custis, 229 letter, April 29, 1857, Tudor Place Archives.

88. Nelligan, *Arlington House*, 339.

89. Nelligan, *Arlington House*, 339; *National Intelligencer*, August 28, 1857, and Custis to T.W.O. Moore, June 6, 1857, Historical Society of Pennsylvania.

90. *Evening Star*, July 10, 1857.

91. J. Augustus Johnson letter to Custis, April 29, 1857, Tudor Place Archives.

92. *Evening Star*, January 16, 1857.

93. Scott and Webb, *Who Is Markie?*, 122.

94. Nelligan, *Arlington House*, 338.

95. *Ibid. Daily National Intelligencer*, July 20, 1857.

96. Custis to Anthony Kimmel, September 4, 1857, Fred W. Smith National Library for the Study of George Washington, Mount Vernon.

97. Custis to Benson Lossing, March 24, 1853, Fred W. Smith National Library for the Study of George Washington, Mount Vernon.

98. Josephine Seaton, *William Seaton: A Biographical Sketch: With Passing Notices of His Associates and Friends* (Boston: James Osgood and Co., 1871), 180.

99. Custis to Lossing, April 4, 1854, Fred W. Smith National Library for the Study of George Washington, Mount Vernon.

100. Background in Benson Lossing, *Harper's Magazine* VII, September 1853, 474.

101. Lossing to Custis, December 7, 1856, Tudor Place Archives.

102. Custis at Arlington House to Lossing in Poughkeepsie, New York, June 19, 1854, Virginia Historical Society.

103. John Perry, *First Lady of Arlington*, 198.

104. Mary Custis Lee to Benson Lossing, November 25, 1857, Arlington House Archives.

105. Nelligan, *Arlington House,* 342.

106. Custis, *Recollections,* 70.

107. *Evening Star,* October 13, 1857.

108. Albany (New York) *Evening Journal,* October 12, 1857.

109. *Irish American* (New York), October 24, 1857.

110. *Harper's Weekly*, October 24, 1857. "The Late G.W.P. Custis," reprinted in 1858, vol. 1, no. 43.

111. Letter from Edward Welch S.J. to Charles B. Kenny, October 12, 1857, Tudor Place Archives.

112. *Pittsfield Sun*, January 21, 1858.

113. *Alexandria Gazette*, January 22, 1858.

114. Custis, *Recollections*, 10–13.

115. Nelligan, *Arlington House*, 343.

116. Richard B. McCaslin, *Lee in the Shadow of Washington* (Baton Rouge: Louisiana State University, 2001), 42, from Lee's Memo Book entries for October 2 and

November 11, 1857; Lee to Mary Custis Lee, November 22, 1857.

117. Nelligan, *Arlington House,* 342. Mary Lee to Robert E. Lee, October 11, 1857, DeButts-Ely Lee Papers, Virginia Historical Society.

118. Mary Custis Lee deButts, ed., *Growing Up in the 1850s,* 97.

119. Benson Lossing to Mary Custis Lee, October 12, 1857, Tudor Place Archives.

120. Mary Custis Lee to Benson Lossing, November 25, 1857, Arlington House Archives.

121. Custis, *Recollections,* 10.

122. Custis, *Recollections,* 11.

123. *Lynchburg Daily Virginian,* April 27, 1860.

124. Custis, *Recollections,* 413.

125. *Ibid.,* 480.

126. Fritz Hirschfeld, *George Washington and Slavery: A Documentary Portrayal* (Columbia: University of Missouri, 1997), 100.

127. See Rosemarie Zagarri, ed., *Life of General Washington* (Athens: University of Georgia Press, 1991).

128. Custis, *Recollections,* 437–438.

129. *Boston Evening Transcript,* March 24, 1860.

130. Nelligan, *Arlington House,* 365; *National Intelligencer,* December 22, 30, 1859.

131. Nelligan, *Arlington House,* 372.

132. Lee to Mary Custis Lee, DeButts-Ely papers, April 4, 1860, and June 3, 1860. Custis-Lee Papers, Library of Congress, Nelligan, 366.

133. Craig Shirley, *Mary Ball Washington: The Untold Story of George Washington's Mother* (New York: Farrar, Straus and Giroux, 2019), 229; Custis, *Recollections,* 135.

134. Mary Custis Lee to Benson Lossing, January 6, 1860, The Society of the Cincinnati.

135. Mary Custis Lee to Benson Lossing, February 20, 1866, Arlington House Archives.

136. Lee to Anna Fitzhugh, November 22, 1857. Duke University, David M. Rubenstein Rare Book and Manuscript Library.

137. Nelligan, *Arlington House,* 354.

138. Mary Lee to W.G. Webster, February 17, 1858, Library of Virginia. Emory M. Thomas, *Robert E. Lee: A Biography* (New York: W.W. Norton & Co., 1995), 177.

139. Emory M. Thomas, *Robert E. Lee: A Biography* (New York: W.W. Norton & Co., 1995), 176.

140. Nelligan, *Arlington House,* 353.

141. Nelligan, *Arlington House,* 350; Emory Thomas, *Robert E. Lee,* 175.

142. Lee to Custis Lee, February 15, 1858, Duke University, David M. Rubenstein Rare Book and Manuscript Library.

143. Emory Thomas, *Robert E. Lee,* 178.

144. *Weekly Union* (Manchester, New Hampshire), December 29, 1857.

145. *Chicago Tribune,* October 19, 1857, cited in Nelligan, *Arlington House,* 351.

146. Charleston *Mercury,* reprinted in *Lafayette Daily Journal* (Indiana,) January 4, 1858.

147. Michael Fellman, *The Making of Robert E. Lee* (Baltimore: The Johns Hopkins University Press, 2003), 70.

148. Emory Thomas, *Robert E. Lee,* 177.

149. Both letters reprinted in *The New York Times,* August 8, 2017. https://www.nytimes.com/2017/08/18/us/robert-e-lee-slaves.html.

150. Rick Murphy and Timothy Stevens, *Section 27 and Freedman's Village in Arlington National Cemetery: The African American History of America's Most Hallowed Ground* (Jefferson, N.C.: McFarland, 2020), 54.

151. The *Randolph County Journal* (Winchester, Indiana), July 7, 1854, told a similar story, adding that Lee punished the slaves for the minor offense of fishing in the river. He allegedly administered 39 lashes to the woman and sent all three escaped slaves to a Richmond jail.

152. April 14, 1866. Reprinted in John W. Blassingame, ed., *Slave Testimony: Two Centuries of Letters, Speeches, and Interviews, and Autobiographies* (Baton Rouge: Louisiana State University Press, 1977), 467–468.

153. Lee to Col. Thomas, June 16, 1859, Lee Papers, Washington and Lee University Library Special Collections.

154. Lee to Custis Lee, February 15, 1858, Duke University, David M. Rubenstein Rare Book and Manuscript Library, Lee Papers. Cited in Elizabeth Brown Pryor, *Reading the Man,* 262.

155. Lee to Custis Lee, December 14, 1860, Duke University, David M. Rubenstein Rare Book and Manuscript Library.

156. *Boston Recorder,* March 23, 1866.

157. Custis to J. Pickett, April 17, 1857, Fred W. Smith National Library for the Study of George Washington, Mount Vernon.

158. *Washington Sentinel,* May 23, 1854.

Bibliography

Institutions Visited

Alexandria Public Library Special Collections
Arlington County Public Library Center for Local History
Arlington House, National Park Service
College of William and Mary, Swem Library
Duke University, David M. Rubenstein Rare Book and Manuscript Library
GealologyBank.com and Virginia Chronicle for 19th-century newspapers.
Historical Society of Pennsylvania, Philadelphia
Historical Society of Washington, D.C.
Library of Congress: Custis-Lee papers, Joseph Schell papers, Ethel Ames collection of Lee
    family papers, DeButts-Ely collection of Lee family papers
Library of Virginia, Richmond
Mount Vernon, Fred W. Smith National Library for the Study of George Washington
New York Public Library, Brooke Russell Astor Reading Room for Rare Books and Manu-
    scripts
Society of the Cincinnati, Library, Washington, D.C.
Tudor Place Archives, Washington, D.C.
University of Virginia, Albert and Shirley Small Special Collections Library
Virginia Historical Society, Richmond
Washington and Lee University Library Special Collections and Archives
(Some punctuation and archaic words in letters and articles have been modernized for clar-
    ity, with care taken to preserve the original meaning.)

Articles and Reports

Allard, Dean C., "When Arlington Was Part of the District of Columbia," *Arlington Histori-
    cal Magazine* 6, no. 2, 1978.

Berard, Augusta Blanche, "Arlington and Mount Vernon 1856 as described in a Letter of
    Augusta Blanche Berard," Edited by Clayton Torrence, *Virginia Magazine of History and
    Biography* 57, no. 2, April 1949, 140–75.

Bly, Antonio T., "Slave Literacy and Education in Virginia," *Encyclopedia of Virginia,* https://
    www.encyclopediavirginia.org/Slave_Literacy_and_Education_in_Virginia.

Brown, Sterling A., "The Negro in Washington," *Washington: City and Capital*, Government
    Printing Office, 1937.

Bryne, Karen, *"We Have a Claim on This Estate": Remembering Slavery at Arlington House,*
    Cultural Resource Management, Interior Department, No. 4, 2002.

Byrne, Karen L., "Our Little Sanctuary in the Woods: Spiritual Life at Arlington Chapel,"
    Arlington Historical Magazine 12, no. 2, October 2002, 39.

Good, Cassandra, "Washington Family Fortune Lineage and Capital in Nineteenth-Century
    America," *Early American Studies,* Winter 2020, 90–133.

Hanna, Jennifer, "Cultural Landscape History," Vol. 2, Interior Department, National Park Service, October 2001.

Harrison, Constance Cary, "Washington at Mount Vernon After the Revolution," *Century Illustrated Magazine* 37, no. 6 (1881–1906); ProQuest, 834.

Harvey, Frederick L., *History of the Washington National Monument and the Washington National Monument Society,* Washington, D.C.: Press of Norman T. Elliott Printing Co., 1902.

Hoyt, William D., Jr., "Self-Portrait: Eliza Custis, 1808." *The Virginia Magazine of History and Biography* 53, no. 2 (April 1945): 95.

Judith M. Jacob, "The Washington Monument: A Technical History and Catalog of the Commemorative Stones," National Park Service, Interior Department, Northeast Region, Design, Construction, and Facility Management Directorate, Architectural Preservation Division, 2005, 54.

Kail, Wendy, "The Court Will Come to Order: Dandridge vs. Executors of Martha Washington's Will," Washington, D.C.: Tudor Place Foundation, 2015.

Kennedy, Roger, "Arlington House, a Mansion That Was a Monument," *Smithsonian* 16 (1985), 156–166.

Keyes, Allison, "How the African-American Syphax Family Traces Its Lineage to Martha Washington," SmithsonianMag.com, March 9, 2018.

National Park Service, *A Guide to Arlington House, the Robert E. Lee Memorial,* 1985.

Nelligan, Murray H., "American Nationalism and the Stage: The Plays of George Washington Parke Custis (1781–1857)," *The Virginia Magazine of History and Biography* 58, no. 3, July 1950.

Philip, D. Morgan, "'To Get Quit of Negroes': George Washington and Slavery," *Journal of American Studies* 39, no. 3, 2005.

Richards, Mark David, "The Debates Over the Retrocession of the District of Columbia, 1801–2004," *Washington History,* Spring/Summer, 2004, 1–29.

Rose, Ruth Preston, "Smith's Island," *Arlington Historical Magazine* 8, no. 1, 1985, 28–30.

Smith, Kathryn Gettings, "Interior Department National Park Service National Register of Historic Places Registration Form," Washington, D.C.: National Park Service, National Capital Region, December 31, 2013.

Streifford, David M., "The American Colonization Society: An Application of Republican Ideology to Early Antebellum Reform," *Journal of Southern History* 45, no. 2, May 1979.

Unpublished Dissertations and Theses

Boettcher, Hannah, "Mary Custis Lee Unpacks the Washington Relics: A Revolutionary Inheritance in Museums, 1901–1918," master's thesis, University of Delaware, 2016.

Nelligan, Murray H., "A Poor Devil of an Author," address given to annual luncheon of Washington chapter of the Association for the Preservation of Virginia Antiquities, Washington, D.C., May 26, 1951, Alexandria Library.

Pielmeier, Douglas Eugene, "Arlington House: The Evolution of a Nineteenth-Century Virginia Plantation," 1996, unpublished dissertation at Arlington House Archives.

Books

Bourne, Miriam Anne, *First Family: George Washington and His Intimate Relations,* New York: W.W. Norton, 1982.

Brady, Patricia, ed., *George Washington's Beautiful Nelly: The Letters of Eleanor Parke Custis Lewis to Elizabeth Bordley Gibson, 1794–1851,* Columbia: University of South Carolina Press, 1991.

Brighton, Ray, *The Checkered Career of Tobias Lear,* Portsmouth, N.H.: Portsmouth Marine Society, Publication Four, 1985.

Bruggeman, Seth C., *Here, George Washington Was Born: Memory, Material Culture, and the Public History of a National Monument,* Athens: University of Georgia Press, 2008.

Callcott, Margaret Law, ed., *Mistress of Riversdale: The Plantation Letters of Rosalie Stier Calvert 1795–1821,* Baltimore: The Johns Hopkins University Press, 1991.

Chernow, Ron, *Washington: A Life,* New York: Penguin, 2010.

Clark, Ellen McAllister, *Martha Washington: A Brief Biography,* Mount Vernon Ladies' Association and University of Virginia Press, 2002.

Costello, Matthew R., *The Property of the Nation: George Washington's Tomb, Mount Vernon, and the Memory of the First President,* Lawrence: University of Kansas Press, 2019.

Coulling, Mary P., *The Lee Girls,* Winston Salem, N.C.: John F. Blair, Publisher, 1987.

Decatur, Stephen Jr., *Private Affairs of George Washington, from the Records and Accounts of Tobias Lear, Esquire, His Secretary,* New York: Houghton Mifflin & Co., 1933.

Decker, Karl, and Angus McSween, *Historic Arlington,* Washington, D.C.: Decker and McSween Publishing Co., 1892.

Dunbar, Erica Armstrong, *Never Caught: The Washingtons' Relentless Pursuit of Their Runaway Slave Ona Judge,* New York: 37Ink/Atria, 2017.

Fields, Joseph E., ed., *"Worthy Partner": The Papers of Martha Washington, with an introduction by Ellen McCallister Clark,* Westport, Connecticut: Greenwood Press, 1994.

Flexner, James Thomas, *George Washington: Anguish and Farewell (1793–1799),* Boston: Little, Brown, 1970.

Foster, John, *A Sketch of the Tour of General Lafayette on His Late Visit to the United States, 1824,* Portland, Maine: printed by A.W. Thayer in the Statesman Office, 1824.

Freeman, Douglas Southall, *George Washington, Vol. Two: Young Washington,* New York: Charles Scribner's Sons, 1948.

Freeman, Douglas Southall, *R.E. Lee, A Biography, Vol.,* New York: Scribner's Sons, 1934–1935.

Glover, Lorri, *Founders and Fathers: The Private Lives of the American Revolutionaries,* New Haven: Yale University Press, 2014.

Gottschalk, Louis, ed., *The Letters of Lafayette to Washington, 1777–1799,* New York: Henry Farhnstock Hubbard, 1944.

Green, Constance McLaughlin, *Washington: Village and Capital, 1800–1878,* Vol. 1; Princeton, N.J.: Princeton University Press, 1962.

Grizzard, Frank E., *George Washington: A Biographical Companion,* Santa Barbara, California: ABC-CLIO, 2002.

Herrick, Carole L., *Ambitious Failure: Chain Bridge: The First Bridge Across the Potomac River,* Reston, Virginia: Higher Education Publications, 2012.

Hinkel, John V., *Arlington: Monument to Heroes,* Englewood Cliffs, N.J.: Prentice-Hall, 1970, 1965.

Hirschfeld, Fritz, *George Washington and Slavery: A Documentary Portrait,* Columbia: University of Missouri Press, 1997.

Horn, Jonathan, *Washington's End: The Final and Forgotten Struggle,* New York: Scribner's, 2020.

King, Julia, *George Hadfield: Architect of the Federal City* (Milton Park, Oxfordshire: Routledge), 2014.

Klaiman, Maria, *The Return of Lafayette 1824/1825,* Charles Scribner's Sons, 1975.

Levasseur, Auguste, *Lafayette in America in 1824 and 1825: Journal of a Voyage to the United States (private secretary to General Lafayette during his trip),* translated by Alan R. Hoffman, Manchester, N.H.: Lafayette Press, 2006.

Lynch, James, *The Custis Chronicles: The Virginia Generation,* Camden, Maine: Picton Press, 1997.

MacIntire, Jane Bacon, *Lafayette: The Guest of the Nation: The Tracing of the Route of Lafayette's Tour of the United States in 1824–25,* Anthony J. Simone Press, 1967.

McDonnell, Michael A., Clare Corbould, Frances M. Clarke, and W. Fitzhugh Brundage, *Remembering the Revolution: Memory, History, and Nation Making from Independence to the Civil War,* University of Massachusetts Press, 2013. Chapters by Seth C. Bruggeman, "More Than Ordinary Patriotism," and Emily Lewis Butterfield, "Lie There My Darling, While I Avenge Ye!," 198–213.

Messing, Christine, John B. Ruddy, and Diane Windham Shew, *A Son and His Adoptive Father,* Mount Vernon Ladies' Association, 2006.

Miller, Donald, *Lafayette: His Extraordinary Life and Legacy,* iuniverse, 2015,

Miller, Helen Hill, *Colonel Parke of Virginia: 'The Greatest Hector in the Town,' A Biography,* Chapel Hill, N.C.: Algonquin Books, 1989.

Nelligan, Murray H., *Arlington House: The Story of the Lee Mansion Historical Monument,* Burke, Virginia: Chateleine Press, 2001, revised version of 1953 edition.

Perry, John, *Lady of Arlington: The Life of Mrs. Robert E. Lee,* Sister, Oregon: Multnomah Publishers, 2001.

Prussing, Eugene E., *The Estate of George Washington, Deceased,* Boston: Little, Brown, 1927.

Pryor, Elizabeth Brown, *Reading the Man: A Portrait of Robert E. Lee Through His Private Letters,* New York: Penguin, 2007.

Quertermous, Grant S., ed., *A Georgetown Life: The Reminiscences of Britannia Wellington Peter Kennon of Tudor Place,* Washington, D.C.: Georgetown University Press, 2020.

Randolph, Mary, *The Virginia Housewife: Or Methodical Cook,* Baltimore, John Plaskitt, 1824, 1836.

Ribblett, David, *Nelly Custis: Child of Mount Vernon,* Mount Vernon Ladies' Association, 1993.

Rose, C.B., Jr. *Arlington County, Virginia: A History,* Arlington, Virginia: Arlington Historical Society, 1976.

Saxton, Martha, *The Widow Washington: The Life of Mary Washington,* New York: Farrar, Straus, Giroux, 2019.

Scott, Frances, and Anne Cipriani Webb, *Who Is Markie? The Life of Martha Custis Williams Carter, Cousin and Confidante of Robert E. Lee,* Westminster, Maryland: Heritage Books, 2007.

Shirley, Craig, *Mary Washington: The Untold Story of George Washington's Mother,* New York: Harper, 2020.

Stetson, Charles W., *Four Mile Run Land Grants,* Washington, D.C.: Mimeoform Press, 1935.

Templeman, Eleanor Lee, *Arlington Vignettes: of a Virginia County* (New York: Avenel Books), 1959.

Thane, Elswyth, *Mount Vernon Family: A Chronicle of the Young People Who Looked to Our First President for Love, Guidance and Support,* New York: Crowell-Collier Press, 1968.

Thompson, Mary V., *"The Only Unavoidable Subject of Regret": George Washington, Slavery, and the Enslaved Community at Mount Vernon,* Charlottesville: University of Virginia Press, 2019.

Torbert, Alice Coyle, *Eleanor Calvert and Her Circle,* New York: The Williams-Frederick Press, 1950.

Vlach, John Michael, "Plantation Landscapes of the Antebellum South," in *Before Freedom Came: African American Life in the Antebellum South,* Edward D.C. Campbell, Jr., with Kym S. Rice, eds., Richmond, Virginia: The Museum of the Confederacy, 1991.

Wiencek, Henry, *An Imperfect God: George Washington, His Slaves, and the Creation of America,* New York: Farrar, Straus, Giroux, 2003.

Index

Numbers in **bold italics** refer to pages with illustrations